LANGUAGE FOR DAILY USE

Phoenix Edition

Curriculum and Instruction

Dr. Dorothy S. Strickland
Professor of Education
Department of Curriculum and Teaching
Teachers College, Columbia University

Consulting Educators

Dr. Richard F. Abrahamson, Consultant for Literature
Professor of Education
Department of Curriculum and Instruction
College of Education, University of Houston

Lexis Allen
Language Arts Curriculum Consultant
Clark County School District
Las Vegas, Nevada

Nola Bacci
Principal
West End Elementary School
Lynbrook, New York

Jennifer Better
Curriculum Coordinator
Cupertino Union School District
Cupertino, California

Dr. Barbara Burke
Assistant Director
Language Education Department
Detroit Public Schools
Detroit, Michigan

Rosemary Coury
Language Arts Supervisor
Ohio County Schools
Wheeling, West Virginia

Barbara L. Everhart
Reading Consultant
Davidson County Schools
Lexington, North Carolina

Betty Gould
Learning Development Specialist
Sachem Central School District
Holbrook, New York

Hildagarde Gray
Librarian
St. John the Baptist School
Pittsburgh, Pennsylvania

Elizabeth Handford
Curriculum Coordinator
Southside Christian School
Greenville, South Carolina

Helen Levy
Librarian
Springdale Elementary School
Princeton City School District
Cincinnati, Ohio

Ozella Nathaniel
Consultant—Elementary Language Arts
Muscogee County Schools
Columbus, Georgia

Delia Stafford
Instructional Specialist, K–3
Houston Independent Schools
Houston, Texas

David Zaslow
Writer-in-Residence
South Oregon Public Schools
Ashland, Oregon

Phoenix Edition

LANGUAGE FOR DAILY USE

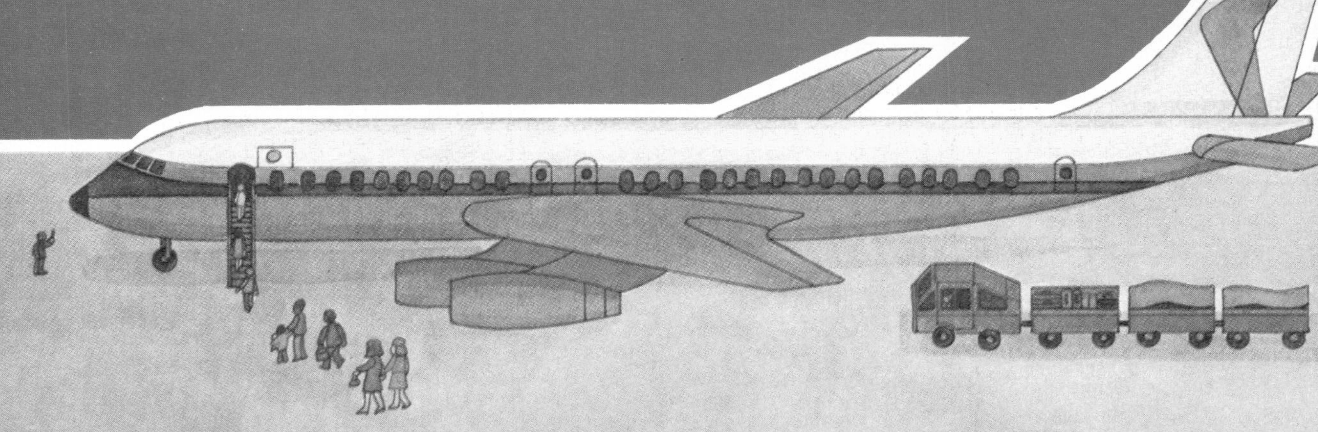

Harcourt Brace Jovanovich, Publishers
Orlando New York Chicago Atlanta Dallas

ACKNOWLEDGMENTS

For permission to reprint copyrighted material, grateful acknowledgment is made to the following sources:

Bradbury Press, Inc., Scarsdale, N.Y., 10583 and Collins Publishers: From *Timothy and Gramps* by Ron Brooks. Copyright © 1978 by Ron Brooks.

Thomas Y. Crowell Publishers: Text of "The Spring Wind" from *River Winding* by Charlotte Zolotow. Copyright © 1970 by Charlotte Zolotow.

The Devin-Adair Company, Inc., 143 Sound Beach Avenue, Old Greenwich, Conn., 06870: Excerpts from *Eat, Drink and Be Healthy: The Joy of Eating Natural Foods* by Agnes Toms. Copyright © 1963 by Agnes Toms.

Gerald Duckworth & Company, Ltd. and Alfred A. Knopf, Inc.: "The Frog" from *Cautionary Verses* by Hilaire Belloc. Copyright © 1941 by Hilaire Belloc.

E. P. Dutton, Inc.: "Galoshes" from *Stories to Begin On* by Rhoda W. Bacmeister. Copyright 1940 by E. P. Dutton & Co., Inc. Renewal copyright © 1968 by Rhoda W. Bacmeister.

E. P. Dutton, Inc. and McClelland and Stewart Limited, Toronto: Stanza from "Sand-Between-the-Toes" from *When We Were Very Young* by A. A. Milne. Copyright 1924 by E. P. Dutton & Co., Inc. Renewal copyright 1952 by A. A. Milne.

Four Winds Press, a division of Scholastic Inc.: "The Six Wise Travellers" in *Little Plays for Little People* by Sally Jarvis. Copyright © 1965 by Parents' Magazine Press.

Hamish Hamilton, Ltd.: Adapted from *The Field of Buttercups: An Irish Story* by Alice Boden.

Harcourt Brace Jovanovich, Inc.: From "Arithmetic" in *Windsong* by Carl Sandburg. Copyright © 1953, 1958, 1960 by Carl Sandburg. "Over the wintry..." by Soseki from *Cricket Songs: Japanese Haiku*, translated and © 1964 by Harry Behn. Pronunciation key and entries from *The HBJ School Dictionary* copyright © 1977 by Harcourt Brace Jovanovich, Inc.

Harper & Row, Publishers, Inc.: Text of "Robert Who Is Often a Stranger to Himself" from *Bronzeville Boys and Girls* by Gwendolyn Brooks. Copyright © 1956 by Gwendolyn Brooks Blakely. Text of "The Park" from *Crickety Cricket! The Best Loved Poems of James S. Tippett* by James S. Tippett. Copyright 1927 by Harper & Row, Publishers, Inc.; renewed 1955 by James S. Tippett.

Alfred A. Knopf, Inc.: "Autumn Thought" from *The Dream Keeper and Other Poems* by Langston Hughes. Copyright © 1932 by Alfred A. Knopf, Inc. and renewed 1960 by Langston Hughes.

J. B. Lippincott Publishers: Second stanza from "Verbs" in *Poems for Children* by Eleanor Farjeon. Copyright 1938 by Eleanor Farjeon.

Macmillan Publishing Co., Inc.: From "Rain Poem" in *Poems* by Elizabeth Coatsworth. Copyright 1957 by Macmillan Publishing Co., Inc.

National Wildlife Federation: "Baby Bird Do's and Don'ts" by Eva Bell, reprinted from *Ranger Rick's Nature Magazine*, © May 1981.

W. W. Norton & Company, Inc.: "Poem" reprinted from *Diversifications* by A. R. Ammons. Copyright © 1975 by A. R. Ammons.

Philomel Books, a division of The Putnam Publishing Group: Untitled poem from *High on a Hill* by Ed Young. Copyright © 1980 by Ed Young.

G.P. Putnam's Sons: "Annie Sullivan," adapted from *Annie Sullivan* by Mary Malone. Copyright © 1971 by Mary Malone.

The Young Naturalist Foundation: Excerpt from "Odd Splash Facts" by Paul Brock in *Owl* magazine, May 1979.

PRINTED IN THE UNITED STATES OF AMERICA

ISBN 0–15–317004–2

PHOTO CREDITS

t—top, b—bottom, r—right, l—left, c—center

Cover: © Leonard Lee Rue III/DPI.

UNIT 1 Openers, page xiv, tl—Phoebee Dunn/DPI, tr—Michal Heron/Woodfin Camp, cr—Michal Heron/Woodfin Camp, bl—L.L.T. Rhodes/Taurus Photos, br—P. Ginsberg/DPI; 5, Ken Yuszkus/Taurus; 13, Joel Greenstein/Omni-Photo Communications; 23, Milton Feinberg/Stock, Boston; 24, John Blaustein/Woodfin Camp; UNIT 2 Openers, 36, tl—Martha Swope, tr—Richard Hutchings, c—Michal Heron/Woodfin Camp, br—Zimbel/Monkmeyer Press Photos, bc—Jason Lauré/Woodfin Camp, bl—Craig Aurness/Woodfin Camp; 45, Hal Yaeger/DPI; 47, Greater Cleveland Growth Association; 63, Lenore Weber/Omni-Photo Communications; 64, all—Wide World Photos; 69, Culver Pictures; 70, Culver Pictures; UNIT 3 Openers, 78, tl—Larry Smith/DPI, tc—Leonard Lee Rue III/DPI, tr—Phil Dotson/DPI, br—American Museum of Natural History, bl—J. M. Barris/DPI; 83, J. Alex Langley/DPI; 101, Daniel Brody/Stock, Boston; UNIT 4 Openers, 114, tl—Focus on Sports, tc—James Sugar/Woodfin Camp, tr—Mimi Forsyth/Monkmeyer Press Photos, cr—G. Cloyd/HBJ Photo, br—Oscar Buitrago/HBJ Photo, bl—HBJ Photo; 117, NASA/Omni-Photo Communications; 119, Tom Wurl/Stock, Boston; 129, Randa Bishop/DPI; UNIT 5 Openers, 152, tl—John Lei/Omni-Photo Communications, tr—Tim Eagan/Woodfin Camp, cr—Chris Reeberg/DPI, br—David Campione/Taurus Photos, bl—Triangli/Palmieri/DPI; 161, K. K. Almond/Stock, Boston; 167, Monkmeyer Press Photo; UNIT 6 Openers, 189, tl—O. Buitrago/HBJ Photo, tr—O. Buitrago/HBJ Photo, cr—S. A. Fernandez/Woodfin Camp, br—Erik Arnesen/HBJ Photo, bl—L. L. T. Rhodes/Taurus Photos; 204, Bruce Silverstein/Peter Arnold; UNIT 7 Openers, 226, l—Springer/Bettmann Film Archive, tr—HBJ Photo, br—HBJ Photo; 241, J. Alex Langley/DPI; 247, Tim Eagan/Woodfin Camp; UNIT 8 Openers, 258, tl—O. Buitrago/HBJ Photo, tr—George Hall/Woodfin Camp, br—O. Buitrago/HBJ Photo, bl—O. Buitrago/HBJ Photo; 270, G. Cloyd/HBJ Photo.

ART CREDITS

Jan Brett: 106, 107, 108, 131, 158, 171; Penny Carter: 10, 11, 102, 120, 121, 234; Carolyn Croll: 39, 40, 228, 229, 273; Susan Dodge: 59, 84, 85, 90, 91, 118, 124, 176, 177, 178, 217, 250-251, 252; Leigh Grant: 42, 103, 144, 216, 287; Kathy Hendrickson: 122-123, 160, 194, 202; Brian Karas: 2, 3, 92, 93, 155; Dora Leder: 8, 9, 88, 135, 188, 189, 261, 281; Lucinda McQueen: 14, 28-29, 142, 143, 205; Diane Paterson: 12, 21, 80, 81, 130, 162, 190-191, 231, 284-285, 286; Ed Renfro: 31, 156, 166, 193, 232, 266-267; Nancy Schill: 4, 6, 46, 168, 169, 172, 173, 211, 283; Bob Shein: 20, 241, 243, 256, 272, 290, 339, 344; Debbie Sims: 7, 57, 60; Judy Sutton: 41, 87, 179, 218, 276; Alexandra Wallner: 19, 133, 201; Lily Yamamoto: 50, 52, 196, 265, 269, 274, 289; Lane Yerkes: 15, 48, 86, 137, 187, 237, 263, 279.

All student handwriting models by Thomas M. Wasylyk.

CONTENTS

UNIT 3 79

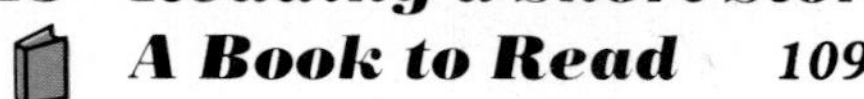

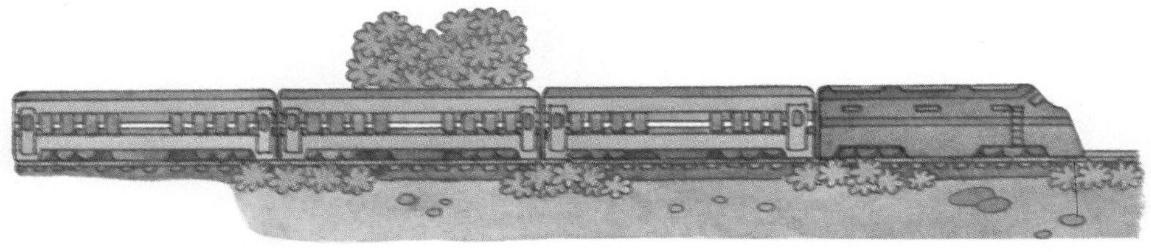

UNIT 5 153

UNIT 6 185

UNIT 8 259

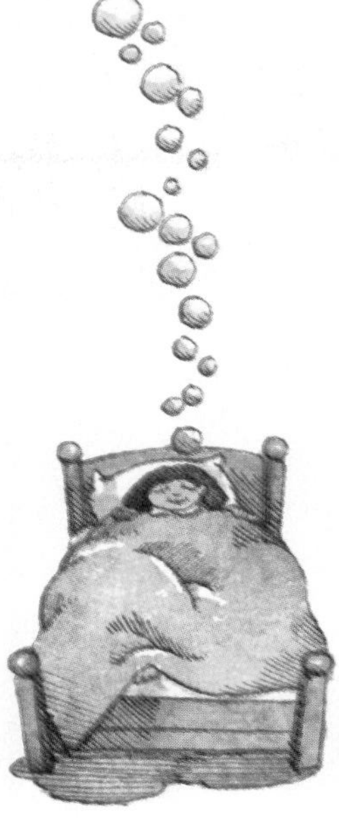

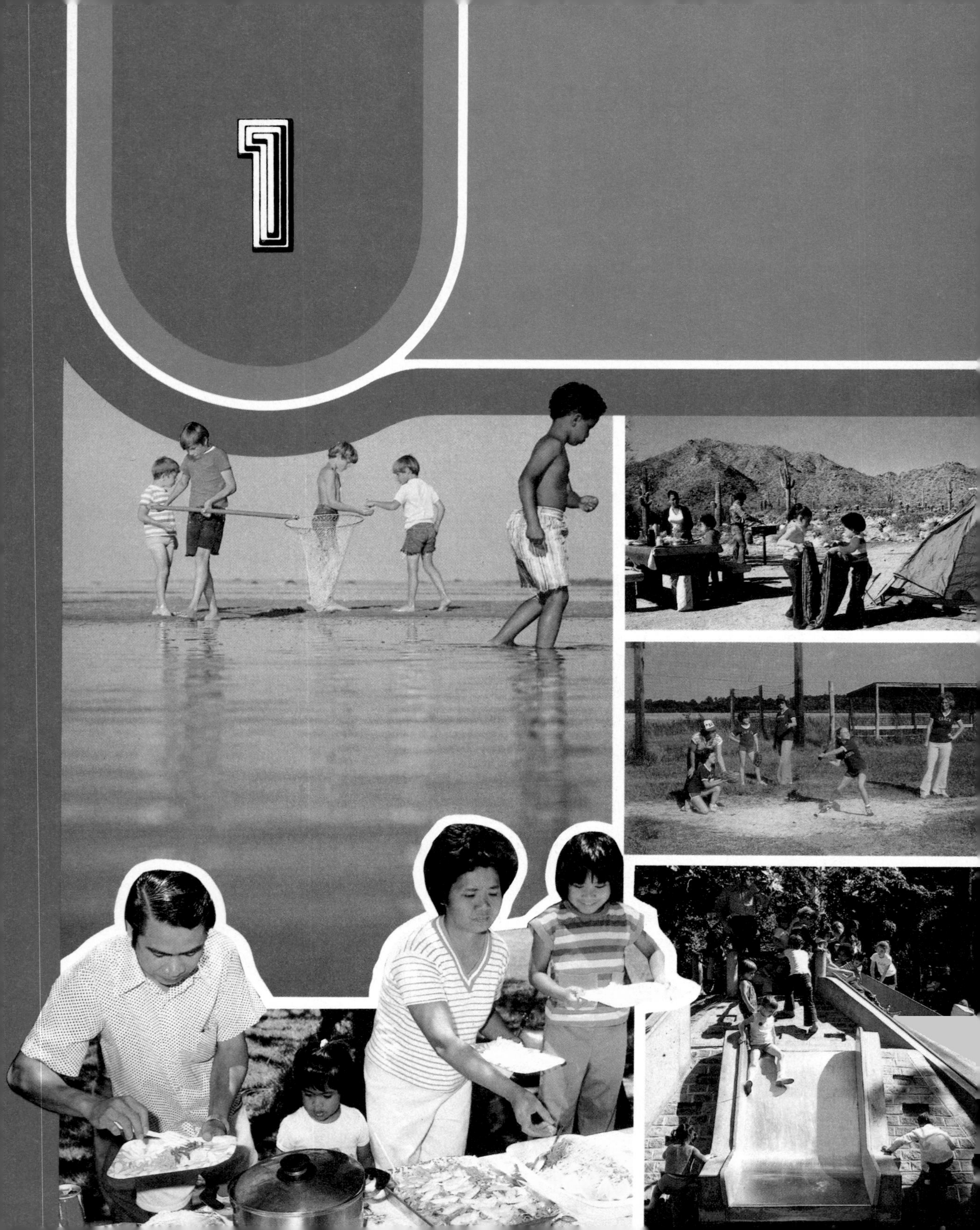
1

LANGUAGE
Learning About Sentences
COMPOSITION
Writing Sentences
STUDY SKILLS
Using the Library
LITERATURE
Reading a Story

Look at the pictures on the opposite page. They show children in summer activities.

Suppose a friend asks you about your summer vacation. How would you tell what you did? You would use sentences.

Which pictures show something you like to do in the summer? Pretend you are in one of the pictures. Think of some sentences that tell what you are doing. See how many different kinds of sentences you can use.

This unit tells about the four different kinds of sentences. You will learn new ways to write sentences. You will see how sentences are put together in a story.

LANGUAGE

Lesson 1: Understanding Sentences

Do you know how to bake sugar cookies? This recipe will show you how.
Crack an egg into the bowl. What great cookies we'll make!

The cookbook and the woman on television are using sentences to tell us something. The sentences are made up of words. Each sentence tells a complete thought. How many sentences are there?

Think and Discuss

Look again at the four sentences. How does each one begin? How does each one end?

Sometimes a group of words looks like a sentence, but it is not one. To know if a group of words is a sentence, read it carefully. Be sure it tells a complete thought.

Look at these groups of words.

1. The cookies.
2. The cookies are hot.

The first group of words does not tell a complete thought. Is it a sentence? The second group of words is a sentence. Why?

- A **sentence** is a group of words that tells a complete thought. Begin a sentence with a capital letter. Finish a sentence with an end mark.

Practice

A. Copy the groups of words that are complete sentences.

1. It was time for breakfast.
2. I sat down at the table.
3. Some corn flakes.
4. Poured a glass of milk.
5. Father gave me a bowl and a spoon.

B. Add words. Make these groups of words into complete sentences. Write the sentences. Remember to begin them correctly.

6. ______ like to bake cookies.
7. Sometimes I ______.
8. ______ helps me bake.
9. ______ are always good when they are hot.
10. I think that cookies ______.

Apply

C. 11.–15. Write five sentences. Tell about a food you like to make or to eat. Be sure to begin and end your sentences correctly.

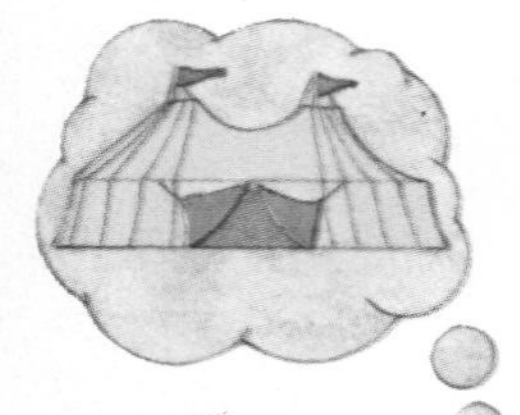

Lesson 2: Understanding Statements and Questions

Read what the boys are saying.

1. The circus will be here tomorrow.
2. Are you going to see it?

Think and Discuss

A sentence that tells something is called a **statement.** It ends with a **period (.)**. Which sentence above is a statement?

A sentence that asks something is called a **question.** It ends with a **question mark (?).** Which sentence above is a question?

What begins both a question and a statement? A capital letter begins every kind of sentence.

- A **statement** tells something. It ends with a period.
- A **question** asks something. It ends with a question mark.

Practice

A. Read these sentences. If the sentence tells something, write *This is a statement.* If it asks something, write *This is a question.*

1. We walked downtown.
2. Where was the circus?
3. We saw many big vans.
4. Lions were in one of them.
5. Did those men come to feed the lions?

B. Write each sentence. Use capital letters and end marks correctly.

6. men led the lions into a building
7. is the circus in that building
8. four elephants walked into the building
9. now we know where the circus is
10. can we go in and look around

Apply

C. 11.–15. Close your book. Write sentences 1–5 as your teacher reads them. Use capital letters and end marks correctly.

HOW OUR LANGUAGE GROWS

Braille is the name of a special alphabet. It was invented by a blind man named Louis Braille. The Braille alphabet is made up of dots. These dots are raised on a sheet of metal or plastic. Blind people can read the Braille letters by running their fingers along the dots. Many books are printed in Braille.

Here are some letters in the Braille alphabet:

A B C D E F G H I

1. What word do these Braille letters spell?
2. Spell these words using the Braille alphabet.

cab fed big head

Lesson 3: Understanding Sentences That Give Orders

Sometimes Maria's mother needs to give Maria orders or directions. On a rainy day Maria's mother might give her these directions.

1. Wear your raincoat.
2. Put on your boots.
3. Take an umbrella with you.

Think and Discuss

A sentence that gives an order or a direction is called a **command.** It ends with a period. Each of the sentences above gives an order or a direction. How do the sentences begin? How do they end?

A command is a third kind of sentence. You have already learned about two others. They are statements and questions. We use all three kinds of sentences every day.

Now read these sentences.

4. Where are you, Maria?
5. Come inside now.
6. It is raining very hard.

Which sentence gives an order? Which one is a statement? Which one asks a question?

- A **command** gives an order or a direction. It ends with a period.

Practice

A. Find the six sentences that give orders. Write them on your paper. Be sure to begin and end each sentence correctly.

1. clean your room, Jody
2. pick up your clothes
3. hang them in the closet
4. make your bed
5. what is all that I see under your bed
6. it looks like junk to me
7. clean under your bed, Jody
8. take out the trash
9. have you dusted the shelves
10. you are doing a great job

Apply

B. Write a command to go with each picture.

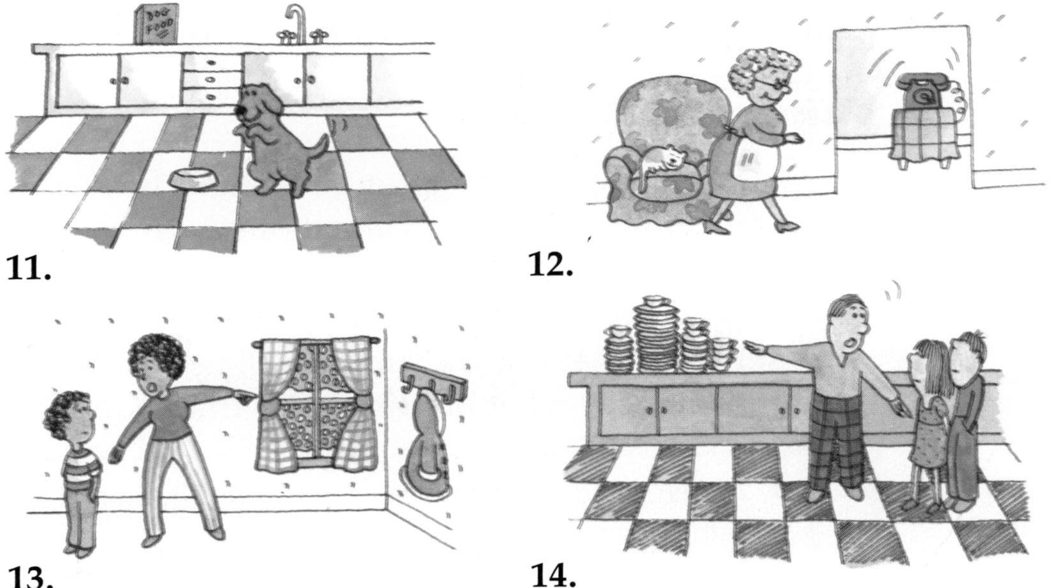

Lesson 4: Understanding Sentences That Exclaim

Sometimes you are glad, excited, surprised, angry, or frightened. At those times what you say may show how you feel.

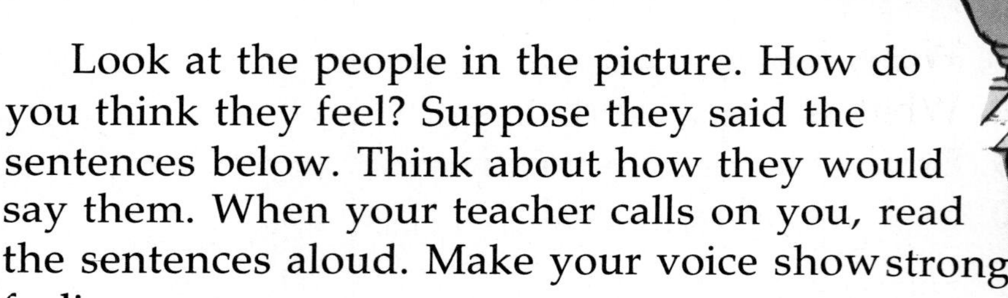

Look at the people in the picture. How do you think they feel? Suppose they said the sentences below. Think about how they would say them. When your teacher calls on you, read the sentences aloud. Make your voice show strong feeling.

1. Hooray, here comes the parade!
2. What a loud noise the drums make!
3. How funny the clowns are!

Think and Discuss

Some sentences show strong feeling. They are called **exclamations.** End exclamations with an **exclamation point (!)**. How do sentences 1, 2, and 3 begin? How do they end?

A sentence that shows strong feeling is another kind of sentence. What are the other three kinds?

- An **exclamation** shows strong feeling. It ends with an exclamation point.

Practice

A. Copy on your paper only the sentences that show strong feeling.

1. Help me find my brother.
2. Hooray, here comes my brother now!
3. He is learning how to ride a bike.
4. He does not ride too well yet.
5. How frightened he looks!
6. Where is my brother going?
7. He should be careful.
8. Wow, he crashed!
9. What an accident that was!
10. I think my brother needs more practice.

B. Correctly write these sentences that show strong feeling. Begin and end each one correctly.

11. what a great day this is
12. wow, we are going to the circus
13. how brave the lion tamer is
14. what big teeth the lions have
15. what beautiful costumes there are

Apply

C. 16.–20. Pretend that you are riding a roller coaster at the park. Think of five sentences to show your strong feelings about the ride. Would you be excited? Would you feel frightened? Write the sentences on your paper. End each one correctly.

Lesson 5: Understanding Parts of a Sentence

Read these word groups.

1. A new store
2. opened yesterday.

If you put word groups 1 and 2 together, you can make a sentence. Try it. What does the sentence say? Every sentence has two parts. When you put them together, you make a complete thought.

Think and Discuss

The part of a sentence about which something is being said is called the **subject.** Subjects can be persons, places, or things. The subject usually comes at the beginning of the sentence. Which word group above could be the subject of a sentence?

A second important part of a sentence is the **predicate.** The predicate says something about the subject. The predicate usually comes after the subject of a sentence. Which word group above could be the predicate of a sentence?

Read this sentence.

3. Susan bought a book at the store.

Which part is the subject? How do you know? Which part is the predicate? How do you know?

- The **subject** of the sentence is the part about which something is being said.
- The **predicate** is all the words that tell something about the subject.

Practice

A. Copy these sentences. Draw one line under the subjects.

1. I walked into the store.
2. The store was very large.
3. Many people walked through the aisles.
4. Dresses hung from big racks.
5. The counters were filled with shirts.

B. Copy these sentences. Draw two lines under the predicates.

6. The store sells many bikes.
7. It has fishing poles too.
8. I saw baseballs and softballs.
9. A tent sat in one corner.
10. I like the toys in that store.

Apply

C. Decide whether these word groups could be used as subjects or predicates. Then write a sentence using each word group.

11. Tim **12.** the cat **13.** can write
14. sits in a chair **15.** that brown book

Lesson 6: Using Subjects and Predicates

Mario is playing with puzzle cards. His baby sister tried to help. Look at the sentence she made. What is wrong with it?

Every sentence has two important parts: the subject and the predicate. The subject and the predicate must go together so that the sentence makes good sense.

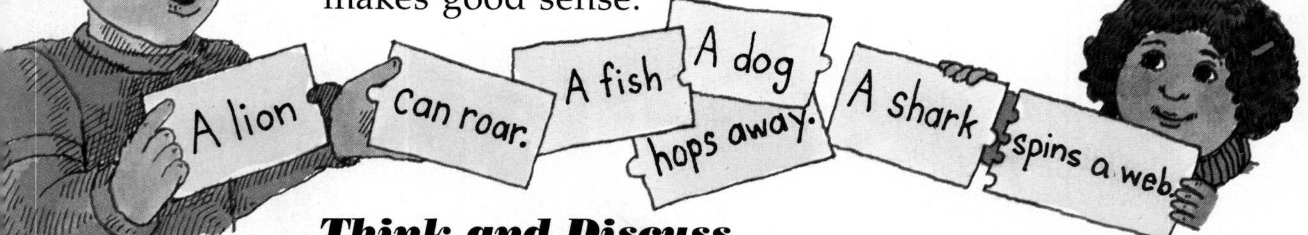

A lion can roar. A fish A dog hops away. A shark spins a web.

Think and Discuss

You need to read a sentence through carefully to see if the subject and the predicate make sense together. Read the sentences below. Do they make good sense?

1. A fish climbs a tree.
2. A fish swims in a bowl.

The subject and the predicate in sentence 1 do not match. The sentence does not make good sense. Sentence 2 does make sense. The subject and the predicate go together.

Suppose you were given this subject to begin a sentence:

3. A tiger . . .

What predicate could you add so that the complete sentence would make sense?

Practice

A. Choose a subject from the box to finish each sentence. Write the sentence on your paper.

A turtle	An elephant	A bird
A shark	A spider	

1. ______ lives in a nest.
2. ______ has a long trunk.
3. ______ hides in its shell.
4. ______ chases fish in the ocean.
5. ______ spins a silky web.

B. Choose a predicate from the box to finish each sentence. Write the sentence on your paper.

purrs and drinks milk.	hides nuts in a tree.
swims in salt water.	hops through the field.
quacks and dives.	shakes its mane.

6. A kitten ______
7. A rabbit ______
8. A whale ______
9. A duck ______
10. A squirrel ______
11. A horse ______

Apply

C. Finish these sentences. Write a subject or a predicate of your own.

12. Roosters ______
13. A goldfish ______
14. Tigers ______
15. ______ live at a zoo.

Lesson 7: Changing Word Order in Sentences

Read sentences 1 and 2.

1. Can you come over to my house?
2. You can come over to my house.

Which sentence is a question? Which is a statement?

Think and Discuss

Sentences 1 and 2 are very much alike. Which words changed places? How does sentence 1 end? How does sentence 2 end?

You can sometimes change the order of words in a question to make a statement. The statement will answer the question.

Read these questions. Change the order of the underlined words. Read the new statement.

3. <u>Is</u> <u>this</u> a new book?
4. <u>Can</u> <u>you</u> watch television now?
5. <u>Should</u> <u>we</u> do our homework first?

Practice

A. Read the questions. Change the order of the underlined words. Write the new statements. Remember to capitalize the first word. Use the correct end mark.

1. <u>Can</u> <u>you</u> make potato salad?
2. <u>Should</u> <u>you</u> boil the potatoes?

3. Will you chop some celery and onions?
4. Did you add the seasoning?
5. Are you ready to eat?

B. Make these questions into statements. Write the statements.

6. Can you make grilled cheese sandwiches?
7. Will you put cheese between two bread slices?
8. Should you melt some butter in a pan?
9. Will you put the sandwich in the pan?
10. Should the heat be low?
11. Is it easy to peek under the sandwich to check it?
12. Will you flip the sandwich over?

Apply

C. 13.–20. Write four questions that can be changed into statements. Then change the order of some words and write the statements.

A Challenge

Some questions cannot be made into statements by changing word order. Here is an example:

Why is Mary unhappy?

Can you think of other examples?

LANGUAGE REVIEW

Sentences pages 2–3

Copy the groups of words that are complete sentences. Write them correctly.

1. in the rain
2. the thunder crashed
3. we ran to the window
4. ran down the roof
5. the storm ended quickly

Statements and Questions pages 4–5

Write the sentences correctly. After each tell whether it is a statement or a question.

6. do you have a kite
7. I have a red one
8. it flies very well
9. can you see it
10. have you ever seen a better kite

Sentences That Give Orders pages 6–7

Copy only the sentences that give orders. Write them correctly.

11. Take this pen
12. Oh, my goodness
13. Are they here yet
14. Please sit down
15. Do not talk

Sentences That Exclaim pages 8–9

Copy only the sentences that exclaim. Write them correctly.

16. Watch out
17. Do you like it
18. Be careful
19. Help, I can't stop
20. This is delicious

Parts of a Sentence pages 10–11

Copy the sentences. Draw one line under the subjects. Draw two lines under the predicates.

21. Karen surprised me.
22. She had a party.
23. My friends were there.
24. We went skating.
25. My older brother fell down twice.

Using Subjects and Predicates pages 12–13

Pick the predicate that goes best with each subject. Write the new sentence.

26. People	is soft.
27. The sofa	grow by the window.
28. My bookcase	can sit in that chair.
29. Plants	open into the garden.
30. Two doors	has three shelves.

Word Order pages 14–15

Change the order of the words in each question to make a statement. Write the statement.

31. Have you read this?
32. Is Josh reading it?
33. May I see the book?
34. Have you finished?
35. Will you let me borrow it?

Applying Sentences

Add words to make these complete sentences. Write at least one of each of the four kinds of sentences.

36. animals in the desert
37. dry, hot weather
38. during the night
39. that small fox
40. snakes and lizards

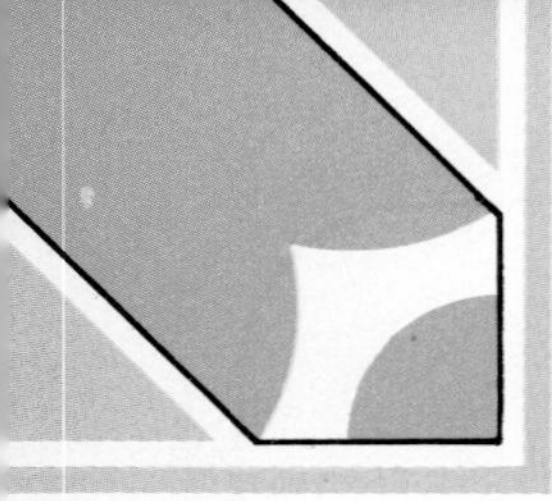

STUDY SKILLS

Lesson 8: Understanding the Parts of a Book

Look at these three pages from a book. The **title page** and **table of contents** are found at the front of a book. The **index** is usually found at the end.

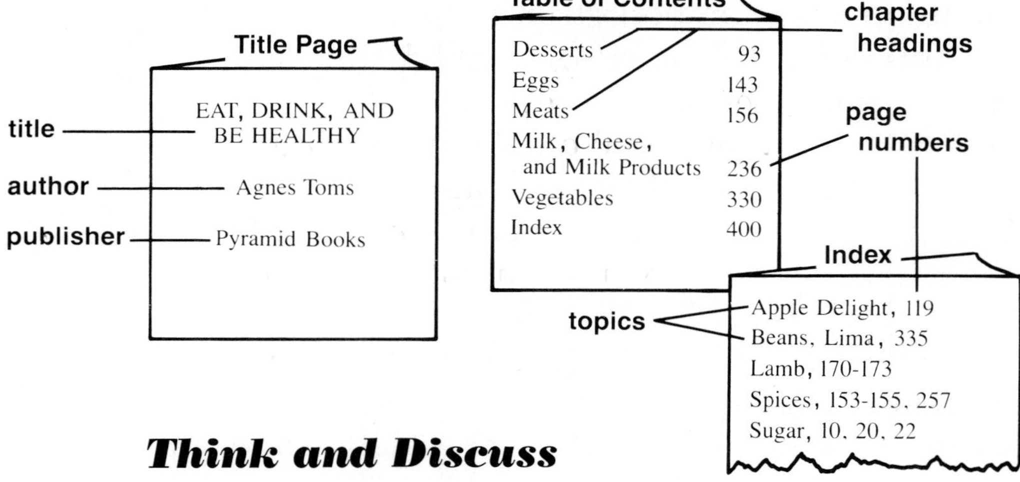

Think and Discuss

What is the name of the book? On what page will you find it? This page also tells you the name of the author. It tells the name of the company that published the book too.

The table of contents lists five chapters and the index. On what page does the chapter on vegetables begin?

Read the alphabetical list on the index page. On what pages would you learn about spices?

Practice

A. Use the three book pages on page 18 to complete each sentence.

1. You can find information about desserts beginning on page ______.
2. The chapter that begins on page 156 is called ______.
3. Information on sugar is found on pages ______, ______, and ______.
4. The chapter called "Eggs" begins on page ______.
5. Information on pork is on page 158. This is part of the chapter called ______.
6. The publisher of the book is ______.
7. To find out the name of the author, you would look on the ______ page.
8. The ______ lists topics in alphabetical order.
9. The ______ lists the page numbers where chapters begin.
10. You would use the ______ to find out the names of chapters.

Apply

B. Use the table of contents and the index of this book. Answer the questions.

11. On what page does Unit 3 begin?
12. On what page does Unit 7 begin?
13. How many lessons are there in Unit 5?
14. On what pages can you read about the encyclopedia?
15. On what pages can you read about maps?

Lesson 9: Using the Library

A library is carefully planned. There are special sections in all libraries. Knowing what is in the library will help you find things quickly.

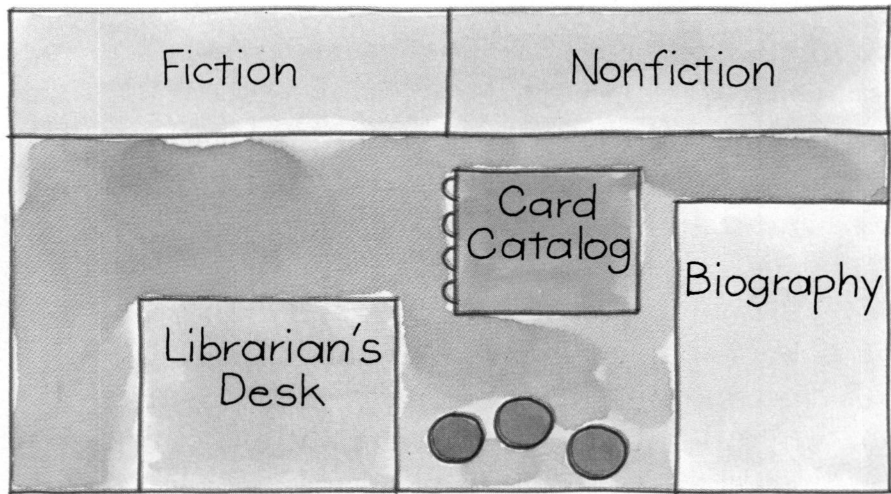

Think and Discuss

Some books tell stories. These books are **fiction.** They tell about make-believe people and things.

Other books tell about real things. They tell facts about people, places, and things. These books are **nonfiction.**

A nonfiction book about a real person is called a **biography.** Biographies are kept in a special section of the library.

Look at the map of the library. In what section would you find a storybook about an unhappy dragon? In what section would you find a book called *Facts About Dinosaurs*?

Librarians know many things about books. They can help you find the books you need.

You may also use the **card catalog** to find books. The card catalog has drawers filled with hundreds of cards. The cards tell you where books are located in the library. When you find the books you want, take them to the **librarian's desk.** The librarian will help you check the books out. Then you may take them home.

LIBRARIAN

Practice

A. Where would you find each of these books? Write *fiction, nonfiction,* or *biography.*

1. a book on birds of the world
2. the story of Peter Penguin and Sammy Seal
3. a book about Richard Byrd, the explorer
4. a book about growing roses
5. a book about a magic garden
6. a book about a talking flower
7. a book about George Washington Carver
8. a book about Beverly Sills
9. a book called *How to Speak Clearly*
10. the story of a singing robot

B. **11.–12.** List two ways you could find the books you need. Write two complete sentences.

Apply

C. **13.–15.** Visit your school or public library. Find a nonfiction book, a fiction book, and a biography. Write the names of each book. Share them with your class.

COMPOSITION

Lesson 10: Combining Sentences with and

Keith wrote two sentences about people who play in a band. Then he made some changes and wrote a third sentence. Read the sentences.

1. The band musicians practiced alone at home.
2. They also practiced together.
3. The band musicians practiced alone at home, and they also practiced together.

Think and Discuss

Keith used the word *and* to join sentences 1 and 2. Two sentences that tell about the same thing can often be joined using the word *and.*

Read sentence 3 again. Find the word *and.* A **comma** appears before the word *and* in sentence 3.

Now read these sentences.

4. The band members worked hard.
5. They enjoyed their work.

How could you combine these two sentences to make one? Where would you put the comma?

- Use a comma before the word *and* when two sentences are joined together.

Practice

A. Copy each sentence and underline the word *and.* Put a comma where it belongs.

1. The concert hall opens and the people walk in.
2. The musicians' chairs are placed on stage and music stands are put nearby.
3. The musicians arrive and they find their seats.
4. The conductor walks on stage and he bows.
5. He turns to the band and he waits for quiet.

B. Combine each pair of sentences with the word *and.* Write the new sentences. Remember to use commas where they are needed.

6. The conductor lifts his baton. The music begins.
7. The violins play first. Soon the flutes join in.
8. The drum beats softly. The trumpets play.
9. The music is beautiful. The people enjoy it.
10. The band finishes playing. The people clap.

Apply

C. Read each sentence. For each one write another short sentence. Be sure the two sentences tell about the same thing. Then join the two sentences.

11. Dave saw the concert.
12. The children found their seats.
13. A piano played first.
14. Dave can play the piano.
15. He enjoyed the concert.

Lesson 11: Varying Sentence Beginnings

Judy wrote about her trip to the city. Read her sentences.

1. We visited our grandmother last weekend. We took a bus to the city. We went to the zoo Saturday. We went sightseeing Sunday afternoon. We took the bus back home last night.

What word begins every sentence?

Think and Discuss

Judy used the word *we* to begin every sentence. Judy decided to write the sentences over. She changed the words around in some of the sentences so that the sentences would begin in more interesting ways.

Read Judy's new sentences.

2. Last weekend we visited our grandmother. We took a bus to the city. Saturday we went to the zoo. Sunday afternoon we went sightseeing. Last night we took the bus back home.

How did Judy begin her first sentence? How did she begin her third sentence? How many sentences begin with the word *we* in example 2?

Read items 1 and 2 again. You can see that Judy used the same words in both. She simply changed the order to improve her sentences.

Practice

A. Think of another way to begin each sentence. Write the new sentences.

1. I went to the beach last summer.
2. I would like to go again this year.
3. I stayed with my cousin last year.
4. I may be able to stay with her next summer.
5. I will write to her tomorrow and ask her.

B. Copy each sentence. Underline the word that could be used to begin the sentence in a different way. Then write the sentence over. Begin it with the word you underlined.

6. Bill and Ellen took a train trip Friday.
7. They visited some friends yesterday.
8. They came back on the train today.
9. They will write to their friends tonight.
10. They are now planning another trip.

Apply

C. 11.–15. Write five sentences about a weekend trip you would like to take. Save your sentences for the next lesson.

To Memorize

Lost time is never found again.

Benjamin Franklin

How can time be lost? Can we ever get it back?

Lesson 12: Editing Sentences

Ellen wrote five sentences. She decided to **edit** the sentences. Editing means finding and correcting mistakes in your writing. What mistakes did Ellen find?

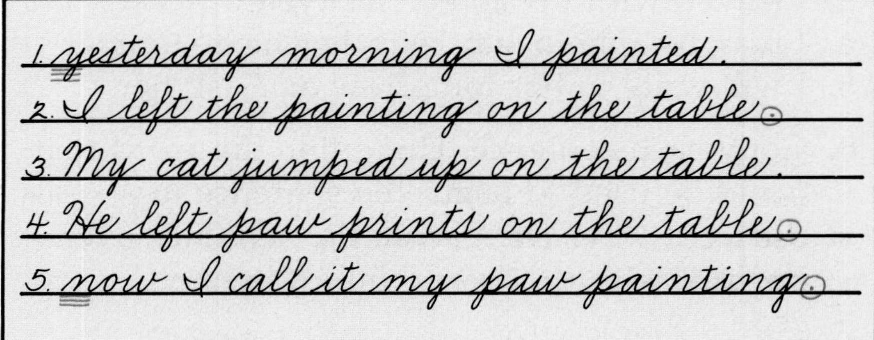

1. yesterday morning I painted.
2. I left the painting on the table
3. My cat jumped up on the table.
4. He left paw prints on the table
5. now I call it my paw painting

- capitalize
- make a period
- add something
- add a comma
- add quotation marks
- take something away
- spell correctly
- indent the paragraph
- make a lowercase letter
- transpose

Think and Discuss

Ellen used editing marks to show her mistakes. Sentences 1 and 5 did not begin with capital letters. Ellen used this mark ≡ to show that. How should all sentences end? This mark ⊙ means to add a period. Where did Ellen add periods?

Practice

A. Rewrite Ellen's sentences correctly.

Apply

B. Edit the sentences you wrote in Lesson 11. Did you begin each sentence with a capital letter? Did you finish each sentence with an end mark? Did you begin your sentences in different ways? Use the editing marks to correct your sentences. When you finish editing them, copy them over.

MECHANICS PRACTICE

Writing Sentences

- Use a period at the end of a statement or command.
- Use a question mark at the end of a question.
- Use an exclamation point at the end of an exclamation.
- Use a comma before the word *and* when two sentences are joined together.
- Begin a sentence with a capital letter.

A. Copy these sentences. Add capital letters and end marks.

1. do you have a pet
2. yes, I have a dog
3. what kind of dog is it
4. it is a beagle
5. what a great dog it is
6. watch it run
7. beagles are very smart
8. is that true
9. where did it go
10. here it is

B. Add capital letters and commas to these sentences. Write the sentences.

11. rats came to Hamelin and they ate all the grain.
12. people saw the piper and he came up with a plan.
13. he led the rats away and the crowds cheered.
14. the piper asked to be paid and the mayor said he would have to wait.
15. the piper played his flute and all the children followed.

LITERATURE

Lesson 13: Reading a Story

You know how to write good sentences. Good sentences can be put together to tell a story. Read this story about Timothy and his grandfather.

Timothy and Gramps

by Ron Brooks

Gramps always took Timothy to school in the mornings and home again in the afternoons.

Timothy didn't like school much. He had no brothers or sisters, and he had no special friends, except for Gramps. They went on walks together. Gramps told Timothy stories, and Timothy told Gramps stories.

At school Timothy played mostly by himself. In the mornings, for *Show and Tell,* other children had pets to show to the rest of the class, and stories to tell about things they had done with friends. Sometimes they just brought something they had found, and talked about that. Timothy had no pet of his own, and he could never seem to find anything special enough to bring and show.

Once or twice, Timothy asked Gramps if he would stay a little while. He wanted to talk about his grandfather, but he could not decide quite how to begin. Gramps did not know what to say either. He just said "Good morning . . . ," and then he went home. He gave it some thought, though, and the next day, he came back. Much to everyone's delight, he sat down and told them all a good long story.

After Gramps had gone, all the other children crowded around Timothy and asked him to tell them more about his grandfather. After a while Timothy did. He told them Gramps's own, special story.

From then on, school didn't seem half so bad.

Think and Discuss

The people in a story are the **characters.** The main character is the person about whom the story is written. Who is the main character in this story?

You learn many things about characters in a story. Some things are told to you. What did the author tell you about Timothy?

You learn other things by the way a character acts. The things the character does tell you more about him or her. What did you learn about Timothy by the way he acts?

Every story has a **setting.** The setting is the place where the story happens. A story may have more than one setting. What is the main setting in the story you read?

Characters and settings are important features of every story. If the author describes them well, they will hold the reader's interest.

Practice

A. Answer these questions in full sentences.

1. Who are the characters in this story?
2. Who is the main character?
3.–4. List two things you learned about Gramps.
5. Part of the story takes place at Gramps's house. What is the other setting in the story?

B. **6.–10.** Write five sentences that describe Timothy. Think about these questions: What kind of person is he? What does he do at home and at school?

Apply

C. 11.–15. Think about the main character in a story you like. How does he or she look or act? Write five sentences that tell about this character. Then draw a picture of the character in a setting from the story.

A BOOK TO READ

Title: **Horace Morris**
Author: Linda Heller
Publisher: Macmillan

The Pottertons have invited Horace to dinner, but nobody is home when he arrives. At last, Emmaline dashes in with a ridiculous excuse for being late. Then Mrs. Potterton rushes in. She claims that strange birds ate her cake while she was on the bus. Finally, Mr. Potterton comes home. He says that his car was flooded with molasses and chased by bees!

Are the Pottertons making silly excuses because they don't like Horace any more? Read this hilarious book and learn the truth.

1 UNIT TEST

Sentences pages 2–3

In each set write the letter for the group of words that is *not* a sentence.

1. a. Bats fly at night.
   b. Sound guides them.
   c. Sleep all day.
2. a. Bats are mammals.
   b. Many different bats.
   c. This is a bat cave.
3. a. Bats scare me.
   b. Their ears are huge.
   c. Darting and turning.
4. a. On a moonlit night.
   b. I heard their squeaks.
   c. Dr. Li studies bats.

Statements and Questions pages 4–5

Copy these sentences. Place a question mark or a period at the end of each sentence.

5. Will you go to the parade this afternoon
6. Three high school bands will be marching
7. My father will ride his horse in the parade
8. Is your sister going to be a baton twirler
9. Do you know at what time the parade begins
10. Are they going to march down Center Street

Sentences That Give Orders pages 6–7

Write only the sentences that give orders or directions.

11. Go to the car.
12. Check the tires.
13. Ali can drive.
14. She takes lessons.
15. Stop at the corner.
16. Mother teaches her.

17. Signal before turning.
18. Pull the hand brake.
19. She tries to park.
20. She hits the curb.

Sentences That Exclaim pages 8–9

Copy these sentences. Add an end mark to make them show strong feeling.

21. Help me
22. Look at them run
23. Slow down
24. That is amazing
25. Here they come
26. He is terrific
27. Watch out
28. I am so excited
29. Hooray for Ed
30. My, this is fun

Parts of a Sentence pages 10–11

Draw one line under the subjects. Draw two lines under the predicates.

31. Linda cooked breakfast for her family.
32. Grandfather toasted some muffins and rolls.
33. Our whole family cooks together.
34. Billy poured orange juice for everyone.
35. My brothers made popcorn last night.

Using Subjects and Predicates pages 12–13

Finish these sentences. Write a subject or a predicate of your own.

36. ______ sails across the lake.
37. The lake ______.
38. ______ goes sailing every Saturday.
39. Our club ______.
40. You and I ______.
41. Charlie ______.
42. ______ painted the sailboat.
43. ______ shone brightly.
44. The sailboat ______.
45. ______ swam to the raft.

Word Order pages 14–15

Change these questions to statements. Write them correctly.

46. Did tribes hunt buffalo for food?
47. Can herds run quickly to escape?
48. Were tribes able to track the buffalo?
49. Can you still find buffalo today?
50. Have you seen herds in Yellowstone Park?

Parts of a Book pages 18–19

Tell where you would look to answer each question. Write *title page, table of contents,* or *index.*

1. What is the title of the book?
2. On what page does chapter two begin?
3. On what page is information about bees?
4. Who is the author of the book?
5. What is the title of the last chapter?

The Library pages 20–21

Finish these sentences. Use the correct word: *fiction, nonfiction,* or *biography.*

6. ______ books are stories that are made up by an author.
7. A ______ tells the life story of a real person.
8. ______ books contain facts about people, places, and things.
9. A book called *Facts About Space* would be found in the ______ section.
10. A book called *The Life of Abraham Lincoln* would be found in the ______ section.
11. A ______ book could be about elves.
12. *The Life of Cecil B. DeMille* is a ______.
13. *How to Carve Wood* would be in the ______ section.
14. *Twyla Tharp* is a ______ of a dancer.
15. *Ghosts and Goblins* would be in the ______ section.

Sentence Combining with <u>and</u> pages 22–23

Combine each pair of sentences with the word *and.* Write the new sentences.

1. Elise kicked the ball. Chris caught it.
2. Keith skates to the goal. Guy follows him.
3. Aileen ran fast. Wendy could not catch her.
4. Lou brings up the anchor. She waves good-by.
5. Sean brought the bat. Stacy brought the ball.

Writing and Editing Sentences pages 26–27

Write a sentence telling about each of these places. Then edit the sentences for capital letters and end marks.

6. a tree house
7. a zoo
8. a toy store
9. a skyscraper
10. an airport

Reading a Story pages 28–31

Read this beginning of a story. Write the answers to the questions in complete sentences.

Mystery by the River

Laura and her younger brother, Jeff, were hiking in a state park in Indiana. They stopped to eat lunch at the river's edge. It was there that Laura found the cave.

It was just a small cave with a tiny opening behind a hedge by the river. Laura wanted to explore it, but Jeff was sure that there were bats inside.

Laura and Jeff went back to their campsite to get a flashlight. Then they returned to the cave.

"You go first," said Laura. "You're smaller."

1. Who are the characters in this story?
2. What is the setting of the story?

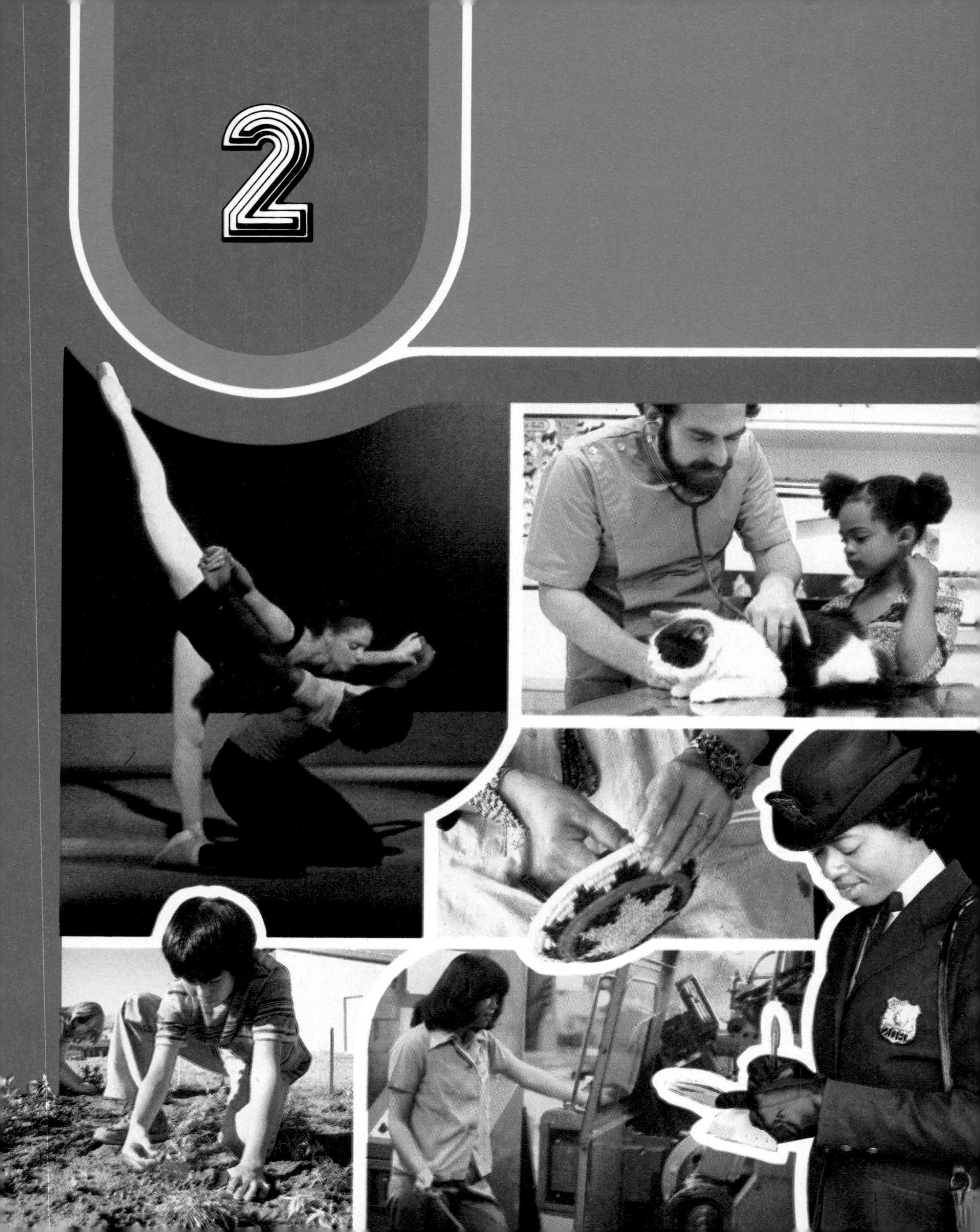
2

LANGUAGE
Learning About Nouns
COMPOSITION
Writing Sentences
STUDY SKILLS
Finding Information
LITERATURE
Reading a True Story

Most people have at least two names. Many people have three or more. What are your first and last names? Do you have a middle name? Which name do you like best?

There are other words you can use to name yourself too. Which of these words name you?

boy	girl	son	daughter
brother	sister	cousin	grandchild
camper	swimmer	runner	reader

In this unit you will learn about words that name people, places, and things. You will write about people. You will read a true story about a real person.

Look at the pictures on page 36. Some show young people. Some show people in places they work. What people, places, and things can you name in each picture?

LANGUAGE

Lesson 1: Understanding Nouns

People have names. Places you visit and things you use have names too. Read these sentences. Look at the words that name a person, a place, and a thing.

1. This is your pilot speaking.
2. We will be landing in Denver soon.
3. Please stay in your seat.

Think and Discuss

Words that name people, places, or things are called **nouns.** In sentences 1–3 the underlined words are nouns. *Pilot* names a person. Which noun names a place? Which noun names a thing?

Airports are interesting places to visit. Imagine that you are at an airport. What are some things you may find at an airport? What kind of people might you find? What are some places to which you would like to fly in an airplane? All of your answers are nouns.

- A **noun** is a word that names a person, place, or thing.

Practice

A. Find the nouns in each group of words. Write only the nouns.

1. Brad	above	Grandmother	Susan
2. yard	Texas	Mexico City	soon
3. jeans	read	toothbrush	camera

B. Each sentence has two nouns. Copy each sentence. Underline each noun.

4. Tom and Sue are very excited.
5. The children are at the airport.
6. Uncle Frank is flying in from Boston.
7. The airplane should arrive in Dallas shortly.
8. Many people are watching the planes land and take off.
9. Tom likes to look out of the large windows.
10. Sue wishes to fly to San Francisco someday.

Apply

C. Use each noun in a complete sentence.

11. fog **12.** Chicago **13.** sailor
14. lake **15.** boat

Lesson 2: Understanding Singular and Plural Nouns

Look at the picture. You will see that the first rancher saw only one coyote. The other rancher saw many coyotes.

Think and Discuss

The word *coyote* is a noun. When we talk about one coyote, the noun is **singular.**

If we talk about more than one coyote, the noun is **plural.** To form the plural of most nouns, you add *s* to the singular noun. What is the plural form for the noun *coyote*? Name some other nouns in the picture. What must you add to each noun to show more than one?

Now read these sentences.

1. The cow is lost by the river.
2. A rancher rides down the hill.

What are the nouns in sentences 1 and 2? What is the plural form of each noun?

- A **singular noun** names one person, place, or thing.
- A **plural noun** names more than one person, place, or thing.
- To form the plural of most nouns, add *s*.

Practice

A. Read each sentence. If the underlined word is singular, write *singular noun.* If the underlined word is plural, write *plural noun.*

1. A desert is a place with little water.
2. Most deserts are hot.
3. The sun and wind make deserts dry too.
4. Many deserts have unusual plants.
5. Desert land has beautiful colors.

B. Write each sentence. Use the plural forms of the nouns in ( ).

6. Desert lands are the homes of ______ and birds. (animal)
7. Some ______ grow in the desert too. (plant)
8. The dune primrose has white ______. (blossom)
9. One plant has bell-shaped ______. (flower)
10. The ______ on the cactus are sharp. (thorn)

Apply

C. Use plural forms of these nouns in sentences.

11. bike **12.** road **13.** rider
14. wheel **15.** mile

Lesson 3: Forming Plural Nouns

The letter *s* is added to form the plural of most nouns. Some plural nouns are formed in other ways. Read these sentences.

1. The walrus swims in its pool.
2. The walruses swim in their pool.

Which sentence has a plural noun?

Think and Discuss

Look at the animals in the zoo. Find an animal whose name ends with *s*. Find an animal whose name ends with *x*.

Here is a list of the animals shown on this page. Read the nouns and their plural forms.

3. walrus—walruses
4. fox—foxes
5. ostrich—ostriches
6. thrush—thrushes

What ending was added to each word to make it plural?

- To form the plural of nouns ending in *s*, *x*, *ch*, or *sh*, add *es*.

Practice

A. Write the plural forms of these nouns.

1. bench	**2.** class	**3.** lunch	**4.** box
5. wish	**6.** sandwich	**7.** kiss	**8.** bush
9. ax	**10.** bus		

B. Copy these sentences. Finish them with plural nouns from Practice A. Use each word only once.

11. Two third-grade ______ went to the zoo.
12. They brought their ______ and ate cheese ______ in the park nearby.
13. Some children sat on the park ______.
14. Others sat near a clump of ______.
15. After the visit, the school ______ took them home again.

Apply

C. Pretend you are in a pet shop. Write five sentences about the things you see. Use plural forms of the nouns below.

16. lynx **17.** leash **18.** finch
19. perch **20.** octopus

To Memorize

Do you ever look in the looking glass
And see a stranger there?
A child you know and do not know,
Wearing what you wear?

Gwendolyn Brooks

What does this poem mean to you? Do you always see the same thing when you look in the mirror?

Lesson 4: Forming Other Plural Nouns

Some nouns change a letter before they add a plural ending. Read these sentences.

1. My puppy played in the field.
2. My puppies played in the field.
3. The boy played with the puppy.
4. The boys played with the puppy.

Which sentences have underlined plural nouns?

Think and Discuss

The noun *puppy* ends with a consonant and *y*. To spell the plural form, the *y* is changed to *i*. What ending is added?

The noun *boy* ends with a vowel and *y*. To spell the plural form, add *s*. Now read these sentences.

5. I see butterflies fluttering by.
6. Daisies bloom in the field.

How do you say the plural form of each noun? How were the nouns *butterfly* and *daisy* made plural? Spell each plural.

- To form the plurals of nouns that end in a consonant and *y*, change *y* to *i* and add *es*.

Practice

A. Write the plural form of each noun below.

1. pony **2.** party **3.** day **4.** lady **5.** fly
6. baby **7.** cherry **8.** sky **9.** dairy **10.** toy

B. Write these sentences. Use plural nouns from Practice A. Use each word only once.

11. My father has 100 cows in his ______.
12. My father also has ______ for me to ride.
13. The cows swish their tails if ______ bother them.
14. My mother has a fruit tree with ______ on it.
15. I feed the pigs and their ______, the piglets.

C. These sentences have singular nouns of all kinds. Make each noun plural. Write the sentences.

16. We visited the city.
17. We saw the tall building.
18. They went to the museum.
19. We sat on the bench outside.
20. We unpacked our lunch box.
21. Everyone enjoyed the lunch.
22. The boy sat with me.
23. We saw the aquarium.
24. I liked the octopus best.
25. He liked the guppy.

Apply

D. Imagine that you are on a trip to a farm in winter. Write five sentences about what you might do there. Use plural forms of these nouns.

26. pony **27.** family **28.** day
29. sky **30.** party

Lesson 5: Understanding Common and Proper Nouns

All of the underlined words in the sentences below are nouns. Read the sentences.

1. My friend lives in the city with her pet.
2. Kristin lives in Durham with Scooter.

Think and Discuss

Look at sentence 1. The underlined words name a person, a place, and a thing. Can you tell who the friend is? Can you tell which city is meant? Can you tell which pet is meant? *Friend, city,* and *pet* are **common nouns.** They name any person, place, or thing.

Some nouns name a special person, place, or thing. Which noun in sentence 2 names a special person? Which nouns name a special place and a special thing? Nouns that name special people, places, and things are **proper nouns.** A proper noun begins with a capital letter.

Read this sentence. Which words are common nouns? Which words are proper nouns?

3. Harry Shaw is a boy who lives on Apple Street in the city of Lincoln.

- A **common noun** names any person, place, or thing. It begins with a small letter.
- A **proper noun** names a special person, place, or thing. A proper noun begins with a capital letter.

Practice

A. Copy these sentences. Each sentence contains a common noun and a proper noun. Underline the common noun. Circle the proper noun.

1. We drove to the state of Ohio.
2. We stopped in the city of Cleveland.
3. A family named Wilson lived there.
4. We stayed in a motel called the Sweet Sleep Inn.
5. It was owned by a woman named Jan Cook.
6. We crossed the Cuyahoga River, a river that flows nearby.
7. Then we stopped in a large park called Metropolitan Park.
8. From there we drove onto a highway, the Ohio Turnpike.
9. Soon we passed by the town of Strongsville.
10. Ohio is an interesting place to visit.

Apply

B. 11.–16. Write one common noun and one proper noun for each of the following. Then use the nouns in sentences.

a person   a place   a thing

Lesson 6: Writing Names and Titles

Read these sentences. Look at the names.

1. Miss Nelson is a new teacher.
2. Ms. Gomez is her assistant.

Are the names common or proper nouns?

Think and Discuss

People's names are proper nouns. Some proper nouns begin with a **title.** The new teacher's title is *Miss.* What is her assistant's title? How does each title begin?

Look at the titles in these pictures.

Each title in the picture is an **abbreviation.** An abbreviation is a short way to write a word. For example, *Dr.* is a short way to write *doctor.* Abbreviations begin with a capital letter when they are used as titles. They end with a period.

Dr. Schatz used the **initial** *L.* on her nameplate. Her first name is *Louise.* An initial can take the place of a name. Initials are always capitalized.

Miss, Ms., and *Mrs.* are titles for women. *Mr.* is a title for men. *Dr.* can name women or men.

- Begin the name of a person with a capital letter.
- Begin titles of a person such as *Ms., Mrs., Mr.,* and *Dr.* with a capital letter.
- Use a period after an abbreviation.
- Capitalize initials that take the place of names.

Practice

A. Write these names correctly on your paper.

1. miss pepe
2. henry field
3. dr pearson
4. mrs pearson
5. ms l. f. cohen
6. dr jane lee

B. Choose a title to give to each person in these sentences. Write the sentences, using the titles.

7. Celia Jones is my neighbor.
8. Bob Jones is her husband.
9. Susan Ling lives two doors down from them.
10. Teresa Perez works in that office.

Apply

C. 11.–15. Write five sentences about people you know. Use a title with each person's name.

A Challenge

Do you know the words for which these abbreviations stand? Look them up in the dictionary.

1. Jr. **2.** Sr. **3.** U.S.A.

Lesson 7: Writing Names of Days, Months, and Holidays

Look at the calendar in the picture. Are the names of the days common nouns or proper nouns?

Think and Discuss

Notice the abbreviations for the days of the week. How does the abbreviation of each day begin? How does each abbreviation end?

Holidays are special days. Names of holidays begin with capital letters. What holiday is marked on the calendar above?

On every calendar page the name of a month also appears. What month is named on the calendar above? The names of some months have abbreviations. Read the list below. Which months do not have abbreviations?

January	Jan.	July	
February	Feb.	August	Aug.
March	Mar.	September	Sept.
April	Apr.	October	Oct.
May		November	Nov.
June		December	Dec.

- Begin the name of a day of the week or its abbreviation with a capital letter.
- Begin the name of a month or its abbreviation with a capital letter.
- Begin each important word in the name of a holiday with a capital letter.

Practice

A. Write these sentences correctly. Then write the abbreviations for each day and month.

1. School opens in september.
2. We do not have classes on saturday.
3. On tuesday we go to the library.
4. In november we have thanksgiving vacation.
5. School ends in june.

Apply

B. 6.–10. Write five sentences about winter.

HOW OUR LANGUAGE GROWS

The days were named long ago. Each day has an interesting meaning.

Sunday is sun day, or day of the sun.
Monday is moon day, or day of the moon.
Tuesday is Tiw's day. Tiw, or Tyr, was the Norse god of war.
Wednesday is Woden's day. Woden was the king of the gods.
Thursday is Thor's day. Thor was Woden's son.
Friday is Frigg's day. Frigg was Woden's sister.
Saturday is Saturn's day. Saturn was a Roman god.

1. Rename the days. Choose names that show what each day means to you.
2. Do you know how the months September, October, November, and December got their names? Use an encyclopedia to find out.

Lesson 8: Writing Names of Places

Joan's family is moving from Carson City to Santa Fe. Look at the map to see where she is going.

Think and Discuss

Read the words on the map that name the city where Joan lives now. Read the words that name the city to which her family is moving. How do these words begin? Are they common nouns or proper nouns?

Find some other proper nouns on the map. Which ones name cities? Which ones name states?

The names of countries are also proper nouns. The name of Joan's country is the *United States of America.* Small words such as *the* and *of* often do not begin with capital letters.

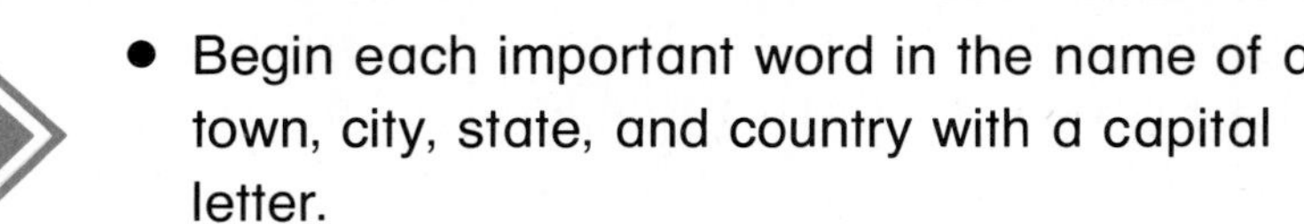

- Begin each important word in the name of a town, city, state, and country with a capital letter.

Practice

A. Study these sentences. Then close your book. Write the sentences as your teacher reads them.

1. Iowa is a state.
2. Canada is a country.
3. Mary lives in Ames.
4. Jack lives in Toronto.

B. Read these sentences. Copy the words that name special places on your paper.

5. My grandmother lives in a city named Helena.
6. The town of Garrison keeps getting bigger.
7. Which country is north of Mexico?

C. Write each sentence correctly on your paper.

8. The capital of georgia is atlanta.
9. The capital of france is paris.
10. london is the capital of england.
11. topeka is the capital of kansas.
12. The capital of delaware is dover.
13. The capital of nebraska is lincoln.
14. The capital of puerto rico is san juan.
15. rome is the capital of italy.

Apply

D. Complete each sentence with the name of a place. Write the sentences on your paper.

16. The city I live in is ______.
17. The state I live in is ______.
18. I was born in (country).
19. I would like to take a trip to (city), (state).
20. The country I would most like to visit is ______.

LANGUAGE REVIEW

Nouns pages 38–39

Copy each sentence. Underline two nouns in each.

1. Alexandra called to her mother.
2. The parade was coming by their house.
3. Two huge balloons were flying above a float.
4. They were shaped like a funny clown and a dog.
5. The girl and her friends enjoyed watching them.

Singular and Plural Nouns pages 40–41

Write the plural forms of these nouns.

6. kitten **7.** donkey **8.** bee
9. giraffe **10.** snake

Plurals That End in es pages 42–43

Write the plural forms of these nouns.

11. guess **12.** ash **13.** lunch
14. box **15.** match

Plurals That End in ies pages 44–45

Write the plural forms of these nouns.

16. pony **17.** poppy **18.** cherry
19. lily **20.** family

Common and Proper Nouns pages 46–47

Copy the sentences. Underline the common nouns. Circle the proper nouns.

21. Mrs. Allen works in the library on Monday.
22. She helps Mr. Mendosa arrange the books.

23. The library is on High Street and First Avenue.
24. Andy and Jeff are here during the summer.
25. Bradley likes books about cars and trains.

Names and Titles pages 48–49

Copy these names correctly on your paper.

26. miss danvers
27. mr g. f. broadstreet
28. dr samuelson
29. ms daniels
30. mrs a. nandi
31. ms king

Names of Days and Months pages 50–51

32.–50. Write the names of the days of the week and the months of the year. After each one, write its abbreviation, if it has one. Remember to use periods.

Names of Places pages 52–53

Write each sentence correctly.

51. Celeste lives in quebec, a city in canada.
52. Her family moved there from paris, france.
53. She will visit the united states of america.
54. Her first stop will be boston, massachusetts.
55. She will spend time in south carolina and kentucky.

Applying Nouns

Write the proper nouns correctly. Use each one in a complete sentence.

56. chicago, illinois
57. hawaii and alaska
58. mexico
59. london, england
60. oregon and idaho

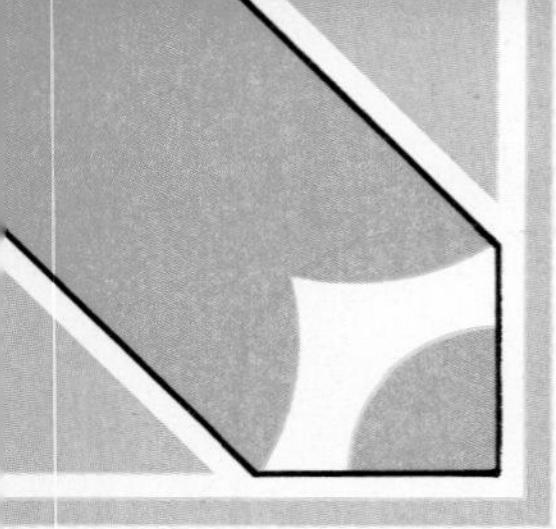

STUDY SKILLS

Lesson 9: Using Alphabetical Order

The order of letters from *A* to *Z* is called **alphabetical order.** We use alphabetical order to find words in the dictionary. Why is alphabetical order helpful?

Think and Discuss

Sometimes we use the first letter to put words in alphabetical order. Are these words in alphabetical order? Look at the first letter of each word to find out.

baker **d**entist **e**ngineer **t**eacher

The words below all begin with the letter *d*. Look at the second letter. The second letter of each word was used to arrange them in alphabetical order.

d**a**ncer d**e**ntist d**o**ctor d**r**iver

What do you do when the first two letters of each word are the same? You must look at the third letter of each word. Arrange these words in alphabetical order.

tr**o**oper tr**a**der tr**u**cker tr**e**asurer

Practice

A. Write each list of words in alphabetical order.

1. engineer, cook, typist, ballerina
2. nurse, pitcher, operator, plumber
3. teacher, barber, baker, artist
4. lawyer, doctor, governor, guide
5. sailor, secretary, soldier, singer

B. Are these job names in alphabetical order? Write *yes* if they are in order. Write the other lists in alphabetical order.

6. captain, carpenter, cashier
7. salesperson, sailor, singer
8. tailor, taster, teacher
9. mother, mover, model
10. coach, counselor, cook

Apply

C. Follow the directions to write each list. Each list must be in alphabetical order.

11. List the first names of five people you know.
12. List the names of the three months beginning with *J*.
13. List the names of three fruits beginning with *p*.
14. List three nouns that begin with *ne*.
15. List three streets near where you live.

Lesson 10: Using Guide Words

Peter is looking up the word *site* in the dictionary. He knows that the dictionary lists words in alphabetical order. Should Peter look at every page to find the word?

Think and Discuss

To find a word in the dictionary, think of its place in the alphabet. Words that begin with the letters *A* through *F* are in the front of the dictionary. Words that begin with *G* through *P* are in the middle. Words that begin with *Q* through *Z* are at the back. In what section will Peter find the word *site*?

Peter turns to page 691. Here is the top of that page.

sister 691 **size**

S

sis·ter [sis′tər] *n.* **1** A girl or woman having the same parents as another person of either sex. **2** A girl or woman associated with another or others, as through membership in a group or shared beliefs: sorority *sisters.*

sit-in [sit′in′] *n.* A demonstration in which people sit down in a public place and refuse to move as a protest against a policy or condition they think unjust.

sit·ting [sit′ing] *n.* **1** The act or position of a

Look at the two words at the top of the page. These are **guide words.** They tell Peter that *sister* is the first word listed on the page. *Size* is the last word listed. Other words on page 691 are listed in alphabetical order. They come between *sister* and *size.* Does *site* come between *sister* and *size* in alphabetical order? *Site* must be listed here.

Now look at these words. Which ones would be listed on page 691?

1. six 2. sink 3. skate 4. sit

Practice

A. Tell where you would find each word in the dictionary. Write *front, middle,* or *back.*

1. nest **2.** teapot **3.** value **4.** bridge
5. flower **6.** other **7.** golden **8.** reason
9. laugh **10.** dream **11.** change **12.** plant

B. Look at the guide words shown below. Write the words in each list that would be on the same page as those guide words.

eaves–eddy

13. ecology effect dune ebb

idyl–illness

14. Iceland igloo imp if

awaken–azure

15. ax awning automobile avenue

dump–duster

16. Dutch dunk dryer during

koala–Labrador

17. kumquat knight Korea ladder

Apply

C. Look up these words in the dictionary. Write the guide words under which each word is listed. Also write the number of the page.

18. owl **19.** hawk **20.** eagle

Lesson 11: Using Entry Words

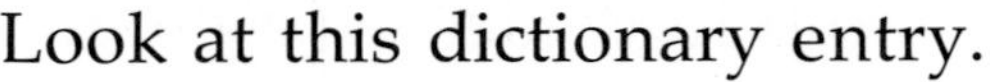

Look at this dictionary entry.

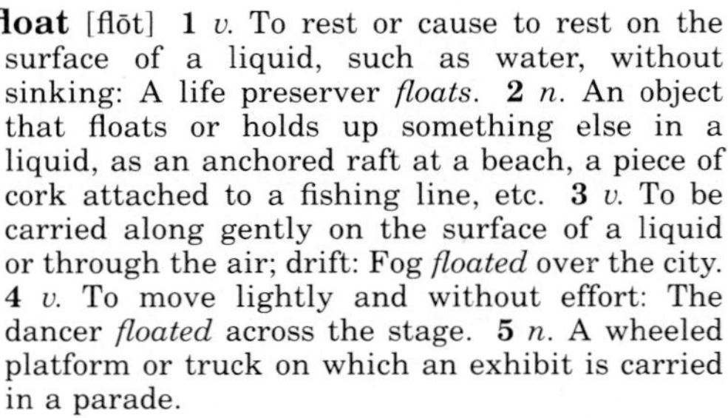

float [flōt] **1** *v.* To rest or cause to rest on the surface of a liquid, such as water, without sinking: A life preserver *floats.* **2** *n.* An object that floats or holds up something else in a liquid, as an anchored raft at a beach, a piece of cork attached to a fishing line, etc. **3** *v.* To be carried along gently on the surface of a liquid or through the air; drift: Fog *floated* over the city. **4** *v.* To move lightly and without effort: The dancer *floated* across the stage. **5** *n.* A wheeled platform or truck on which an exhibit is carried in a parade.

What is the word in dark black type?

Think and Discuss

The word *float* is an **entry word.** The dictionary lists information about entry words. It lists the **definition**, or meaning, of each word. Many words have more than one definition. Look at the numbered definitions above. How many definitions are listed for *float*? Can you find a picture on this page to match each definition?

The dictionary also tells how to pronounce words. Inside the brackets after the entry word is the **respelling** for that word. The respelling for *float* is [flōt]. The **pronunciation key** shows how the respelling is pronounced. Look at the key below. It shows that the *oa* in *float* [flōt] is pronounced like the *o* in *open.*

add, **ā**ce, **câ**re, p**ä**lm; **e**nd, **ē**qual; **i**t, **ī**ce; **o**dd, **ō**pen, **ô**rder; t**oo**k, p**oo**l; **u**p, b**û**rn; ə = a in *above,* e in *sicken,* i in *possible,* o in *melon,* u in *circus;* **yōō** = u in *fuse;* **oi**l; p**ou**t; **ch**eck; ri**ng**; **th**in; **th**is; **zh** in *vision.*

Practice

A. Use these entries to answer the questions.

> **cut·ter** [kut′ər] *n.* **1** A person or instrument that cuts: a paper *cutter.* **2** A small, armed ship, especially one used by the Coast Guard. **3** A boat carried by a ship to go to and from the ship. **4** A small sleigh. **5** A sailboat having a single mast.
>
> **dug·out** [dug′out′] *n.* **1** A boat made by hollowing out a log. **2** A shelter hollowed out in the earth. **3** A low, covered shelter at a baseball diamond, in which players sit when not in the field.
>
> **kay·ak** [kī′ak] *n.* An Eskimo canoe made of a light frame fully enclosed by skins, with an opening for the user.

1. What is the second entry word?
2. How many definitions does *cutter* have?
3. Which entry word has this respelling: [kut′ər]?
4. What is the third definition of *dugout*?
5. Is the *ay* in *kayak* pronounced like the *a* in *āce*?

B. Use the entries to answer these questions.

6. How many masts does a cutter have?
7. What kind of athlete would rest in a dugout?
8. Which Native Americans use a skin canoe?
9. Which boat is used by the Coast Guard?
10. Where could you take shelter from a storm?

Apply

C. Look up these words in a dictionary. Write the respelling and one definition for each word. Use each word in a sentence.

11. mast **12.** raft **13.** keel **14.** tugboat **15.** anchor

COMPOSITION

Lesson 12: Combining Subjects with and

Matt wrote a report about tugboats. Here are two sentences from his report.

1. Great ships use tugboats.
2. Barges use tugboats.

Matt thought of a better way to write the sentences. Here is what he wrote.

3. Great ships and barges use tugboats.

Think and Discuss

Matt combined the subjects of the two sentences. He used both subjects—*great ships* and *barges*—in his new sentence. *Great ships and barges* is the complete subject of sentence 3.

What is the predicate of sentences 1 and 2? When two sentences have the same predicate, the subjects can often be combined.

What word joined the subjects in Matt's new sentence? The word *and* is often used to combine the subjects of two sentences.

Now combine the subjects of these sentences.

4. Steamships wait in the harbor.
5. Tugboats wait in the harbor.

Practice

A. Underline the complete subject in each sentence.

1. The captain and her crew run the tugboat.
2. The captain and her assistant steer the boat.
3. The engineer and his helper keep the engines running.
4. The deck hands and a cook work on the tugboat.

B. Combine the subjects from each pair of sentences. Use the word *and.* Write the new sentences.

5. Shipowners met to have a tugboat built.
   Designers met to have a tugboat built.
6. The captain met with them.
   The engineers met with them.
7. Builders began to make the tugboat.
   Their workers began to make the tugboat.
8. The engines were put in place.
   The controls were put in place.
9. Ropes were placed on deck.
   Ladders were placed on deck.
10. The builders finished the little tugboat.
    Their workers finished the little tugboat.

Apply

C. Use each pair of common nouns in the subject of a sentence. Combine each pair with *and.*

11. oceans, lakes
12. ships, tugboats
13. ropes, sails
14. sailors, passengers

Lesson 13: Writing Sentences About People

Everyone has a name. Look at the famous Olympic stars in the pictures. What are their names?

Dorothy Hamill Wilma Rudolph Mark Spitz

How does each person's name begin?

Think and Discuss

The name of a person is a proper noun. Proper nouns are always capitalized. Read these sentences telling about the Olympic stars in the pictures.

1. In the 1960 Olympic Games Wilma Rudolph won three gold medals in track.
2. Dorothy Hamill received a gold medal in figure skating in 1976.
3. In 1972 Mark Spitz won seven gold medals in swimming.

Are the names in the sentences capitalized? Does each sentence begin with a capital letter? How does each sentence end?

Practice

A. These sentences are missing capital letters and end marks. Write the sentences correctly.

1. have you ever heard of dick fosbury
2. dick fosbury invented a new way to high jump and won a gold medal in 1968
3. rafer johnson won the decathlon in Rome in 1960
4. in 1976 nadia comaneci received seven perfect scores in gymnastics
5. emil zatopek and his wife, dana zatopek, won gold medals in the 1952 Olympics

B. Use the information about famous people. Write complete sentences.

6. John Curry—1976 Olympics—won gold medal in men's figure skating
7. Ruth Fuchs—won gold medal in women's javelin
8. Bruce Jenner—entered the decathlon, won for the United States
9. Nadia Comaneci—first perfect score of 10 in gymnastics
10. Rosi Mittermaier—won gold medal in skiing

Apply

C. **11.–15.** Write five sentences about famous people. Write one sentence about each person. Use the person's name in the sentence. Be sure to use capital letters correctly.

Lesson 14: Editing Sentences

Mary wrote some sentences about famous inventors. She edited the sentences before she copied them over. Read her edited sentences.

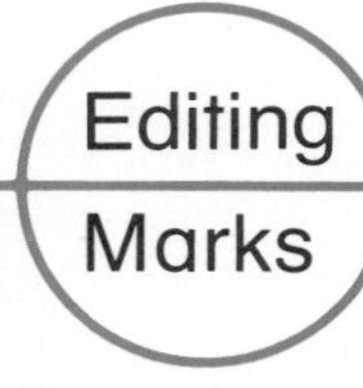

- ≡ capitalize
- ⊙ make a period
- ^ add something
- ^, add a comma
- ^“ ” add quotation marks
- take something away
- ◯ spell correctly
- ¶ indent the paragraph
- / make a lowercase letter
- ∿ tr transpose

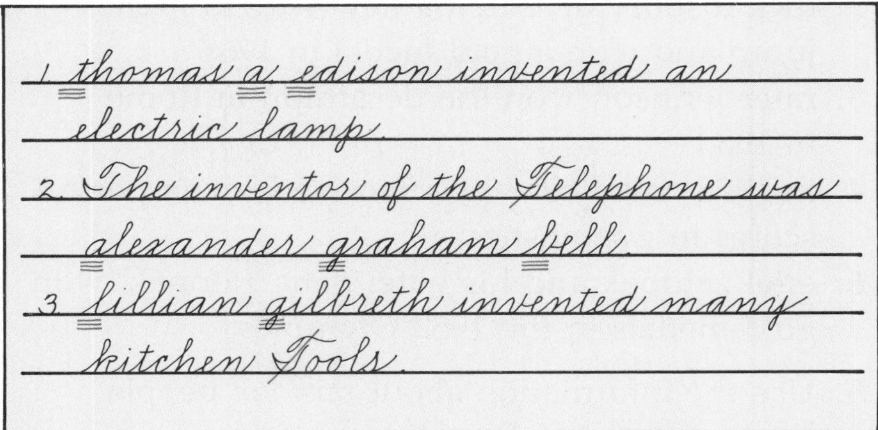

1 thomas a edison invented an
electric lamp.
2. The inventor of the Telephone was
alexander graham bell.
3 lillian gilbreth invented many
kitchen Tools.

Think and Discuss

In sentence 1 Mary did not remember to use capital letters for the inventor's name and initial. Where were capitals needed in sentences 2 and 3?

This editing mark / shows that a capital letter must be changed to a small letter. Why did Mary use this mark in sentences 2 and 3?

Practice

A. 1.–3. Rewrite Mary's sentences correctly.

Apply

B. 4.–8. Look back at the sentences you wrote in Lesson 13. Did you capitalize each person's name? Edit and rewrite your sentences.

MECHANICS PRACTICE

Writing Proper Nouns and I

- Begin proper nouns and titles with capital letters.
- Capitalize initials that take the place of names.
- Always capitalize the word *I*.
- Use a period after an abbreviation.

A. Write these proper nouns correctly.

1. lucy adams
2. dallas
3. mr t. alvarez
4. california
5. mrs pearl ames
6. sue reston
7. indiana
8. miss lucy smith
9. burlington
10. ohio

B. Write these sentences correctly.

11. alan b. shepard, Jr., was our first astronaut.
12. john glenn was the first person from the united states to orbit the Earth.
13. valentina tereshkova was the first woman in space.
14. edward h. white made the first space walk.
15. neil armstrong and edwin aldrin walked on the moon.
16. i would love to meet mr armstrong.
17. i would ask him how i could become an astronaut.
18. The astronauts train in houston, texas.
19. If possible, i would like to go to houston to visit dr wolf, a space scientist.
20. i hope to see a space flight at cape canaveral.

LITERATURE

Lesson 15: Reading About a Famous Person

Think of a famous person you admire. How would you find out more about this person? One way is to read about his or her life in a **biography.**

Think and Discuss

A biography tells the life story of a real person. Almost every famous person has a biography written about him or her. Many biographies have pictures of the person too.

The details in a biography are true. The events in a person's life are usually told in the order in which they happened. What part of a person's life would begin a biography? Most biographies start by telling about the person as a child. Then a biography gives facts about the person's later life. You learn why the person is famous. Some people make the world a better place in which to live. Some have great adventures. Others are the very best at what they do.

Read this true story about a famous teacher named Anne Sullivan. Her student, Helen Keller, became a famous American author. She was known throughout the world.

Annie Sullivan

by Mary Malone

When Annie Sullivan was ten she was an orphan. She was nearly blind, but she wanted to learn. She was able to go to the Perkins Institute for the Blind. She worked hard to learn to read Braille. Braille is the way blind people read by feeling raised dots on a page. She also learned how to talk to people who could not hear or see. She could tap words very quickly on their hands.

Annie was graduated from Perkins when she was twenty. She was first in her class. Soon after she graduated, she was offered a job.

Captain and Mrs. Keller of Tuscumbia, Alabama, wanted a teacher for their little girl, Helen. Helen was six years old. She was blind and deaf. She could not speak. Before she was two years old, an illness took away her sight, hearing, and speech. She lived in a world of darkness.

Annie struggled to teach Helen. She began by spelling words into Helen's hands. Helen did not understand what words were. She did not know that everything has a name. She did not know that words can be put into sentences.

Annie taught Helen to know many things by touching and smelling them. Her fingers kept tapping the words for them into Helen's hand. Still Helen didn't understand.

Annie thought of a way to help Helen. She took Helen to the outdoor water pump. Helen held a mug while water was pumped into it. The cold water spilled over Helen's hand. Annie spelled *water* as

this happened. Suddenly Helen's face changed. She spelled *water* by herself many times. She pointed to the pump, then to the ground, and asked for names. Quickly Annie spelled words into Helen's hand. Helen wanted to know the name of every object she touched. She learned thirty new words in a very short time. Annie was overjoyed. She knew that she had broken through the darkness at last. She had given Helen a key to the world around her—the key of language.

Why do you think a biography was written about Anne Sullivan?

Practice

A. Answer these questions in complete sentences.

1. Who is the main character in this biography?
2. Is this a true story?
3. Are the facts in this story told in order?
4. Tell some facts about Annie as a child.
5. Most of this biography tells about Annie as a teacher. Write some facts you learned about this time in her life.

B. Write *true* if the statement is true. Write *false* if it is not true.

6. Biographies are about real people.
7. Biographies tell facts about people's lives.
8. Every famous person writes biographies.
9. Biographies only tell about famous children.
10. The facts in a biography are usually in order.

Apply

C. 11. Pretend you are writing a biography. It is about a person you know. Tell some facts about the person's life. Put the facts in the order they happened. Tell why this person is special and important.

A BOOK TO READ

Title: **Shark Lady: True Adventures of Eugenie Clark**
Author: Ann McGovern
Publisher: Four Winds Press

At the New York Aquarium, nine-year-old Eugenie Clark first saw a great shark. She knew then that someday she would "walk with the fish" deep in the murky green sea.

Her mother had taught her to swim before she was two. Genie loved the ocean and all creatures in it.

The first time she put on the heavy underwater helmet that divers wore then, her dream came true—she was truly walking with the fish! Danger, excitement, and pleasure were all part of Eugenie's career. She worked in the South Sea Islands and in her marine laboratory in Florida. She visited the Prince of Japan to give him a trained shark. The only shark bite she ever suffered came from the jaws of a *dead,* stuffed tiger shark lying on the front seat of her car.

Today, in her 50's, Genie says: "I hope I will still be diving when I'm 90."

2 UNIT TEST

Nouns pages 38–39

One word in each sentence is a noun. Write the letter of the word that is a noun.

1. A yellow (a) butterfly (b) swooped toward (c) us.
2. Its delicate (a) wings (b) fluttered (c) slowly.
3. Bright (a) green grasshoppers (b) chirped (c) loudly.
4. Thousands of them (a) live (b) in our backyard (c).
5. One by (a) one the fireflies (b) flashed (c) on and off.
6. Scientists (a) have studied (b) and written (c) about them.

Singular and Plural Nouns pages 40–41

Copy the sentences. Underline the nouns. Above each noun write *S* if it is singular. Write *P* if it is plural.

7. Bring your knees to your chest slowly.
8. Stretch your arms above your head.
9. Fall to the floor like a floppy doll.
10. Let your body sway to the music.
11. Sarah will do somersaults.

Plural Nouns pages 42–43

Write the plural form of each noun.

12. dress **13.** bus **14.** watch **15.** bush **16.** ranch
17. guess **18.** rash **19.** glass **20.** fox

Other Plural Nouns pages 44–45

Write the plural form of each noun.

21. berry **22.** bunny **23.** lady
24. story **25.** bakery **26.** spy
27. puppy **28.** jelly **29.** penny
30. hobby **31.** lily **32.** butterfly

Common and Proper Nouns pages 46–47

Write the sentences. Underline the common nouns. Circle the proper nouns.

33. Will Dr. Thomas visit our school on Tuesday?
34. She lives in Lombard, a town near Chicago.
35. Jason and Flora are in my class.
36. My teacher owns a house in New Mexico.
37. In October our class will have a party.

Names and Titles pages 48–49

Write these names and titles correctly.

38. mrs r. s. fernandez **39.** dr alicia granger
40. dr walter haas **41.** miss joanie sudo
42. mr b. w. warshaw **43.** ms diana lord

Names of Days, Months, and Holidays pages 50–51

Write these proper nouns and abbreviations correctly.

44. august **45.** september **46.** wednesday
47. tues **48.** labor day **49.** friday

Names of Places pages 52–53

Write these sentences correctly.

50. We visited georgia and florida last month.
51. My favorite cities were atlanta and orlando.
52. My mother was born in warsaw, poland.
53. Her family came to new york city and bought a house in bayonne, new jersey.
54. Now we live in tulsa, oklahoma.
55. My brother's school is in ames, iowa.

Alphabetical Order pages 56–57

Write these lists of words in alphabetical order.

1. coin, penny, money, dollar, nickel
2. city, store, street, corner, sidewalk
3. shell, salmon, seaweed, shark, sand
4. party, package, paint, paste, paper
5. wishbone, wind, wild, wizard, wicked

Guide Words pages 58–59

The guide words on one page of a dictionary are *bamboo* and *baton.* Write the words that would appear on that page.

6. bark	**7.** bay	**8.** base
9. basket	**10.** bank	**11.** badger

Entry Words pages 60–61

Use these entries to answer the questions.

can·yon [kan′yən] *n.* A deep, narrow valley or gorge with very steep sides.

pla·teau [pla·tō′] *n.* **1** A broad stretch of high, level land; a high plain. **2** A time when change or progress stops for a while: a *plateau* in the city's growth.

12. What entry words are shown?
13. How many definitions does *plateau* have?
14. What is the respelling of *plateau*?
15. What is another word for *canyon*?

Combining Subjects with and pages 62–63

Combine each pair of sentences. Use the word *and* to combine the subjects. Write the new sentences.

1. Amy cooked dinner. Jerry cooked dinner.
2. Joe peeled potatoes. Cal peeled potatoes.
3. Li had some punch. Maria had some punch.
4. Cal took some peas. His father took some peas.
5. Jerry loved the dinner. His friends loved the dinner.

Writing and Editing Sentences pages 64–67

6.–10. Write five sentences about different people you know. Then edit the sentences for capital letters and end marks.

Reading About a Famous Person pages 68–71

Read this true story about a famous person. Then answer the questions that follow.

Samuel Langhorne Clemens was born in Missouri in 1835. He grew up in a town on the Mississippi River. He and his friends swam, fished, and sailed the river.

Later, Mr. Clemens wrote books about his adventures as a boy. One of his most famous books, *The Adventures of Tom Sawyer,* is really about him. He became one of America's greatest writers.

1. What is this kind of story called?
2. Who is the main character?
3. Why is this person famous?
4. Write two facts about this person.

MAINTENANCE and REVIEW

Sentences pages 2–3

Decide which groups of words are complete sentences. Write them correctly.

1. babies grow and change very quickly
2. crying or eating all morning long
3. a baby in a large blue stroller
4. sometimes I baby-sit for my aunt's twins
5. active babies may crawl a mile each day
6. very young babies sleep many hours a day
7. only wake up to eat or take a bath
8. two little babies in matching shirts

Four Kinds of Sentences pages 4–9

Write the sentences correctly. Add capital letters and end marks where they are needed.

9. why do babies cry
10. how fast he crawls
11. find the toy doll
12. my brother is growing
13. his eyes are blue
14. do you see his bib
15. what a loud cry
16. will you dress him

Parts of a Sentence pages 10–11

Copy the sentences. Draw one line under the subjects. Draw two lines under the predicates.

17. Julie makes a mask for the party.
18. The colored mask glows in the dark.
19. Other students come to the party.
20. One friend dresses in a long gown.
21. Philip wears a cowboy hat and boots.
22. Sara's best friend pretends to be a bear.

Nouns pages 38–39

Copy these sentences. Underline the two nouns in each one.

23. My father is helping me paint my room.
24. I want to use blue paint on the walls.
25. My best friend has a lovely blue blanket.
26. It is the same color as my paint.
27. Daddy bought me my own paintbrush.
28. I can paint the door and the windowsill.
29. This room will be beautiful by next week.
30. Even Barbara does not have such a nice bedroom.

Plural Nouns pages 40–45

Write the plural form of each noun.

31. tree
32. boy
33. match
34. bus
35. body
36. lash
37. sky
38. truck
39. dress
40. watch
41. party
42. penny
43. fox
44. cup
45. knee

Common and Proper Nouns pages 46–53

Write the sentences. Underline the common nouns. Use capital letters with the proper nouns.

46. Mrs. schwartz is having a large party on the last friday in november.
47. She lives on a narrow road in topeka, kansas.
48. Her family moved to topeka from a small town in alabama called lenora.
49. miss follett will show the guests her slides of paris, france, and dublin, ireland.
50. miss follett just returned to the city after a trip to france, ireland, and england.

3

LANGUAGE
Learning About Verbs

COMPOSITION
Writing Sentences

STUDY SKILLS
Using the Dictionary

LITERATURE
Reading a Story

Animals cannot talk or write, but you can. You can use words to tell about the pictures on page 78. What is each animal doing? Think of good action words to describe each picture.

Action words are called **verbs.** Some verbs tell about action that is happening now. Other verbs tell about action that happened in the past. Which picture shows an animal that lived long ago? The action in this picture happened in the past.

In this unit you will work with action words. You will write sentences about action and see how action words are used to tell a story.

Without action verbs, you could not *run,* or *read,* or *eat.* Worst of all, you could not *learn.* Are you ready to learn about action words? Lights, camera, ACTION!

LANGUAGE

Lesson 1: Understanding Verbs

Read these sentences.

1. The children walk through the woods.
2. The children see the gingerbread house.
3. The children eat part of the roof.

The director yells, "ACTION!" and the children begin to act. *The children* is the subject of each sentence above. The predicate tells what the children *do.*

Think and Discuss

Words that show actions are called **action verbs.** Verbs appear in the predicate part of a sentence.

Look at sentence 1. Which word shows the action? What do the children do? What are the verbs in sentences 2 and 3?

Which words show the actions in these sentences?

4. The children sleep in the woods.
5. The children run from the house.

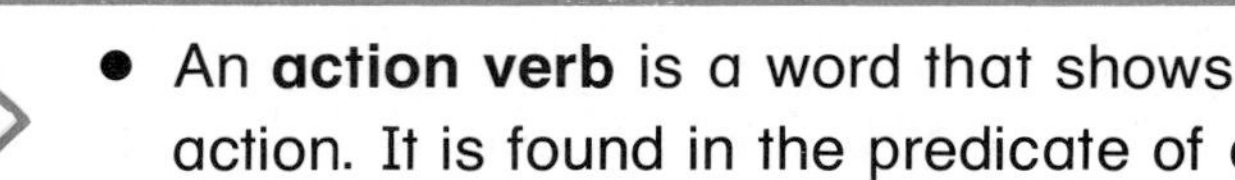

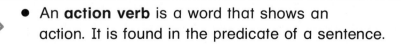

- An **action verb** is a word that shows an action. It is found in the predicate of a sentence.

Practice

A. Copy these sentences. Draw two lines under the predicates. Circle the action verbs.

1. Actors climb up on stage.
2. They read their lines slowly.
3. The director shouts orders.
4. Some people watch from the seats below.
5. One man claps after each line.

B. Copy these directions for making an egg-carton garden. Draw two lines under the action verbs.

6. We get an egg carton, soil, and seeds.
7. You fill each cup with some soil.
8. I put two or three seeds in each cup.
9. You cover the seeds lightly with soil.
10. We sprinkle water in each cup.
11. You place the garden on a windowsill.
12. We watch our plants.
13. I cut the cardboard carton in half.
14. You plant each row in the garden.
15. The cardboard cups slowly crumble into the soil.

Apply

C. Write five sentences. Use these action verbs in your sentences.

16. crawl **17.** hide **18.** scream
19. fly **20.** see

Lesson 2: Understanding Past Time and Present Time

Read these sentences.

1. The girls climb the mountain.
2. The girls climbed the mountain.

What are the action verbs in these sentences?

Think and Discuss

Action verbs show actions. They also can tell *when* the action happened. Look at sentence 1. The verb *climb* tells about an action that is happening *now.* It tells about **present time.**

In sentence 2 the verb *climbed* tells about **past time.** It tells you that the girls have finished climbing the mountain. The action is in the *past.*

How does the verb in sentence 2 end? Most past time verbs end in *ed.*

Now read these sentences.

3. They rest at the campsite.
4. They rested at the campsite.

Which sentence tells about something that happened in the past? What is the past time verb used? Which verb is a present time verb?

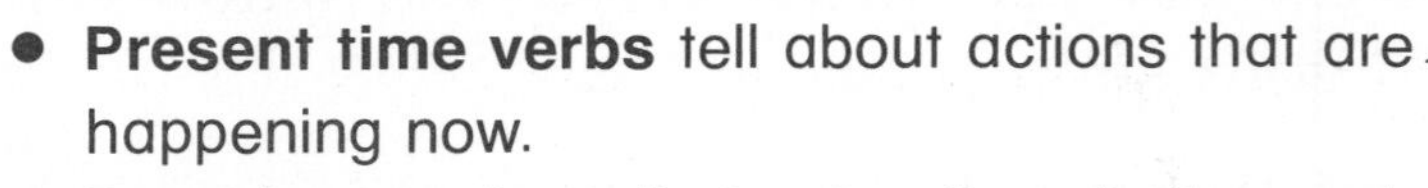

- **Present time verbs** tell about actions that are happening now.
- **Past time verbs** tell about actions in the past. Most past time verbs end in *ed.*

Practice

A. 1.–5. Listen as your teacher reads some sentences. Write the sentences.

B. Copy each sentence. Draw two lines under the action verb. Then tell whether each verb tells about past time or present time.

6. Those baby elephants weigh 250 pounds.
7. The young elephants play together.
8. The elephant herd watched the lion.
9. Two large elephants flap their ears.
10. The herd stayed near the river.

C. Add an ending to these verbs. Make them tell about past time. Then use them in sentences.

11. bark **12.** toss **13.** wait **14.** chew **15.** call

There are many exciting action words and phrases used in sports. Each sport has its own words and phrases. In baseball you *throw a curve.* In basketball you *dribble.* Here are some more sports words and phrases: *steal a base, serve, rebound, lay up, sprint.*

1. In what sports are these words used? Use a dictionary to help you find out.
2. Can you dribble a curve? Can you throw a goal? Is it possible to strike out in football?

Lesson 3: Making Subjects and Verbs Agree

Every sentence has two parts. The subject tells whom or what the sentence is about. The predicate tells something about the subject.

Read these sentences.

1. The bird sings. 2. The birds sing.

Think and Discuss

What is the subject of sentence 1? This sentence tells about one bird. We say that the subject is **singular.** What is the subject of sentence 2? This sentence tells about more than one bird. The subject is **plural.**

Both sentences have verbs that tell about present time. Verbs must work together with their subjects. Subjects and verbs must agree. What are the verbs in sentences 1 and 2?

An *s* was added to the verb in sentence 1. This verb now agrees with its singular subject. The verb in sentence 2 has no *s* at the end. It agrees with a plural subject.

Now read these sentences.

3. The little boy fishes. 4. The little boys fish.

Which sentence has a plural subject? There is no ending on the verb in that sentence. What is the verb ending in sentence 3? Add *es* to verbs that end in *sh, ch, ss,* or *x* to make them agree with singular subjects. Add *s* to most other verbs to make them agree with singular subjects.

- To make most verbs agree with singular subjects, add *s.*
- To make verbs that end in *sh, ch, ss,* or *x* agree with singular subjects, add *es.*

Practice

A. Write the verb from each sentence. If the sentence has a singular subject, write *singular.* If it has a plural subject, write *plural.*

1. Magnets turn inside compasses.
2. The magnet picks up a paper clip.
3. Ms. Barney teaches about magnets.
4. That woman shows us many kinds of magnets.
5. The students watch her carefully.

B. Copy each sentence. Complete each one with the correct spelling of the present time verb in ( ).

6. The cow ______ flies with its tail. (swat)
7. My dog ______ its tail when it is happy. (wag)
8. The robin ______ on a branch. (perch)
9. The bird ______ its tail to balance. (use)
10. The beavers ______ the water with their tails. (slap)

Apply

C. Write five sentences. Use the words below as subjects. Be sure your verbs agree with them.

11. The pilot **12.** Explorers **13.** A space suit
14. Their adventures **15.** That radio

Lesson 4: Forming Past Time Verbs

Read these sentences.

1. Last night Mika dreamed about a time machine.
2. Her friends traveled back in time.

Do the sentences tell about present or past time?

Think and Discuss

How do the verbs in sentences 1 and 2 end? Most action verbs add *ed* to form past time. This is true whether the subjects are singular or plural. Now read these sentences.

3. She hoped the machine would never stop.
4. It hopped through time.

Look at the underlined verbs. *Hoped* is the past time form of the verb *hope*. *Hope* ends with an *e*. It drops the *e* and adds *ed* to form the past time. *Hopped* is the past time form of the verb *hop*. *Hop* is a one-syllable word. It ends with a consonant. It doubles that consonant and adds *ed* to tell about past time.

- Some verbs end with *e*. To form the past time, drop the *e* and add *ed*.
- Some verbs have one syllable and end with a consonant preceded by a vowel. To form the past time, double the final consonant. Then add *ed*.

Practice

A. Copy each sentence. Finish it by using the past time form of the verb in ( ).

1. People of long ago ______ simple tools. (invent)
2. They ______ them to make life easier. (use)
3. Some people ______ for miles to find trees. (hike)
4. They ______ the trees back to their camp. (drag)
5. Then they ______ the trees up for firewood. (chop)

Apply

B. Use the past time form of each verb in a sentence.

6. rush **7.** tag **8.** move **9.** skip **10.** chase

To Memorize

Verbs are things I do, and make,
And feel, in one way or another.
Thanks to verbs, I eat my Cake,
And throw my Ball, and hug my Mother.

Eleanor Farjeon

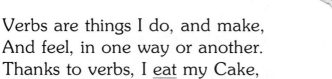

What is your definition of a verb? Be a poet. Change the underlined verbs to verbs of your own.

Lesson 5: Forming Other Past Time Verbs

Sakie wrote some sentences about a fish dinner. She could not decide whether to write about past time or present time. Read her first two sentences.

1. We fry some fish in oil.
2. We fried some fish in oil.

Which sentence tells about past time?

Think and Discuss

What is the verb in sentence 2? *Fried* is the past time form of the verb *fry*. It ends in *ed*. The *y* in *fry* has been changed to an *i*. Some verbs end in a consonant followed by *y*. The *y* must be changed to *i* before *ed* is added.

Sakie decided to write with past time verbs. Read her sentences. Look at the underlined verbs.

3. We washed some lettuce leaves, and then we dried them.
4. We carried the dishes to the dining room.
5. My family hurried to the table.

Which verb in sentence 3 changed *y* to *i* before *ed* was added? Look at sentences 4 and 5. What are the present time forms of the underlined verbs?

- Some verbs end in a consonant and *y*. To form the past time, change the *y* to *i*. Then add *ed*.

Practice

A. Change the underlined verbs from present time to past time. Write the sentences.

1. The dogs <u>bury</u> bones in the garden.
2. They <u>try</u> to steal toys from the twins.
3. The twins <u>cry</u>.
4. The dogs <u>scurry</u> away.
5. We <u>carry</u> the twins inside.

B. Some verbs in these sentences change *y* to *i* to form the past time. Some do not. Write the sentences so that they tell about past time.

6. Pirates bury treasure in the sand.
7. My friends and I search for treasure.
8. We move slowly through the sand.
9. We spy a small tin box.
10. We pry the lid open, and my friends gasp.

Apply

C. Use the past time form of each verb in a sentence.

11. worry **12.** marry **13.** carry **14.** fry **15.** try

A Challenge

Would these sentences take present time or past time verbs? How can you tell? Finish each sentence.

1. Long ago he ______.
2. Now they ______.
3. Last year we ______.
4. Once we ______.
5. Today people ______.

Lesson 6: Using Forms of Have

Most verbs show past time by adding *ed.* Some do not. Read these sentences.

1. We have a beach ball.
2. We had a beach ball last year.

Which sentence tells about the past time?

Think and Discuss

Have is a verb with an unusual past time form. The past time form is *had.*

Have has an unusual present time form too. Read these sentences.

3. The girl has some seashells.
4. The girls have some seashells.

Which sentence has a singular subject? Most verbs agree with singular subjects by adding *s.* The form of *have* that agrees with singular subjects is *has.* How would you make sentence 3 show past time? How could sentence 4 show past time?

Verb	Present	Past
have	have, has	had

Forms of *have* often help other verbs show past time. The forms of *have* are then called **helping verbs.** Read these sentences.

5. Joanne walked on the sand.
6. Joanne has splashed through the water.

7. Her brothers have returned on the boat.
8. They had fished in the ocean.

Which sentences use forms of *have*? Look at the action verbs in those sentences. How do they end?

- A **helping verb** helps the main verb tell about an action.

Practice

A. Complete each sentence with *have* or *has.*

1. Mrs. Chang ______ a new car.
2. The car ______ two doors.
3. The Changs ______ an old car too.
4. Both cars ______ room for four people.
5. The new car ______ more room for packages.

B. Copy the verbs. Two words form the verb in each sentence. Label each one *helping verb* or *action verb.*

6. Trees have shaded this street for years.
7. People have cared for the trees.
8. Mr. Bradley has chopped down one tree.
9. The leaves had turned brown.
10. The tree had died.

Apply

C. Use *have* or *has* as helping verbs with each verb below. Write a sentence using each verb.

11. dried **12.** traced **13.** danced
14. stitched **15.** pasted

Lesson 7: Using Irregular Verbs

The verb *go* shows present and past in unusual ways. Read these sentences.

1. The farmer goes to the market.
2. The farmer went to the market yesterday.
3. The farmer has gone to the market before.

Which sentences tell about past time?

Think and Discuss

Sentence 1 tells about present time. It has a singular subject. What form of *go* is used here?

Sentence 2 tells about past time. What form of *go* is used here?

Sentence 3 uses a helping verb to tell about past time. What form of *go* is used with a helping verb?

The chart below shows different forms of the verbs *go, come,* and *run*.

Verb	Present	Past	Past with *Have*, *Has*, or *Had*
go	go(es)	went	gone
come	come(s)	came	come
run	run(s)	ran	run

Look at the verbs *come* and *run.* They change only one letter to spell their past time forms. They spell their present time and helping verb forms the same way.

Now read this sentence.

4. Some chickens <u>run</u> in the grass.

How would you make this sentence show past time with *have*?

Practice

A. Write each sentence. Underline all the verbs. Then tell whether they show *present time, past time,* or *past with have.*

1. The horses ran through the barnyard.
2. Some ducks have come to the pond.
3. A piglet runs toward the fence.
4. The farmer has gone into the field.
5. His dog went across the road.

B. Write the sentences. Change the underlined verb to the form shown in ( ).

6. Rabbits <u>go</u> into their hutch. (past)
7. A turkey <u>comes</u> through the bushes. (past)
8. Kittens <u>ran</u> past the oak tree. (present)
9. The cows <u>come</u> for their dinner. (past with *have*)
10. Two cats <u>go</u> into the barn. (past with *have*)

Apply

C. Use these forms of *go, come,* and *run* in sentences of your own.

11. has gone **12.** have run **13.** came
14. goes **15.** went

LANGUAGE REVIEW

Verbs pages 80–81

Copy the sentences. Draw two lines under the action verbs.

1. The motorboat raced across the lake.
2. Its powerful motor roared noisily.
3. Ducks and wild geese flapped their wings.
4. They flew to a quiet part of the lake.
5. The captain of the boat waved at me.

Past Time and Present Time pages 82–83

Copy the sentences. Underline the verbs. Decide whether the verbs show *past time* or *present time.* Write *present* or *past* to indicate which time each verb shows.

6. The monkeys scamper around their cage.
7. They grab branches with their tails.
8. Yesterday I listened to them at the zoo.
9. They chattered madly to each other.
10. Monkeys eat fruits and vegetables.

Subject-Verb Agreement pages 84–85

Choose the correct answer. Write the sentences. Make each verb agree with the subject.

11. Tanya (play, plays) the violin beautifully.
12. Mark and Tanya (perform, performs) with a youth orchestra.
13. The students (practice, practices) long hours together.
14. Tanya (watch, watches) the conductor.
15. Mark (fix, fixes) the string on his cello.

Past Time Verbs pages 86–87

Change the verbs to show past time. Write the sentences.

16. Alani kicks the ball to the other team.
17. She trots down the field after her teammates.
18. David tackles the runner out of bounds.
19. Chris injures himself in the third quarter.
20. He trips over his own feet on the field.

Other Past Time Verbs pages 88–89

Change the verbs to past time forms. Write them.

21. bury **22.** copy **23.** carry **24.** reply **25.** marry

Forms of Have pages 90–91

Complete the sentences with present time forms of *have.*

26. The children ______ a dance class after school.
27. Maria ______ her ballet shoes with her.
28. Kim ______ his shoes in a bag.
29. Kim and Maria ______ classes every Tuesday.
30. Kim's sister ______ dance classes each day.

Irregular Verbs pages 92–93

Change the underlined verb to the form shown in ( ).

31. The Smiths go to the lake in July. (past)
32. Uncle George comes along. (past)
33. The children run to the water. (past with *have*)

Applying Verbs

Make these verbs show past time. Then use them in sentences.

34. cross **35.** hurry **36.** have **37.** run **38.** go

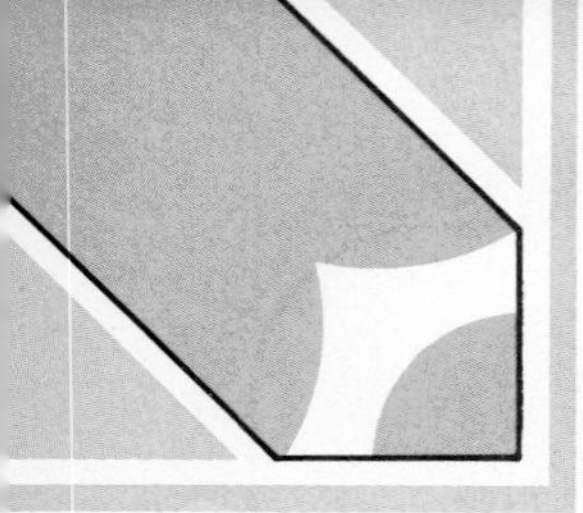

STUDY SKILLS

Lesson 8: Choosing the Right Meaning

Krista found these two sentences in her book.

1. The monkey climbed up the tree trunk.
2. The man slammed the door of the trunk and drove away.

Does the word *trunk* have the same meaning in sentences 1 and 2?

Think and Discuss

Krista looked up the word *trunk* in the dictionary. Here is the listing she found.

> **trunk** [trungk] *n.* **1** The main stem or stock of a tree, not including the limbs or roots. **2** The human body, apart from the head, neck, and limbs. **3** A main or central section of anything, as the main section of a nerve or blood vessel. **4** A long, flexible snout, as that of the elephant. **5** A large piece of luggage used for packing and carrying clothes, etc., as for a journey. **6** A compartment of an automobile for storing luggage, etc. **7** *(pl.)* Very short pants or trousers, worn by swimmers, athletes, etc.

She was surprised to see that *trunk* has seven different definitions. Each definition has a number.

Which definition fits sentence 1 from Krista's book? Only definition 1 tells about the trunk of a tree. Which definition fits sentence 2?

Practice

Use these dictionary entries to answer Practice A and B.

point·er [poin′tər] *n.* **1** A hand, finger, or other indicator, as on a clock or meter. **2** A slender rod used to point out things on maps, charts, etc. **3** A smooth-haired dog trained to point out game.

shut·ter [shut′ər] *n.* **1** A hinged board for shuttering a window. **2** A part of a camera that opens to admit light through the lens.

script [skript] *n.* **1** Handwriting. **2** A printing type that looks like handwriting. **3** A copy of a play, for the use of actors.

A. Read these sentences. Notice the underlined words. Copy the definition that fits each sentence.

1. Jenny clicked the shutter and took a picture.
2. I wrote my paper in script.
3. The teacher used a pointer to show us the map.
4. Each actor has a copy of the script.
5. A loose shutter banged on the window.

B. Copy each sentence. Finish each one with *pointer, script,* or *shutter.* Then write the number of the definition that fits the sentence.

6. The ______ barked at the birds.
7. I wrote the ______ for our class play.
8. The ______ on my camera is broken.
9. The letter was written in ______.
10. One green ______ covered the window.

Apply

C. 11.–15. Write five sentences that use the word *horn.* Use at least three different definitions.

horn [hôrn] *n.* **1** One of a pair of hard, hollow growths, usually curved and pointed, on the heads of cattle, sheep, goats, etc. **2** One of a pair of branched, solid growths on the heads of deer, shed each year; antler. **3** The material of a horn. **4** Something made from a horn: a powder *horn.* **5** A musical wind instrument, once made from a horn, now usually of brass. **6** A device for sounding a warning: an automobile *horn.*

Lesson 9: Understanding Homographs

Krista found that many words have more than one meaning. Some words have more than one dictionary entry. Read the three entries for *bat.*

> **bat**[1] [bat] *n., v.* **bat·ted, bat·ting** **1** *n.* A sturdy stick or a club, especially one used for hitting a ball. **2** *v.* To hit with or as if with a bat. **3** *n.* A sharp blow **4** *v.* To use a bat. **5** *n.* In baseball, a turn at batting. **6** *v.* To take a turn at batting.
> **bat**[2] [bat] *n.* A small, mouselike animal with wings of thin skin supported by bones. Bats fly at night.
> **bat**[3] [bat] **bat·ted, bat·ting** To wink.

Think and Discuss

Words that have the same spelling but different meanings are called **homographs.** Homographs are listed one after the other in the dictionary. A number is after each entry word.

Look at entry *bat*[1]. How many definitions are listed for that entry? Read the first definition.

What is the definition for entry *bat*[2]? *Bat*[2] has a very different meaning than *bat*[1].

Homographs are spelled the same way. Some homographs are pronounced differently. Here is an example.

> **tear**[1] [târ] *v.* **tore, torn, tear·ing,** *n.* **1** *v.* To pull apart or rip by force: to *tear* a letter open. **2** *n.* A rip or hole: There's a *tear* in the mattress. **3** *v.* To make by tearing: He *tore* a hole in his shirt. **4** *v.* To become torn: cloth that *tears* easily. **5** *v.* To make one or more deep scratches in: Briers *tore* his skin. **6** *v.* To divide by fighting: The committee was *torn* over the issue.
> **tear**[2] [tir] *n.* A drop of salty liquid in or shed from the eye, as in crying.

How do you pronounce entries *tear*[1] and *tear*[2]? Which entry has to do with *crying*?

Practice

bow[1] [bou] *v.* **bowed, bow·ing,** *n,* **1** *v.* To bend the head or body, as in greeting or saying yes. **2** *n.* A bending of the head or body, as in greeting. **3** *v.* To give up; yield: They *bowed* to the king's wishes. **4** *v.* To bend or curve: He was *bowed* by the heavy load.

bow[2] [bō] **1** *n.* A strip of springy wood bent by a string, used for shooting arrows. **2** *n.* A knot with loops in it. **3** *n.* Anything bent or curved, as a rainbow. **4** *n.* A rod holding tightly stretched horsehair, used to play a violin or other instrument. **5** *v.* To play with a bow.

bow[3] [bou] *n.* The forward part of a ship, boat, etc.

wind[1] [wind] **1** *n.* A movement of air of any speed. **2** *n.* Air that carries some scent: The dogs got *wind* of the fox. **3** *n.* The power of breathing, breath. **4** *v.* To make short of breath: The long run *winded* him. **5** *n.* Useless talk: That's a lot of *wind.* **6** *n. (pl)* Wind instruments, as in an orchestra.

wind[2] [wīnd] *v.* **wound, wind·ing,** *n.* **1** *v.* To coil or pass (thread, rope, etc.) around itself or around something else: to *wind* thread. **2** *v.* To coil or twine, as around some object: The rope *winds* on this drum. **3** *v.* To cover with something by coiling: to *wind* a spool with thread. **4** *v.* To make (a machine, as a clock) go by coiling a spring or raising a weight. **5** *v.* To run or move in a turning, twisting path: The road *winds* through town.

A. Use the dictionary entries for *bow.* Complete these sentences.

1. Entry ______ means part of a ship.
2. Entry ______ means to bend the body.
3. Entries ______ and ______sound the same.
4. Entry ______ has four definitions.
5. Definition 2 for entry *bow*[2] says ______.

B. Write *entry wind*[1] or *entry wind*[2] to tell which is used in each of these sentences.

6. A wild west *wind* was blowing.
7. Help me *wind* the hose up.
8. Can you *wind* your watch?
9. An oboe is a *wind* instrument.
10. The paths *wind* up the hill.

Apply

C. 11.–15. Write a sentence of your own for each entry for *bow* and *wind.*

COMPOSITION

Lesson 10: Combining Predicates With and

Karen wrote some sentences explaining the work farmers do. She looked over the sentences and decided to write them in a different way.

Read the sentences Karen wrote.

1. Farmers grow crops.
2. Farmers harvest them.
3. Farmers grow crops and harvest them.

Think and Discuss

The word *farmers* is the subject in each sentence. What is the predicate of sentence 1? What is the predicate of sentence 2? When two sentences have the same subject, the predicates can often be combined. The word *and* can be used to combine the predicates of the two sentences.

Check over the sentences you write. If the subjects of two sentences are the same, the predicates can often be joined with the word *and*.

Now read these sentences.

4. Farmers dig holes.
5. Farmers plant seeds.

How would you combine these sentences?

Practice

A. Copy each sentence. Draw two lines under the complete predicate.

1. Farmers prepare the soil and ready it for planting.
2. They plow the ground and roll it smooth.
3. They add fertilizer and plant the seeds.
4. Farmers weed the crops and protect them from insects and disease.
5. Farmers harvest the crops and sell them at the market.

Apply

B. Combine the predicates of each pair of sentences with the word *and*. Write the new sentence for each pair.

6. Farm machines help farmers.
   Farm machines do much of their work.
7. Tractors pull farm machines.
   Tractors carry the workers.
8. Plows cut into the soil.
   Plows turn it over.
9. Cultivators loosen the soil clumps.
   Cultivators take the soil apart.
10. Planting machines drop seeds in the ground.
    Planting machines cover the seeds.

Lesson 11: Writing Sentences with Interesting Verbs

Dull verbs make dull sentences. Interesting verbs create lively sentences.

Read these sentences.

1. Cheryl went out of the room.
2. Cheryl tiptoed out of the room.
3. Cheryl stumbled out of the room.
4. Cheryl dashed out of the room.

What is the verb in each sentence?

Think and Discuss

The verb *went* in the first sentence does not clearly explain how Cheryl moved. The verbs in the other sentences describe Cheryl's actions better. These verbs help the reader better understand Cheryl's movements. Can you think of some other interesting verbs that might be used to describe Cheryl's actions? Name the verbs.

When you write sentences, take time to use interesting verbs. Interesting verbs make sentences that are exciting to read.

Practice

A. In each of these sentences there are two verbs. Read each sentence. Choose the verb in ( ) that is clearer. Write the sentence.

1. The clouds (went, floated) across the sky.
2. A door (moved, rattled) in the wind.
3. A black bird (swooped, flew) to the ground.
4. A flag (fluttered, moved) in the breeze.
5. A woman (walked, hurried) down the street.

B. The verb in each sentence below is underlined. Think of another verb that would tell more clearly what happened. Write the sentences using the verbs you chose.

6. Large trees <u>were</u> on the hillside.
7. Swift water <u>ran</u> over the rocks.
8. Heavy raindrops <u>fell</u> on the path.
9. The frightened deer <u>ran</u> away.
10. A rabbit <u>came</u> around the curve.

Apply

C. Write sentences that tell about these things. Choose interesting verbs for your sentences.

11. a cat under the sofa
12. a fast horse in a race
13. a leak in the roof
14. a lion in the jungle
15. an ice cream cone on a hot day

Lesson 12: Editing Sentences

Josh wrote some sentences about the first time he made popcorn. Then he edited the sentences to make them more interesting to read. Read his sentences.

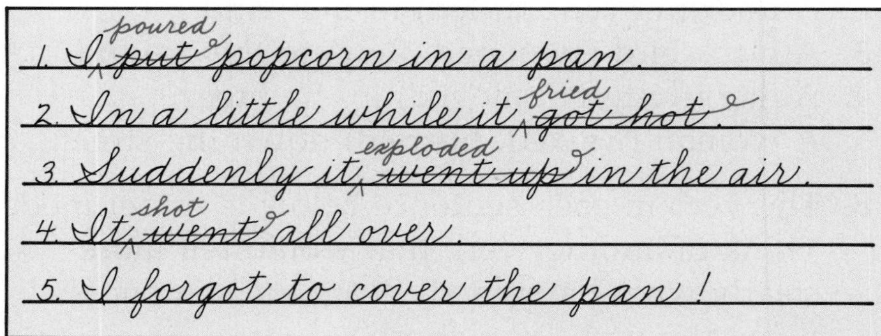

1. I ~~put~~ poured popcorn in a pan.
2. In a little while it ~~got~~ fried hot.
3. Suddenly it ~~went up~~ exploded in the air.
4. It ~~went~~ shot all over.
5. I forgot to cover the pan!

Think and Discuss

Josh used this mark ⌐ to take some words away. Which words did he take away?

He then added some interesting verbs. This mark ∧ means to add something. What verbs did Josh add? How did these changes improve Josh's sentences?

Practice

A. Write Josh's sentences over. Use the changes he made.

Apply

B. Edit the sentences you wrote in Lesson 11. Could you make your verbs more interesting? Did you begin and end each sentence correctly? Write the sentences again.

 capitalize

⊙ make a period

∧ add something

add a comma

add quotation marks

take something away

spell correctly

indent the paragraph

/ make a lowercase letter

tr transpose

MECHANICS PRACTICE

Writing Names of Days, Months, and Holidays

- Use a period after an abbreviation.
- Begin the name of a day of the week or its abbreviation with a capital letter.
- Begin the name of a month or its abbreviation with a capital letter.
- Begin each important word in the name of a holiday with a capital letter.

A. Write these sentences correctly.

1. My birthday is january first.
2. I start planning my party in november or december.
3. halloween is on friday, october 31.
4. On monday, september 3, we begin school.
5. Spring vacation will start on wednesday, april 21.
6. I usually go to camp in june or july.
7. We will drive to camp on saturday or sunday.
8. My camp always has a big independence day party.
9. mother's day is in may, but father's day is in june.
10. We must do all our swimming in june, july, and august.

B. Write the abbreviations for these nouns.

11. Tuesday
12. February
13. January
14. Sunday
15. Thursday
16. August
17. April
18. Friday

LITERATURE

Lesson 13: Reading a Short Story

You know that people in a story are called **characters.** The main character is the person the story is about. The place where the story happens is called the **setting.**

Think and Discuss

The action in a story is called the **plot.** Often a main character has a problem. The plot of a story shows the steps the character takes to solve the problem.

The action in this story takes place long ago. Do you think the author used present or past time verbs to tell the story?

The Field of Buttercups

by Alice Boden

One fine morning in Ireland Michael O'Grady thought he would take a day's holiday. He walked through the village and then went along the land that led up the hill.

It was a lovely day. The air was fresh and Michael was enjoying himself. All of a sudden he heard a noise—a funny tap-tapping, coming from behind the wall.

Quietly he climbed up and peeped over the wall into the field. What a surprise! There was a little man, sitting on a stone mending a shoe. It was the tap-tap of his hammer that Michael had been hearing.

Michael knew that he was looking at a leprechaun, and everyone in Ireland knows that a leprechaun has a pot of gold hidden away in a secret place.

Michael remembered that they say if you take your eyes off a leprechaun he disappears, so he kept watching him all the time. He climbed carefully over the wall, crept across the grass, stretched out his arm and grabbed the leprechaun tightly by the arm.

"Now," he said, "where is your pot of gold?"

The leprechaun twisted and turned, but he could not get free. He knew that in the end he would have to take Michael to the place where he kept his gold.

They walked a long way, across the fields and over bogs and ditches and walls. Michael kept his eyes on the little man all the time.

On and on they went until they came to a field that was yellow with buttercups. At last the leprechaun stopped. He gave a big sigh and pointed to a buttercup.

"Dig under that buttercup," he said, "and you will find the pot of gold."

Michael looked at the hard stony ground. He

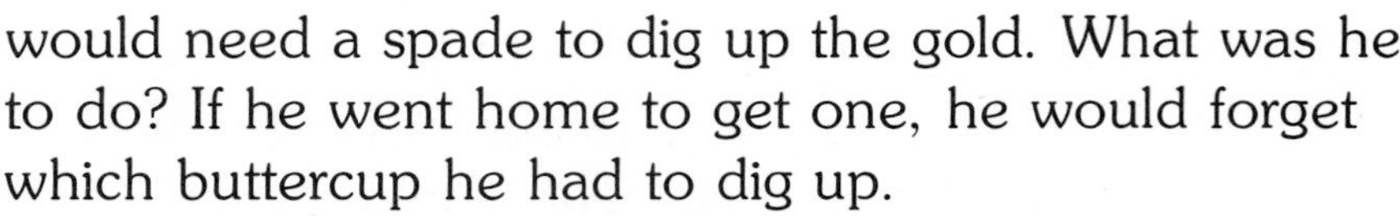

would need a spade to dig up the gold. What was he to do? If he went home to get one, he would forget which buttercup he had to dig up.

Then he had an idea. He took off one of the red garters he was wearing. Then he tied it around the stem of the buttercup so that he would be sure to know which was the right flower when he came back.

He looked hard at the leprechaun. "Promise you will not take that garter away from the flower," he said.

"I promise," said the leprechaun, crossing his heart. "May I go now?"

"Yes," said Michael, "now you have promised not to touch my mark." He let go of the leprechaun, who vanished into the air.

Michael ran home as fast as his legs could carry him. He was in through the front door and out through the back to pick up a spade before his mother could do more than shout, "Michael O'Grady, come back! You have not eaten your dinner!"

Michael just kept running all the way back to the buttercup field. And then—what did he see?

It was true that the leprechaun had not touched the garter. Now, on every single buttercup there was a red garter just like Michael's.

What was he to do? He could not very well dig up every buttercup in the whole field.

Michael went off home. As he walked along he began to laugh. He laughed and laughed. It was a good trick that the leprechaun had played on him.

Practice

A. Answer the questions in full sentences.

1. Name three characters in this story.
2. Who is the main character?
3. The main character has a problem. He wants something. What is it?
4. What is the setting of the story?
5. How would you describe the character of the leprechaun? What kind of person is he?

Apply

B. 6.–10. Make up a character who could be in a story. Write five sentences that tell about your character.

A BOOK TO READ

Title: **Anna's Magic Broom**
Author: Barbara Westman
Publisher: Houghton Mifflin

One day, Anna had a strange visitor—a flying broom! Off she rode with her pet cat to explore the city. She was sorry to see that the city was a mess. With the help of the broom, she swept the whole town clean.

The people of the town were delighted—all but mean Marvin. He tried to steal the broom. The town grew dirtier, and Anna grew sadder and sadder.

Find out how the people of the town helped Anna solve her problem. Read *Anna's Magic Broom.*

3 UNIT TEST

Verbs pages 80–81

One word in each sentence is a verb. Write the letter of the word that is a verb.

1. Hoshi walked quickly toward the pool.
   (a: Hoshi, b: walked, c: quickly)
2. Joyce and Stefan waded in the shallow end.
   (a: and, b: waded, c: shallow)
3. Freddie splashed Jonathan near the steps.
   (a: Freddie, b: splashed, c: Jonathan)
4. Miriam dives for pennies with Barbara.
   (a: Miriam, b: dives, c: pennies)
5. The older girls swim laps until noon.
   (a: older, b: girls, c: swim)
6. We jumped off the board into the water.
   (a: jumped, b: board, c: water)

Past Time and Present Time pages 82–83

Copy the sentences. Underline the verbs. After each sentence write whether the verb tells about *past* or *present* time.

7. Cows march toward their milking barn in a line.
8. Our rooster crowed in the morning sunshine.
9. Four ducks waddled lazily near the pond.
10. The farmer drives his tractor through the field.
11. Five kittens tumbled in the barn hayloft.
12. We collect fresh brown eggs in the henhouse.

Subject-Verb Agreement pages 84–85

Choose the correct verb. Write the sentences.

13. Keiko (cross, crosses) a log over the stream.
14. Her sisters (find, finds) mushrooms in the woods.
15. A hawk (circle, circles) in the sky above.

Past Time Verbs pages 86–87

Change the verbs to show past time. Write the sentences.

16. Carol opens the typewriter case.
17. She plugs the typewriter cord into the socket.
18. The big blue machine hums.
19. Carol taps out her name on the keys.
20. She erases one little mistake.

Other Past Time Verbs pages 88–89

Change the verbs to show past time.

21. study	**22.** worry	**23.** dry
24. marry	**25.** copy	**26.** reply
27. hurry	**28.** cry	**29.** scurry
30. try	**31.** carry	**32.** ferry

Forms of <u>Have</u> pages 90–91

Choose the correct answer. Write the sentences.

33. Mother (has, have) promised us a trip.
34. Tom (has, have) explored this area already.
35. David and Sue (has, have) looked for a table.
36. The boys (has, have) wandered away somewhere.
37. Lou (has, have) decided to come back next year.
38. Kai (has, have) visited the garden in back.
39. Her parents (has, have) ordered sandwiches.
40. The smiling waiter (has, have) poured some milk.

Irregular Verbs pages 92–93

Choose the correct word. Write the sentences.

41. The child has (gone, went) downstairs already.
42. She has (run, ran) hot water for a bath.
43. Lani (come, comes) in to kiss me goodnight.
44. The boys (go, goes) to bed early.
45. Lani (gone, went) to bed at eight o'clock.

Choosing the Right Meaning pages 96–97

Read the dictionary entry. For each sentence tell which definition number is correct.

> **steam·er** [stē′mər] *n.* **1** A machine, engine, etc., worked or driven by steam, as a steamship. **2** A pot in which something is steamed: a *steamer* for vegetables. **3** A soft-shell clam cooked by steaming.

1. We ate *steamers* and fresh corn.
2. I saw a *steamer* passing on the river.

Homographs pages 98–99

Read the entries. Answer the questions below.

> **bluff**[1] [bluf] **1** *v.* To fool or frighten. **2** *n.* The act of bluffing. **3** *n.* A person who bluffs.
> **bluff**[2] [bluf] **1** *n.* A broad, steep bank or cliff. **2** *adj.* Broad, steep: a *bluff* seacoast. **3** *adj.* Gruff but kindly.

3. Are these homographs pronounced the same way?
4. Which entry could mean *a high cliff*?
5. Which entry could mean *someone who fools*?

Combining Predicates with and pages 100–101

Combine each pair of sentences. Use the word *and* to combine the predicates. Write the new sentences.

1. The leaves trembled. The leaves fell.
2. The wind moaned. The wind howled.
3. My umbrella twisted. My umbrella broke.
4. The branches creaked. The branches swayed.
5. The river swelled. The river flooded.
6. The storm raged. The storm roared.

Writing and Editing Sentences pages 102–104

Use lively verbs in place of these overused verbs. Write them in four sentences. Edit your sentences for capital letters and end marks.

7. go **8.** walk **9.** talked **10.** moved

Reading a Story pages 106–109

Read the story. Answer the questions that follow. Write complete sentences.

Horace Jones wanted to be a sailor. Finally his uncle allowed him to work on his ship.

The sailors on the ship learned that Horace was the captain's nephew. They gave him extra work to do. They teased him and told him he was too young and skinny to be a sailor.

Horace wanted to prove that he could be a good sailor. He worked very hard. One morning he was high in the rigging of the ship. He spotted a ship far in the distance. It had a black flag. "Pirates!" cried Horace. He called to the sailors. They came running.

Captain Jones's ship chased the pirate ship. The sailors captured the pirates. Horace had saved the day! The sailors never teased him again.

1. Who is the main character in this story?
2. What problem does this character have?
3. Where does the story take place?

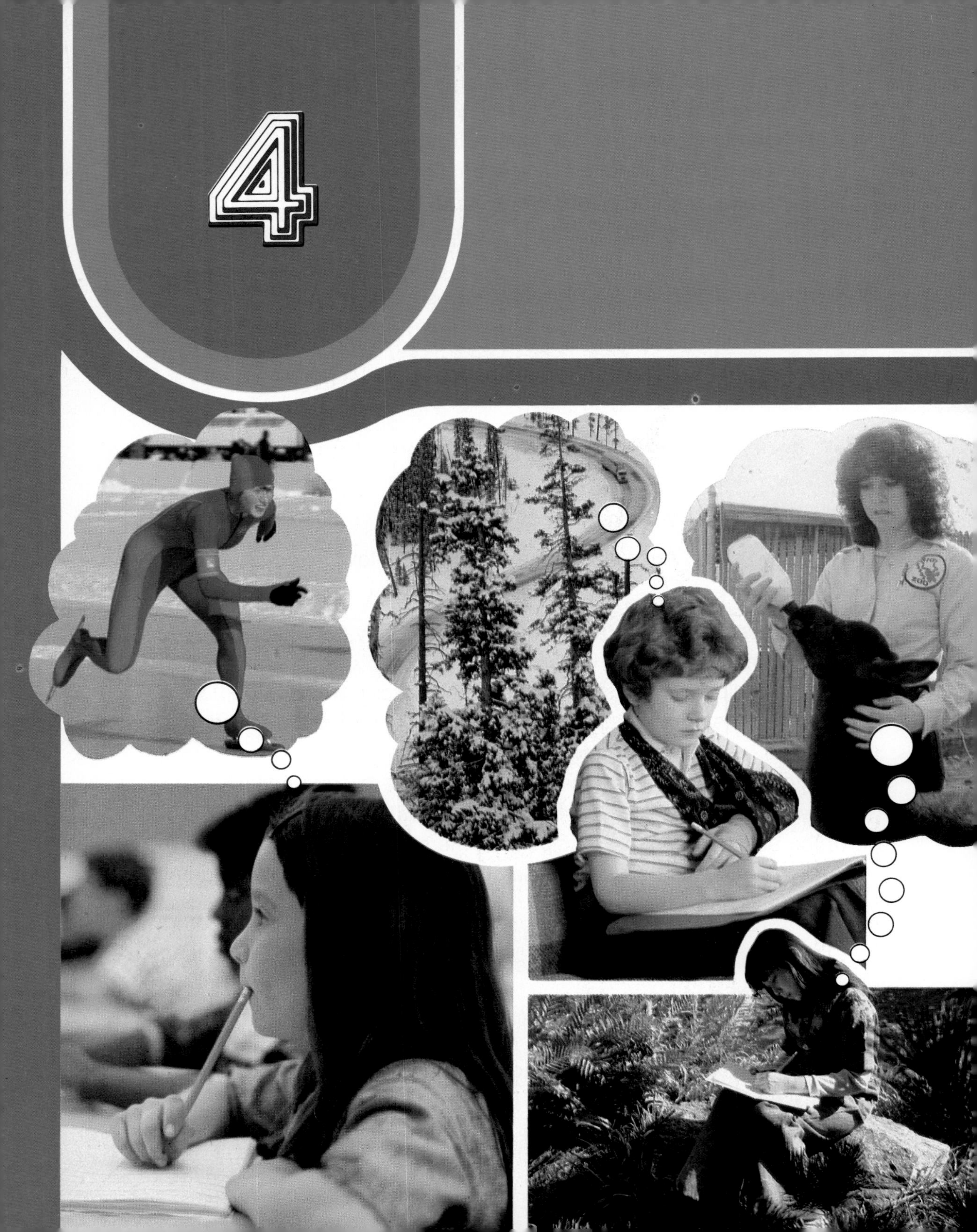

LANGUAGE
Learning About Paragraphs

COMPOSITION
Writing Paragraphs That Tell a Story

STUDY SKILLS
Organizing Your Writing

LITERATURE
Reading a Fable

Do you like to write stories? Writing a story can be as much fun as reading one.

You must plan the parts of your story before you begin. Decide what is going to happen in the beginning, the middle, and the end. Write the events in order so the story makes sense.

You have already learned about some important elements of stories. Your stories, too, must have characters, settings, and plots.

You should also try to make the words in your story as interesting as you can. The *way* you tell your story is as important as the story itself.

In this unit you will learn about writing stories. Perhaps one day you will become a story writer yourself.

LANGUAGE

Lesson 1: Understanding Paragraphs

Read these sentences about the moon.

The moon does not give light to the earth. It does not have its own light. The moon reflects the light of the sun.

Think and Discuss

All the sentences you have just read are about the same **main idea.** That main idea is *the moon gives no light.* Sentences that tell about the same main idea can be written in a group. That group of sentences is called a **paragraph.**

Look at the first word in the paragraph about the moon. The word *The* is indented. It is set in a few spaces from the left margin. The first word in a paragraph is always indented.

What other words on this page are indented? How many paragraphs are in this Think and Discuss section?

- A **paragraph** is a group of sentences that tell about one main idea.
- The first line of a paragraph is indented.

Practice

A. Read each paragraph. Then write the main idea of each paragraph.

1. Do you know what a comet looks like? A comet has a head and a tail. The head is made of gases and small solid pieces. The tail is made up of gases.

2. The nine planets are different distances from the sun. Mercury and Venus are closer to the sun than Earth is. Mars, Jupiter, and Saturn are farther from the sun than Earth. Uranus, Neptune, and Pluto are even farther away.

3. A meteor is a piece of matter from outer space. It looks like a streak of fire shooting across the sky. Another name for a meteor is a shooting star.

4. Our earth is made of many layers. The solid rock covering of the earth is called the crust. The second rock layer is called the mantle.

Apply

B. Read the following sentences. Choose the four sentences that tell about the same main idea. Write them in paragraph form.

5. Our sun is a star.
6. The sun is made up mainly of two gases.
7. There is no water on Mercury.
8. The sun gives the earth light and heat.
9. Pluto is a small planet.
10. Sunlight is needed for growing plants.

Lesson 2: Understanding the Topic Sentence

All the sentences in a paragraph are about one main idea. Read the following paragraph.

Every type of rock has a special name. Granite is the name of a hard rock. Limestone is a soft rock found in the walls of many caves. Shale is a flat smooth rock.

Think and Discuss

Some paragraphs have a sentence that states the main idea or topic. That sentence is called the **topic sentence.**

The paragraph above has a main idea. What is the main idea? Which sentence states the topic of the paragraph? That is the topic sentence.

A topic sentence is usually the first sentence of a paragraph. It may also be at the end. Where is the topic sentence in the paragraph about rocks?

- The **topic sentence** tells the main idea of the paragraph.

Practice

A. Read this paragraph carefully. Then close your book. Write the paragraph as your teacher reads it. Use correct paragraph form.

1. This house is made of rock. Large flat stones were used to build the chimney. Big rocks were used for the walls. Small flat stones cover the roof of the house.

B. Copy each paragraph below. Underline the topic sentence.

2. Rocks are different sizes. Pebbles are little rocks. Boulders are big rocks. Mountains may be giant rocks.
3. Rocks are found in many places. They are in river beds and on the beach. They are in vacant city lots. They are hidden underground.
4. Many things are made with rocks. Homes and buildings are made of rocks. Roads are built with rocks. Some rocks are made into beautiful jewelry.

Apply

C. Add a topic sentence to each paragraph. Then write the paragraphs.

5. Ruby stones are deep red in color. Jade stones are green. Moonstone is milky-white.
6. The Museum of Natural History in New York has a large rock collection. The Field Museum in Chicago has one too.
7. Large stone quarries for granite are found in Vermont. White marble is another important stone found in Vermont. Limestone and slate are also important Vermont products.
8. Diamonds are precious gems. Rubies and emeralds are gems too.

Lesson 3: Identifying Supporting Details

Read this paragraph.

The aquarium is a good place to learn about animals. You can take a tour with a guide. The guide will tell you the names of the fish. You will learn how sharks live in the ocean. You may watch a whale being fed.

What is the topic sentence of this paragraph?

Think and Discuss

The topic sentence tells the main idea of the paragraph. The other sentences give **details** about the topic. They help the reader understand more about the main idea. Which sentences in the paragraph tell about learning at the aquarium?

Practice

A. Copy the following paragraphs. Draw one line under each topic sentence. Draw two lines under the sentences that give more details.

1. Libraries are quiet places to study. No loud noises are allowed. There are chairs and tables for working. The librarian will make sure that nobody bothers the students.

2. It is best to go to our supermarket on Friday morning. The lines are not long then. The fruits and vegetables are fresh. It is easy to find everything you need.

3. A trip to the fire station can be exciting. When our class went, we learned many things. We heard the firebell ring. We tried on the fire chief's hat. He even let us ride on the engine.

Apply

B. 4.–8. Copy the topic sentence. It tells the main idea of the picture. Then write five details from the picture that tell more about the topic sentence.

A hospital is a busy place.

A Challenge

Write a paragraph about your day at school. First plan your topic sentence. Is your school day exciting? Do you work hard? Did anything unusual happen that you want to write about? Write the topic sentence. Then plan detail sentences. Make sure that they tell more about the topic sentence.

Lesson 4: Ordering Sentences in Paragraphs

Each paragraph has a main idea. It also has sentences with details that explain the main idea. All the sentences have to be put in the right order so that the paragraph will make sense.

Think and Discuss

Time-clue words help you put your sentences in order. Some time-clue words are *first, second, third, next, then, soon,* and *last* or *finally.*

Read the following paragraph.

Maria wanted to grow a sweet potato vine. First she placed the fat end of a sweet potato in a jelly jar. She checked to be sure the top of the sweet potato stuck out of the jar. Next she filled the jar with water. Soon she could see roots starting. Then the vine began to grow.

The main idea of this paragraph is written in a topic sentence. What is it? The detail sentences are written in the order in which they happen. What time-clue words did the writer use? The sentences are written in order. The paragraph makes good sense.

Practice

A. In each paragraph the topic sentence comes first. One sentence in each paragraph is out of order. Write the paragraphs. Put the sentences in the right order.

1. It is not easy to plant roses. First the soil must be prepared. Finally the bushes may be planted. Then holes must be dug one or two feet apart.

2. Quince can be grown from a small branch. Part of the branch is placed under the ground. At last a small yellow fruit appears. Soon the branch begins to grow.

Apply

B. Put the following sentences in order. Then write them in paragraph form. Underline the time-clue words in each paragraph.

3. Beans are easy to grow.
Last put the pot in a sunny window.
First cover lima beans with soil in a pot.
Next water them well.

4. Farmers plant different vegetables at different times of year.
First they plant cabbage and peas.
Tomatoes and eggplant are planted last.
Such vegetables as spinach and carrots are planted second.

Lesson 5: Keeping to the Topic

Suppose you were reading a paragraph about birds. Suddenly the author told you the best way to make mashed potatoes. How would you feel?

Think and Discuss

Every sentence in a paragraph should keep to the topic. An author who switches from birds to potatoes in a single paragraph confuses his or her readers. A single sentence that does not keep to the topic weakens the paragraph. It makes the paragraph harder to understand.

Read the following paragraph.

> There are over 300 kinds of parrots. They come in all sizes and colors. I have a birdcage in my room. Different kinds of parrots are found in different countries.

What is the main idea of this paragraph? Which sentence does not keep to the topic?

Practice

A. Copy each paragraph. Leave out the sentence that does not keep to the topic.

1. Parrots come in all sizes. Some parrots are 40 inches (101 centimeters) long. I am learning how to measure in centimeters. Others are less than 4 inches (10 centimeters) long.

2. Macaws are interesting birds. They are the largest parrots. Parakeets are small. Macaws have brightly colored feathers.

3. Parrots are smart. They learn quickly. Many parrots can be taught to speak. Fran's father bought her a cat for a pet.

Apply

B. 4.–8. Pick one of these topic sentences. Write five detail sentences that tell more about it. Be sure all your sentences keep to the topic.

My pet can do some tricks.
A bird feeder can help birds in the winter.
Pets can be good friends.

HOW OUR LANGUAGE GROWS

Have you ever asked friends to give you a hand? Did they *really* give you their hands? No, not really. You used a *figure of speech.* Figures of speech help us to say things in interesting ways. Many figures of speech use the word *hand. Hand* is a very *handy* word.

What do these figures of speech mean?

1. Please give me a *hand.*
2. The audience gave her a big *hand.*
3. The noise was getting *out of hand.*
4. I have a lot of time *on my hands.*
5. He has the *upper hand* in the argument.

LANGUAGE REVIEW

Paragraphs pages 116–117

Write the following sentences in paragraph form. Then write the main idea of the paragraph.

1. When you swim, remember important safety rules.
2. Never go in the water alone.
3. Do not run around the edge of the pool.
4. Before diving, be sure the water is deep enough.

The Topic Sentence pages 118–119

Copy the topic sentence in each of the following paragraphs.

5. The jungle is full of life. Its wet warm climate makes things grow quickly. One tree may be the home for hundreds of living things.
6. Many jungle animals are only active at night. Jungle bats use a kind of radar to fly at night. Jungle leopards have large eyes to help them hunt in the dark.
7. The weather in the Yucatan jungle is hot and steamy. Plants grow well in the dampness. Sudden rains keep the jungle damp.

Supporting Details pages 120–121

Copy the sentences that give supporting details for this topic sentence.

I learned to ski.

8. I went to a ski school in January.
9. My sister taught me to skate last winter.
10. My first snow skis were short.
11. I had to ski on the smallest hill.

Sentence Order in Paragraphs pages 122–123

Put these sentences in order. Write the paragraph.

12. Yesterday I watched a squirrel getting ready for winter. It carried nuts inside its mouth as it ran up a tree. First it ran here and there collecting nuts. Then it disappeared inside a hole in the tree.

Keeping to the Topic pages 124–125

Copy each paragraph. Leave out the sentence that does not keep to the topic.

13. Washington, D.C. is our nation's capital. The President lives there. Congress meets there to make laws. Another important city is Philadelphia. People come from all over to see the government at work in Washington.

14. Yesterday was Election Day. My parents went to the polling place to vote. They voted for people to become judges in our town. They voted for a new mayor too. While they were gone, I made dinner for my little brother and sister.

Applying Paragraphs

15. Write a paragraph about one of these main ideas. Write a topic sentence first. Your other sentences should give details in the correct order. Be sure to indent the first word.

the best time of day
a game I play
making breakfast
feeding a pet
a dream I had
trying on new clothes
a letter from a friend
visiting a farm

STUDY SKILLS

Lesson 6: Finding the Main Idea

The main idea in a paragraph is the most important idea in the paragraph. The sentences in the paragraph explain the main idea. They may also give details about it.

Think and Discuss

Read the paragraph below.

Some trains travel under the ground. They are called subway trains. They travel through large tunnels that have been dug in the earth and rock. Often people riding and walking above ground cannot hear the trains.

What is the main idea of this paragraph? What is the topic sentence? Which sentences give details about the main idea?

Practice

A. Read the following paragraphs. Then choose the main idea, *a, b,* or *c,* and write it.

1. Some airplanes are huge. They can carry hundreds of people. They may have five or more doorways. One big plane carried our first space shuttle on a test flight.

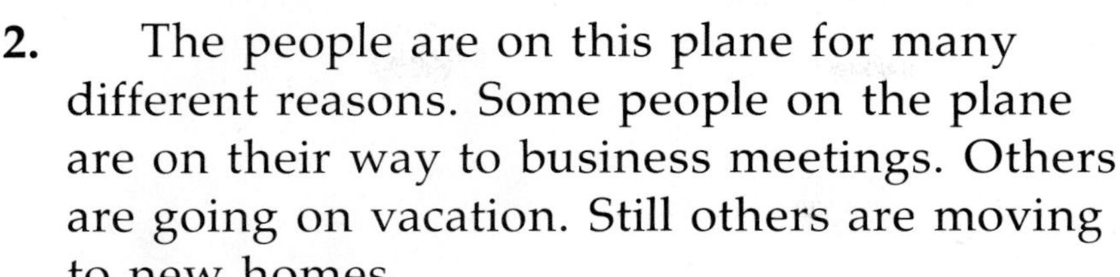

a. the space shuttle
b. huge airplanes
c. many doorways

2. The people are on this plane for many different reasons. Some people on the plane are on their way to business meetings. Others are going on vacation. Still others are moving to new homes.

a. high above the ground
b. going on vacation
c. different reasons for traveling

3. Mr. Brown takes many plane trips. He travels on his job. He went to North Carolina last week. Next week he will go to Massachusetts. In October he will fly to Los Angeles, California.

a. a trip to Massachusetts
b. Mr. Brown travels a lot
c. the many jobs of Mr. Brown

4. Diane took a flying lesson. She rode in a small plane. The pilot showed her how to steer. Then she flew for three minutes alone. She had a wonderful time.

a. Diane's flying lesson
b. learning to steer
c. small planes

Apply

B. 5. Find a good paragraph in your science or social studies book. Copy it. Then tell what the main idea of that paragraph is.

Lesson 7: Choosing and Limiting the Topic

Brenda has decided to write a paragraph about her dog. She has a lot of topic ideas. Will she be able to put all her topic ideas in one paragraph?

Think and Discuss

A paragraph must have only one main idea. How many topics should Brenda write about in one paragraph?

Brenda wanted to write about playing with her puppy. She found that she had too much to say. She could not fit it all into one paragraph. She then decided to write about swimming with her puppy. This topic is not too big. Brenda could write one good paragraph about swimming with her puppy. She has **limited** her topic.

Practice

A. Which topic in each group is the best size for a paragraph? Choose *a, b,* or *c.* Write the topic on your paper.

1. a. Aesop's fables
   b. fairy tales and fables
   c. how to read a fable aloud
2. a. plants
   b. leaves of an apple tree
   c. trees in America
3. a. songs of many countries
   b. a famous American folk song
   c. music in our time
4. a. how to make cocoa
   b. hot drinks
   c. coffee, tea, and cocoa
5. a. calendars in history
   b. months of the year
   c. how July got its name

Apply

B. For each topic think of a more limited topic. The first one has been done for you.

6. hamsters (what hamsters look like)
7. doctors
8. furniture
9. games
10. movies

To Memorize

Whoever is happy will make others happy too.

Anne Frank

Are you happiest when you are with happy people? What do you do to make other people happy?

COMPOSITION

Lesson 8: Writing a Story Beginning

The beginning of a story is very important. It makes us curious. We read the story because we want to know what is going to happen. We want to know what the characters will do.

Think and Discuss

Erica wrote a story about something that happened to her. This is how she began.

Last summer Dad and I were fishing at the lake. Suddenly we heard a loud crash.

The beginning of a story tells the reader *who* the story is about. It tells *what* is happening. It tells *where* it is happening and *when* it is happening. *Who, what, where,* and *when* are called the 4 *W's.*

There is one more *W.* We have to read the story to find out *why* certain things are happening.

Erica told us the 4 *W's* in the beginning of her story. Find the answers to these questions.

Who is in Erica's story?
When did it happen?
Where did it happen?
What happened?

A story beginning introduces the characters. It gives the setting for the story.

Practice

A. Read these beginning sentences. Write what the underlined words tell: *who, what, where,* or *when.*

1. Last week I bought an elephant <u>at the fair</u>.
2. Mara <u>found a gold ring</u> on the street yesterday.
3. <u>My brother</u> yelled to me from downstairs.
4. <u>Today</u> the train whistled three times.
5. <u>Neka and Dena</u> are going to the cave now.

B. The following beginning sentences are missing one of the 4 *W's.* Copy them. Add the missing part.

6. The ______ crawled through the grass in the field. (who)
7. Colleen won the race ______. (when)
8. My mother ______ at the park yesterday. (what)
9. Tomorrow I will learn to bake bread ______. (where)
10. The lion tamer ______ at the circus yesterday. (what)

Apply

C. 11. Write a story beginning using one of these topics. Include the 4 *W's.*

The Prize-Winning Pig
Caught in a Snowstorm
Finding a Wallet Full of Money
A Wish That Came True

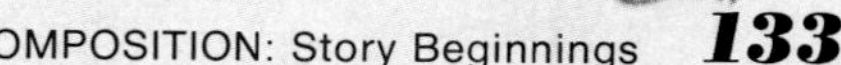

Lesson 9: Writing Stories in Order

Here is the story Erica has written so far. Read her story beginning.

Last summer Dad and I were fishing at the lake. Suddenly we heard a loud crash.

What might Erica tell about next?

Think and Discuss

The story beginning sets the scene for the action in the story. The main part of a story tells what happens to the characters. Sentences in a story must be in order so that the story makes sense.

Here is the main part of Erica's story. What happened first after she heard the noise? What happened next?

I thought a big animal was coming through the woods toward us. We waited for a few minutes. Then we went to see what had happened. A tree had fallen across the path in the woods. The top of the tree was in the lake. Something had chewed through the trunk of the tree near the bottom.

Are Erica's sentences in order? Does the story make sense?

Erica's story is not finished. You will see how she ends the story in Lesson 10.

Practice

A. Copy the following story events in the right order.

1. **a.** Koko lived next to a city lot that was full of trash.
b. They prepared the soil in the lot and planted the seeds.
c. She and her friends worked hard to clear away the trash.
d. Koko and her friends earn money selling the vegetables they grow.

2. **a.** The airplane circled the airport.
b. Slowly, the door opened.
c. It landed on the runway.
d. She saw her uncle standing at the airport window.
e. Maria was the first person to leave the plane.
f. She ran to greet him.

3. **a.** With one quick move he pulled the cloth away.
b. Marc had practiced his magic trick for days.
c. He put glasses and plates on the tablecloth.
d. He placed a cloth over the table.
e. The children gasped and cheered.
f. The glasses and plates stayed on the table.

Apply

B. **4.** Look at the story beginning you wrote in Lesson 8. What is going to happen to the characters? Write a main part for your story. Tell about what the characters do.

Lesson 10: Writing a Story Ending

Here is the story Erica has written so far.

Last summer Dad and I were fishing at the lake. Suddenly we heard a loud crash. I thought a big animal was coming through the woods toward us. We waited for a few minutes. Then we went to see what had happened. A tree had fallen across the path in the woods. The top of the tree was in the lake. Something had chewed through the trunk of the tree near the bottom.

What question has not been answered?

Think and Discuss

The end of a story tells how the characters solve their problems. It finishes the story.

Erica wanted to end her story. She thought of three ways to do it. Which ending is the best one?

1. The beavers were building again.
2. Now no one could cross the path.
3. We wondered who had done this.

Sentence 1 is the best ending. It answers the problem in the story. The other endings do not say why the tree fell down.

A good ending fits the story. It makes what happened clear. It finishes the story. The reader is left with a satisfied feeling because everything has been explained.

Practice

A. Copy each story. Then choose the best ending. Add it to the story.

1. One Saturday Jimmy and Bill dressed up like tramps. They put patches on their shirts. Their clothes were torn. Mrs. Hill was very surprised when two ragged tramps came to her door.

a. She had forgotten it was Halloween.
b. She did not know the boys.
c. She told them to wash up.

2. Betsy was delivering papers on her bike early one morning. She saw a light in Ben's store. Betsy rode closer to the light. The light became bigger and brighter. Betsy stopped her bike and looked in the store window.

a. The light came from the headlight on her own bicycle.
b. She could not see the light anymore.
c. The light was brighter than moonlight.

Apply

B. 3. Read over the story you wrote in Lessons 8 and 9. How should the story end? How can the characters solve their problems? Think of a few ideas. Then write the story ending you like best. Check to make sure that the ending fits the story. Will it leave the reader feeling satisfied?

Lesson 11: Writing a Story

Sandra wrote a story about something that happened at camp. Read her story.

The Missing Cookies

Something strange happened at camp today. My parents sent me a box of cookies. I left them on my bed. When we all came back to the bunk after lunch, the cookies were gone. Who had taken them? Suddenly we heard a noise from the closet. I opened the door very slowly. A skunk was happily eating Joyce's crackers. On the floor beside him was the last of my cookies.

Think and Discuss

Does Sandra's story have a beginning, a main part, and an end? Who are the characters in the story? What is the story's setting?

Sandra added a **title** to her story. The title is "The Missing Cookies." This title gives the main idea of the story. It interests the reader. Notice that the words in the title begin with capital letters. When you write titles, begin the first, last, and all important words with capital letters.

How to Write a Story

1. Plan your story. Think of characters, setting, a problem, and an ending to solve the problem.
2. Write an interesting beginning. In it, introduce the main character and the setting.
3. Tell the problem the main character will face. Then write the main part of the story.
4. Write an ending. Tell how the main character solves the problem.
5. Think of a good title for your story. Begin the important words of the title with capital letters.

Practice

A. Think of something that has happened to you or to someone you know. Plan a story about it. Write the answers to these questions.

1. Who is in your story?
2. Where will the story take place?
3. When does it happen?
4. What is the problem in the story?
5. What do the characters do about the problem?
6. How should the story end?
7. What is the title of the story?

Apply

B. **8.** Look back at your answers for Practice A. Use those answers and the rules in this lesson to write your story.

Lesson 12: Editing a Story

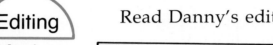

- capitalize
- make a period
- add something
- add a comma
- add quotation marks
- take something away
- spell correctly
- indent the paragraph
- make a lowercase letter
- tr transpose

Read Danny's edited story.

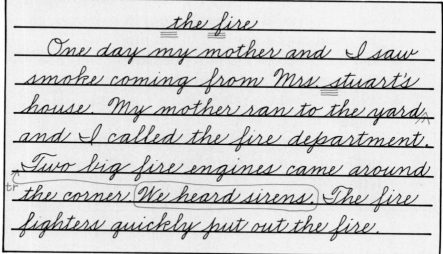

the fire

One day my mother and I saw smoke coming from Mrs. stuart's house. My mother ran to the yard and I called the fire department. Two big fire engines came around the corner. We heard sirens. The fire fighters quickly put out the fire.

Think and Discuss

Danny used the letters *tr* to show that he needed to **transpose** two sentences. Transpose means to make words or sentences change places. Danny circled the sentence he wanted to move and drew an arrow to show where it should go. Why did Danny make this change?

He used this mark ^, to add a comma. Where did he put the comma? What other editing mark did he use? Why did he need to use it?

Danny's changes made his story clearer and easier to read. Now he will copy the story over.

Practice

A. Write Danny's story correctly. Include all the changes he made.

Apply

B. Edit the story you wrote in Lesson 11. Did you follow the rules for writing stories? Rewrite your story.

MECHANICS PRACTICE

Writing Paragraphs

- Begin sentences with capital letters.
- Indent the first line of a paragraph.

Write these paragraphs correctly.

1. Mexico is a country with many large cities. the capital of Mexico is Mexico City. It is the largest city in Mexico. other large cities are Guadalajara, Monterrey, and Acapulco.
2. Jai alai is a game played in Mexico. the players hit a ball with a racket. the racket looks like a small basket. jai alai is an exciting game to watch.
3. Mexico is south of the United States. the weather there is usually warm. in January some parts of Mexico are warm enough for swimming.
4. Texas is a state. it was once part of Mexico. the people in Texas fought with Mexico. in 1845 Texas became part of the United States.
5. mountains cover parts of Mexico. some of the mountains have mines for silver and iron. others are used for growing coffee. many of the mountains are really volcanoes.

LITERATURE

Lesson 13: Reading a Fable

Long ago very few people knew how to read or write. Parents told stories to their children. Some stories were used to teach lessons. They were always short so that children could remember them. These short stories are called **fables.**

Think and Discuss

Often the characters in fables are animals. They think, talk, and act like people. They make the mistakes people make. A fable is a short animal story with a lesson for people.

Now read this fable.

Fox and Crow

by Aesop

A big black crow sat high in a tree. In his beak he held a delicious hunk of cheese. A fox passed by. Looking up, he spotted Crow. He noticed what Crow was holding, and he decided to get some of the cheese for himself.

"How are you, dear Crow?" called Fox. Crow, of course, could not answer. His beak was full of cheese.

"You look lovely today," said the crafty fox.

Crow puffed up his feathers a bit and peered down at Fox.

"My, my," Fox went on, "I certainly admire the way your feathers shine in the sunlight. Black is my favorite color, you know."

Crow did not answer, but he listened carefully to every word.

"There is nothing as handsome as a crow in flight," said Fox. "Your wings are so huge! You are so graceful!"

Crow spread his wings and fluttered them in the breeze. Fox was right; they were lovely. He was very pleased with Fox's flattery.

"Oh, it is true," Fox smiled. "You are a stunning creature. It is all the sadder, then, that you have no voice. If only you could sing, I believe you could be the finest bird in the forest!"

Poor, silly Crow. He wanted so much to be the finest bird in the forest. It was true that his voice was usually quite loud and scratchy, but he simply needed to practice. Perhaps Fox enjoyed loud songs. Crow tilted his head back, opened his beak, and let out a shrill "Caw! Caw!"

With that, the cheese fell out of his beak and dropped to the ground. Fox gulped it down in one bite and ran off into the forest.

Never listen to flattery.

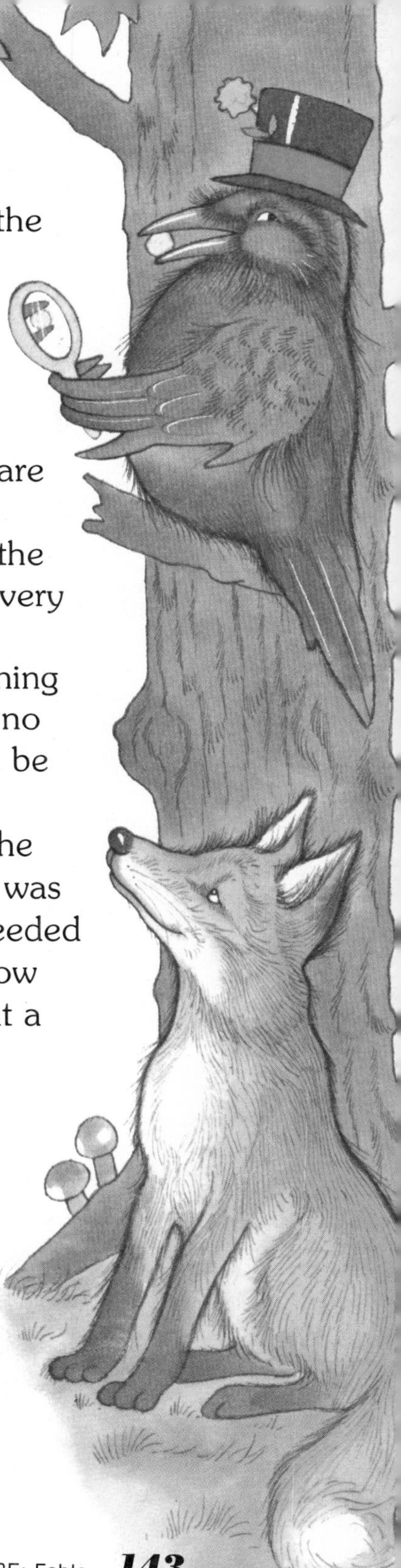

The last sentence in this fable teaches the lesson of the fable. Such a lesson is called the **moral** of the fable. Can you explain the moral of this fable in your own words?

Practice

A. Write *true* if the statement is true. Write *false* if it is not true.

1. All animal stories are fables.
2. Animals in fables behave like people.
3. Fables are short stories.
4. The main character in a fable is usually a person.
5. A fable teaches a lesson.

B. Read this story. Answer the questions that follow.

Ant and Dove

by Aesop

One day, little Ant went to the pond for a drink of water. As she leaned over, she slipped and fell in. Dove was resting on a branch, admiring her reflection in the pond. She heard Ant's cries for help. Thinking quickly, she pulled a leaf from the branch and dropped it in front of Ant. Ant crawled aboard and was saved.

The following week, Dove and Ant were at the pond again. A man came by with a net. When he saw Dove, he spread the net and tried to catch her. Ant raced over and bit the man on his toe. With a squeal of dismay, the man dropped the net and ran off. Dove wriggled out of the net and flew away, free.

One good turn deserves another.

6. Is this a fable? How can you tell?
7. What is the moral of "Ant and Dove"?
8. Explain the moral in your own words.

Apply

C. 9. Choose one moral. Explain it in your own words. Then write a fable that teaches that lesson. Use animals as your characters.

Don't cry over spilled milk.
Don't put off until tomorrow what you can do today.
Tricky people should not complain when they themselves are tricked.

A BOOK TO READ

Title: **Fables**
Author: Arnold Lobel
Publisher: Harper & Row

Can a lumpy, humpy camel in a tutu dance in a ballet? What would you think of a crocodile in sunglasses and a bathrobe? Is it possible for a cat, in a hat, to catch a fish for his dish?

These are brand-new, full-of-fun fables by a man who draws pictures every bit as well as he writes stories. Each crab, lobster, beetle, and lion in these fables will teach you a lesson. Don't forget, however, "*Advice From Friends Is Like The Weather. Some Of It's Good; Some Of It's Bad.*"

4 UNIT TEST

Paragraphs pages 116–117

One thing is wrong with each of these paragraphs. Write the letter of the item that tells what it is.

1. Joe Namath was a great football player. He threw many touchdown passes. He was able to make quick decisions to win games.

   a. The paragraph is not indented.
   b. The paragraph does not keep to the topic.
   c. The paragraph has groups of words that are not sentences.

2. Wilma Rudolph was a champion runner. Ran for the United States Olympic team. Weak and sickly as a child. Fought against her sickness and won.

   a. The paragraph is not indented.
   b. The paragraph does not keep to the topic.
   c. The paragraph has groups of words that are not sentences.

The Topic Sentence pages 118–119

Copy the paragraph. Underline the topic sentence.

3. Animals have many different defenses. The bony armor plates of an armadillo protect it. The wild boar has sharp tusks. The claws of a lobster can crush other animals.

Supporting Details pages 120–121

Read the topic sentence. Copy only the details that support the topic sentence.

Topic sentence: The Pony Express delivered mail between Missouri and California.

4. The swift ponies and expert riders were faster than stagecoaches.
5. The young riders rode at top speed.
6. Today most mail travels by air.
7. The Pony Express lost the mail only once.
8. The news of Abraham Lincoln's election was carried to California by the Pony Express.
9. Horses are some of the fastest animals.

Sentence Order in Paragraphs pages 122–123

The sentences in this paragraph are in the wrong order. Rewrite the paragraph correctly.

10. Frogs grow very strangely. The little tadpoles begin to grow legs. Tadpoles hatch from eggs. Some months later, the tadpoles become frogs.

Keeping to the Topic pages 124–125

Rewrite the paragraph. Leave out the sentences that do not keep to the topic.

11. Trees have many uses. They are homes for birds, insects, animals, and even other plants. Pine cones are interesting. Trees make oxygen. They protect other growing things from sun and wind. Some apple trees are growing in my backyard. Many useful things such as paper and matches are made from trees.

Finding the Main Idea pages 128–129

Write the letter of the item that tells the main idea of each paragraph.

1. My favorite color is red. It is a bright, cheerful color. Apples and strawberries are red. My bicycle is red too.

a. a color I like **b.** colors
c. fruits that are red

2. We play games outside after school. If we have enough people, we play baseball. *Hide-and-seek* is good for smaller groups. *Tag* is also a good outdoor game.
   a. my neighborhood **b.** outdoor games we play
   c. games for large groups

Choosing and Limiting the Topic pages 130–131

Study each pair of topics. Write the best choice for a paragraph topic on your paper.

3. Famous Waterfalls
   Niagara Falls
4. The Life of Columbus
   Columbus as a Boy
5. Your Amazing Heart
   The Human Body
6. Importance of Plants
   Medicine from Plants

Story Beginnings pages 132–133

Write the one sentence that tells the four *W*'s: *who, what, where,* and *when.*

1. The little man laughed and ran up the hill.
2. Mr. Lupo played the piano for me on Saturday.
3. A strange bird landed in Ima's yard last night.

Stories in Order pages 134–135

Write this story in an order that makes sense.

4. One winter night Sam heard a howl outside his cabin. He was worried that it might be a wolf. He tramped through the snowdrifts to the river. When the snow stopped, Sam went to look.

Story Endings pages 136–137

Write the sentence that would best end the story above.

5. Sam was very surprised at what he saw.
6. A small beagle pup was howling at the moon.
7. There were no wolves to be seen.

Writing and Editing a Story pages 138–140

8. Write a story with a beginning, a middle, and an end. Think of an interesting way to begin your story. Be sure the end of your story solves the characters' problems. Edit your story for capital letters and end marks. You may use this list of story ideas.

The Secret Room	Night in a Toy Store
Airport Adventure	How Bear Tricked Fox
Escape of the Animals	A Message in a Bottle

Fables pages 142–145

Read this fable. Then answer the questions below.

The Cat and the Pig

A cat was walking along the road. She stepped carefully around the puddles, and she held her tail high so that it would not get dusty. As she walked, she met a pig, who touched the cat's paw as she passed.

"Get away!" snapped the cat. "Pigs are dirty, disgusting creatures!" The pig said nothing.

On her way home that night, the cat slipped on a stone and fell into a muddy bog. She dripped mud from every whisker as she ran howling to the nearest lighted doorway.

The pig opened the door. Inside the cat could see a spotless, cheerful room. "Please let me come inside and clean up," she begged.

The pig laughed. "You may clean yourself at my well in the yard," she said, "but I cannot allow you to track mud in my clean house. Cats are dirty, disgusting creatures!"

Never judge someone whom you do not know.

1. Who are the characters in this fable?
2. What lesson did the cat learn? Explain it in your own words.

MAINTENANCE and REVIEW

Parts of a Sentence pages 10–11

Copy the sentences. Draw one line under the subjects. Draw two lines under the predicates.

1. My dog shakes hands with visitors.
2. Uncle Burt and Cousin Robin came to my house.
3. They greeted my dog at the door.
4. The silly dog held out its paw and shook hands.

Proper Nouns and Abbreviations pages 46–53

Write these sentences correctly. Use capital letters and periods.

5. mrs goldstein is our nearest neighbor.
6. She lives in westport, connecticut.
7. dr goldstein works in the town of bridgeport.
8. Last thanksgiving the goldsteins visited norway.

Verbs pages 80–81

Copy the sentences. Underline the action verbs.

9. Peter belongs to the track team at school.
10. He runs in the cross-country races.
11. Last year Peter won a gold cup and a medal.
12. He beat the best runner at Farley School.
13. His family watched him from the grandstand.

Subject-Verb Agreement pages 84–85

Choose the correct verb in ( ). Write the sentences.

14. The girls (dress, dresses) in old clothes.
15. Michelle (wash, washes) the car with Father.
16. Her sisters (spray, sprays) the windows with water.
17. Ann (wax, waxes) the car, and Beth (shine, shines) it.

Past Time Verbs pages 86–89

Change the verbs to show past time. Write the sentences.

18. Mr. and Mrs. Lopez own a small bakery.
19. Mr. Fiorelli repairs furniture in his shop.
20. My sister cooks in a health-food restaurant.
21. I carry shopping bags for people at the market.
22. Many people shop at the market on Main Street.
23. My sister and I like our jobs very much.

Helping Verbs pages 90–91

Copy the sentences that use forms of *have* as helping verbs.

24. We always have a wonderful time at the beach.
25. John has carried his blanket onto the sand.
26. Rita and Kay have changed into swimsuits.
27. They have waded into the shallow water.
28. Carol has a beachball and a small radio.

Irregular Verbs pages 92–93

Choose the correct verb in ( ). Write the sentences.

29. Kanoa (go, goes) to school by herself each day.
30. Yesterday she (run, ran) all the way there.
31. Today Lia (runs, run) with Kanoa.

Topic Sentence and Keeping to the Topic pages 118–119, 124–125

Copy the paragraph. Leave out the sentence that does not keep to the topic. Underline the topic sentence.

32. People were excited when Prince Charles visited our city. Many people lined the street to see him. The prince lives in England. People cheered when he arrived.

5
ONE WAY
DONT
WALK

LANGUAGE
Learning About Adjectives

STUDY SKILLS
Building Vocabulary

COMPOSITION
Writing Descriptions

LITERATURE
Reading Poetry

Look at the pictures on page 152. They show a rainy day. The word *rainy* tells about the noun *day*. It describes the kind of day that is pictured.

Pretend you are in the pictures. What kinds of sounds would you hear? How would you feel? What kinds of buildings would you see? What are some of the different colors you would see? How many people would you see? How would those people feel? The words you used are describing words.

You will learn more about describing words in this unit. You will use them to write a paragraph. You will see how they are used in poetry. Describing words add variety to the language you use every day.

LANGUAGE

Lesson 1: Understanding Adjectives

Read these sentences.

1. That tall woman lives here.
2. She lives in this tiny town.
3. The white house belongs to her.

What are the nouns in sentences 1, 2, and 3?

Think and Discuss

Nouns name people, places, and things. A word that describes a noun is called an **adjective.** Look back at sentences 1, 2, and 3. What kind of woman does sentence 1 tell about? In what kind of town does she live? What kind of house does she own? The words that answer these questions are describing words, or adjectives.

Now read these sentences. Think of a describing word to finish each one.

4. The ______ chair is mine.
5. We bought the ______ mirror yesterday.
6. It will hang over the ______ sofa.

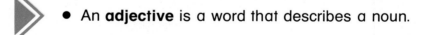

- An **adjective** is a word that describes a noun.

Practice

A. Copy the sentences. Circle the adjective that describes each underlined noun.

1. The dog is not allowed on our new rug.
2. Do you like my orange bedspread?
3. I hung a framed picture on the wall.
4. That striped wallpaper matches the rug.
5. The metal desk will fit against the wall.

B. Copy the sentences. Circle the adjectives.

6. A gray squirrel dropped a small acorn.
7. My neighbors play interesting games.
8. This is a pleasant neighborhood.
9. The streets are lined with green trees.
10. My best friend lives down the block.
11. Our new house is on a shady street.
12. A wooden fence surrounds the lovely garden.
13. Yellow roses and white carnations grow there.
14. I picked a big bouquet for my little sister.
15. Friendly people live here.

Apply

C. 16.–25. Copy this paragraph. Add adjectives in each blank.

We needed a ______ person to help us move. One ______ man carried my ______ desk. Another carried the ______ chair and the ______ table. They were careful not to break our ______ china. The hardest thing to move was the ______ piano. It took ______ people to move it up the ______ stairs. We were very ______ by the end of the day.

Lesson 2: Understanding Kinds of Adjectives

It is ten o'clock. The department store opens. People crowd in. Read about things that happen inside.

1. Martin sees ten hats on a rack.
2. They are purple hats.
3. They are large hats.
4. He finds a soft hat he likes.

Think and Discuss

Which adjective tells *how many* hats? *What color* are the hats? *What size* are the hats? How do the hats *feel* to the touch?

Adjectives can tell many things about nouns. They can tell *how many (five, some).* They can tell *what color (red, blue).* Some adjectives tell *what size or shape (big, round).*

Some adjectives tell about how an object *feels (fluffy, rough)* or *sounds (loud, shrill).* Others tell how an object *smells (musty, perfumed)* or *tastes (juicy, sweet).*

Now read these sentences. Think of adjectives to add that tell *how many, what size,* and *what color.*

5. June tried on ______ jackets.
6. Alex looked at ______ television sets.
7. Lucia found ______ sunglasses.

Practice

A. Write the adjective in each sentence that describes the underlined noun. Tell whether it tells *how many, what color,* or *what size.*

1. I see the green coat I want.
2. It has eight buttons down the front.
3. We went down the long hallway.
4. This store has four floors.
5. There Martin found some gloves he liked.

B. Write the adjective that describes each underlined noun. Tell whether it tells how something *feels, smells, sounds,* or *tastes.*

6. We ate lunch in a noisy restaurant.
7. It was nice to relax on the soft chairs.
8. I had a sandwich and a sour pickle.
9. The sweet odor of cakes made me hungry.
10. I enjoyed every bit of my delicious lunch.

Apply

C. Copy these sentences. Add adjectives that tell the things stated in ( ).

11. This store is ______. (what size)
12. It has ______ interesting things on display. (how many)
13. On weekends it is a ______ place. (sound)
14. The restaurant serves ______ hamburgers and ______ soup. (taste, feel)
15. ______ people can fit in its ______ booths. (how many, what color)

Lesson 3: Understanding Articles

What are the nouns in these sentences?

1. A trumpet announces the acrobats.
2. An acrobat bows to the king.

Think and Discuss

The underlined words in sentences 1 and 2 are special adjectives. They do not really describe the nouns. Just as the trumpet announces the acrobats, these adjectives announce the nouns. These adjectives are called **articles.**

The article *the* can be used with all singular and plural nouns. Which singular noun does *the* signal in sentence 2 above? Which plural noun does it announce in sentence 1?

The articles *a* and *an* are used with singular nouns. *A* goes with nouns that begin with consonant sounds. *An* goes with nouns that begin with vowel sounds.

Would you use *a* or *an* in these sentences?

3. The juggler gave the queen ______ rose.
4. He tossed ______ apple up and caught it.

- *A, an,* and *the* are adjectives called **articles.**
- When a singular noun begins with a consonant sound, use *a.*
- When a singular noun begins with a vowel sound, use *an.*
- *The* is used with singular and plural nouns.

Practice

A. Choose the correct article. Write the sentences.

1. (The, A) audience is very quiet.
2. One acrobat does (a, an) somersault.
3. He juggles (a, an) orange and (a, an) ball.
4. (An, The) acrobats build (a, an) pyramid.
5. (An, The) queen enjoys (an, the) acrobatics.

Apply

B. Copy each word. Write *a* or *an* before it. Then use each word group in a sentence.

6. dance **7.** throne **8.** elf **9.** crown **10.** actor

HOW OUR LANGUAGE GROWS

Mountains and rivers are often given names that describe them.

The *Rocky Mountains* are known for their rocky peaks.
The *Smoky Mountains* were named for the mist that covers their peaks. It looks like smoke.
The *Sawtooth Mountains* have peaks that look like the sharp teeth of a saw.
The *Colorado River* winds through deep canyons of red stone. The word *colorado* means *red colored* in Spanish.

1. List some mountains, towns, or rivers that are near your home. Try to guess how they got their names.
2. Pretend you have discovered a river. Describe it and give it a name.

Lesson 4: Making Comparisons with er and est

Look at the pictures. Read the sentences.

1. Mount Snow is high.
2. Mount Elbert is higher than Mount Snow.
3. Mount Everest is the highest mountain of all.

Which adjective describes Mount Snow?

Think and Discuss

Adjectives can describe nouns. They can also describe by comparing two or more nouns. The adjective in sentence 2 compares two nouns—*Mount Elbert* and *Mount Snow.* What is the adjective? What two letters end it?

The adjective in sentence 3 compares more than two nouns. What three letters end that adjective?

The word *high* has one syllable. Most one-syllable adjectives add *er* or *est* to make comparisons.

Now read these sentences. What adjectives should complete each one?

4. The top of Mount Snow is *cold.*
5. The top of Mount Elbert is ______ than that.
6. The top of Mount Everest is the ______ of the three mountain tops.

- Add *er* to most one-syllable adjectives when they are used to compare two things.
- Add *est* to most one-syllable adjectives when they are used to compare more than two things.

Practice

A. Copy this chart. Write the missing adjectives.

1.	old	________	oldest
2.	tall	taller	________
3.	small	________	smallest
4.	long	________	longest
5.	warm	warmer	________

B. Choose the correct adjective in ( ). Write the sentences.

6. The lake is (deeper, deepest) than the river.
7. I am the (slower, slowest) hiker in the group.
8. Even Jeff is (faster, fastest) than I am.
9. The field is (warmer, warmest) than the forest.
10. This is the (longer, longest) trail I know.
11. The lake water is (colder, coldest) than the air.
12. This hill must be the (higher, highest) one in the whole world.

Apply

C. 13.–20. Add *er* and *est* to each adjective. Use each of the eight adjectives you make in a sentence of your own.

low young strong sharp

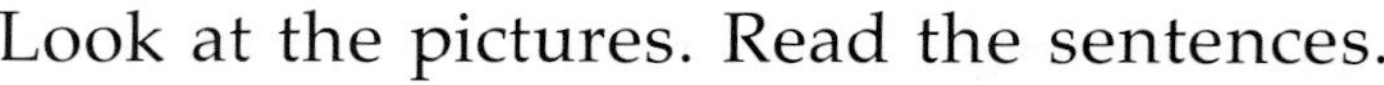

Lesson 5: Making Comparisons with More and Most

Look at the pictures. Read the sentences.

1. Football is exciting.
2. Baseball is more exciting than football.
3. Hockey is the most exciting sport of all.

Which sentence compares two things? Which compares more than two things?

Think and Discuss

One-syllable adjectives add *er* or *est* to compare. Adjectives with two or more syllables compare in a different way. These adjectives use the word *more* to compare two things. What word do they use to compare more than two things?

- Use *more* with many adjectives of two syllables. Use *more* with adjectives of three or more syllables. *More* is used to compare two things.
- Use *most* with many adjectives of two syllables. Use *most* with adjectives of three or more syllables. *Most* is used to compare more than two things.

Practice

A. 1.–5. Listen as your teacher reads some sentences. Write the sentences correctly as they are read. Be sure to begin and end each sentence correctly.

B. Copy this chart. Add the missing adjectives.

6.	difficult	______	most difficult
7.	unusual	more unusual	______
8.	beautiful	more beautiful	______
9.	frightening	______	most frightening
10.	terrible	more terrible	______

C. Finish each sentence with *more* or *most.*

11. Flo is ______ powerful than Ted is.
12. She is the ______ amazing skater I know.
13. She can do ______ difficult turns than I can.
14. Hockey is a ______ dangerous sport than soccer.
15. Skaters are the ______ wonderful athletes of all.

Apply

D. Add *more* or *most* to each adjective. Use each adjective in a sentence.

16. charming **17.** harmful **18.** careful
19. active **20.** interesting

To Memorize

Lovely! See the cloud, the cloud appear!
Lovely! See the rain, the rain draw near!
Who spoke?
It was the little corn ear
High on the tip of the stalk.

Zuñi Corn-grinding Song

Why would the corn find the rain lovely?

LANGUAGE REVIEW

Adjectives pages 154–155

Copy the sentences. Circle the describing adjectives. Underline the nouns they describe.

1. The hot sun beat down on the desert.
2. The thirsty camels walked slowly.
3. The travelers stopped at a small well.
4. Hungry jackals howled at the full moon.
5. The tired people slept under warm blankets.

Different Kinds of Adjectives pages 156–157

What does each underlined adjective tell about the noun it describes? Write *color, sound, size,* or *number.*

6. <u>Huge</u> dinosaurs once roamed the earth.
7. They lived in wet <u>green</u> jungles and swamps.
8. Large <u>buzzing</u> insects flew everywhere.
9. <u>Many</u> dinosaurs were plant-eaters.

Articles pages 158–159

Copy the sentences. Underline the articles.

10. The ear is a sense organ.
11. The ears of an elephant have large flaps.
12. The ear of an antelope turns to catch sounds.

Comparisons with <u>er</u> and <u>est</u> pages 160–161

Choose the correct adjective in ( ). Write the sentences correctly.

13. Sheila's necklace is the (longer, longest) of the three.
14. Is this color (lighter, lightest) than that color?
15. Isn't this the (softer, softest) yarn you ever felt?

16. I think your sweater is (warmer, warmest) than mine.
17. Sam's jacket is (shorter, shortest) than his sweater.

Comparisons with More and Most pages 162–163

Choose the correct adjective in ( ). Write the sentence.

18. The potato salad is the (more delicious, most delicious) part of the picnic.
19. Her kite is the (more colorful, most colorful) of the two.
20. This is the (more confusing, most confusing) game I have ever seen.
21. The rules are (more complicated, most complicated) than the rules in football.
22. I still think that this is the (more wonderful, most wonderful) picnic we have had all year.
23. The weather is (more beautiful, most beautiful) than it was last summer.
24. This is the (more exciting, most exciting) group of people I have ever met.

Applying Adjectives

Add an adjective to each sentence. Write the sentences. Underline the noun that each adjective describes. Circle the adjective.

25. A child cried.
26. Flowers grew.
27. Jets roared.
28. Dogs barked.
29. Fish swam away.
30. Smoke drifted up.
31. Boys shouted.
32. A woman sang.
33. Kittens played.
34. Cars drove by.
35. Hamburgers broiled.
36. Runners jogged.
37. A telephone rang.
38. Music was playing.
39. Horses trotted by.
40. Doors opened.

STUDY SKILLS

Lesson 6: Understanding Synonyms and Antonyms

How do these children feel?

Think and Discuss

Read the underlined adjectives. What do you notice about their meanings? Words that have almost the same meaning are called **synonyms.**

Now look at this picture.

What do you notice about the meanings of the underlined adjectives? *Hot, steamy,* and *warm* are synonyms. They mean almost the same thing.

Look at both pictures again. In the first picture the children are *outside.* In the second picture they are *inside. Outside* and *inside* are called **antonyms.** They are words with opposite meanings.

- A **synonym** is a word that has almost the same meaning as another word.
- An **antonym** is a word that means the opposite of another word.

Practice

A. Read these pairs of words. Write *synonyms* if the words are synonyms. Write *antonyms* if they are antonyms.

1. tall, high
2. shop, store
3. wild, tame
4. bumpy, smooth
5. choose, pick
6. open, close

B. Write the sentences. Use a synonym in ( ) to take the place of the underlined word.

7. <u>Fall</u> comes before winter. (autumn, summer, cold)
8. We had a very <u>rainy</u> spring. (dry, dull, wet)
9. I <u>saw</u> the first robin. (ran, noticed, lost)

C. Write the sentences. Use an antonym in ( ) to take the place of the underlined word.

10. It is becoming <u>dark</u>. (windy, cold, light)
11. The ground is <u>hard</u>. (wet, soft, firm)

Apply

D. 12.–15. Think of one synonym and one antonym for each word. Use the synonyms and antonyms in sentences.

near pretty

Lesson 7: Understanding Homophones

Read these sentences.

1. Manuel went to the grocery store.
2. He bought two cartons of milk.
3. He picked up some butter too.

What does each underlined word mean?

Think and Discuss

To, two, and *too* sound alike. They are spelled differently. They mean different things. These words are called **homophones.**

Find the homophones in these sentences.

4. Manuel met Chaka there.
5. They put their groceries in the same cart.
6. Chaka went to the deli to buy some rolls.
7. Manuel waited for her by the freezer.

What does each homophone mean?

- **Homophones** are words that sound alike. They are spelled differently and have different meanings.

Practice

A. Write the homophone in ( ) that goes with each word.

1. ate (eight, at, eat) **2.** know (cow, now, no)
3. one (on, won, two) **4.** sent (rent, scant, cent)

B. Choose the correct homophone in ( ). Write the sentences.

5. May I have (one, won) more apple?
6. You just ate a (pair, pear) and a peach.
7. This picnic was a (great, grate) idea.
8. We should have one next week (to, too).
9. (Their, There) are still some sandwiches left.
10. Feel the (wait, weight) of this watermelon.
11. It must (weigh, way) as much as you do!
12. Kaya and Anne brought (to, too, two) melons.
13. The melons came from (their, there) garden.

C. Choose the correct homophone in ( ). Write the paragraph.

14.–20. (To, Two) brothers lived in a (would, wood). They liked to (right, write) to the king. Every day they (cent, sent) him a letter. They told him (their, there) sad story. They wanted (too, to) be sailors and go to (sea, see).

Apply

D. Use each of these words in a sentence.

21. to **22.** too **23.** two **24.** their **25.** there

A Challenge

Use each pair of homophones in a single sentence. Check the dictionary if you need help.

Example: see, sea I *see* the ships in the *sea.*

1. blue, blew
2. deer, dear
3. sail, sale
4. their, they're
5. its, it's
6. to, two

COMPOSITION

Lesson 8: Writing a Descriptive Paragraph

Read the following paragraphs.

1. It was a rainy day. Fog was over the river. Umbrellas were everywhere. Raindrops were on the street and the grass.
2. It was a dark, rainy day. Gray fog hung over the river. Big black umbrellas were everywhere. Heavy raindrops fell on the street and the new green grass.

Which paragraph uses more describing words?

Think and Discuss

Both writers saw the same thing. The second writer used adjectives and interesting verbs to tell about the day. Which adjectives describe the umbrellas? What other adjectives were used? These adjectives help the reader picture the scene. They make paragraph 2 more interesting to read.

A paragraph that describes a person, place, or thing is called a **descriptive** paragraph. Descriptive paragraphs use many adjectives and interesting verbs. They paint pictures in the reader's mind. They help the reader see exactly what the writer saw.

How to Write a Descriptive Paragraph

1. **Indent the first sentence.**
2. **Begin with a topic sentence telling what the paragraph is about.**
3. **Add detail sentences. In them use interesting words to describe the topic.**
4. **Keep to the topic.**
5. **Use good sentence order.**

Practice

A. 1.–10. Add adjectives to the paragraph below. Make the paragraph paint a picture in the reader's mind. Write the paragraph.

It was a ______ day. The ______ corn stood tall in the ______ field. ______ clouds hung overhead. A ______ wind was rising. It blew the ______ hat off the ______ scarecrow. Two ______ crows flapped by. Their ______ wings beat hard against the ______ breeze.

B. Write a descriptive sentence about each object.

11. a tree	**12.** a cow	**13.** a fence
14. a path	**15.** a rainbow	**16.** a building

Apply

C. 17. Write a descriptive paragraph about one of these topics. Follow the rules given above.

My Favorite Fruit	Outside My Window
An Unusual Person	A Secret Place

Lesson 9: Writing a How-to Paragraph

Kwayo wanted to teach his sister how to make scrambled eggs. Read his paragraph.

It is easy to make scrambled eggs. First break two eggs into a bowl, add a little milk, salt, and pepper, and beat. Second put a frying pan on the stove and melt butter in it. Third pour the eggs into the hot pan. Next stir the eggs around the pan with a spoon until they are cooked. Last turn off the fire and serve the eggs.

Think and Discuss

A how-to paragraph tells all the things you have to do in the order in which you must do them. A how-to paragraph has **time-clue words** such as *first* and *next* to help the reader follow the correct order. What are the time-clues in Kwayo's paragraph?

Suppose Kwayo listed the directions in the wrong order. Would his sister's eggs turn out well?

How to Write a How-to Paragraph

1. **Write a topic sentence. This tells the reason for the directions.**
2. **Add detail sentences. Use time-clue words to show the correct order.**
3. **Tell what materials are needed.**
4. **State information simply and clearly.**
5. **Keep to the topic.**

Practice

A. 1.–5. Add time-clue words to this paragraph. Then copy the paragraph.

Here's how to make rice. ______ put 1 cup of rice in a pot. ______ cover the rice with 2 cups of water. ______ bring the water to a boil. Put a cover on the pot. ______ steam the rice for 20 minutes. ______ fluff the rice with a fork.

B. 6. These directions for making fried rice are out of order. Write them in the correct order.

First melt butter in a frying pan. Last cook all ingredients until they are hot. Fried rice is easy to make. Second add pieces of green pepper and bean sprouts. Next mix in the cooked rice, an egg, and soy sauce. Third fry the vegetables for one minute.

Apply

C. 7. Choose a serious or funny topic from the list below. Write a how-to paragraph. Follow the rules in this lesson.

How to Make the World's Biggest Pancake
How to Tie a Shoelace
How to Train a Goldfish
How to Ride a Bicycle

Editing Marks

- capitalize
- make a period
- add something
- add a comma
- add quotation marks
- take something away
- spell correctly
- indent the paragraph
- make a lowercase letter
- transpose

Lesson 10: Editing a How-to Paragraph

Sally wrote a how-to paragraph about shoveling snow. Read her edited paragraph.

You must keep your sidewalks clear in winter. First dress warmly, and get your shovle (shovel) then shovel the snow near the dorr (door). Sprinkle salt on the cleared walk. Next shovel snow off the sidewok (sidewalk). tr

Think and Discuss

Sally circled words that were not spelled correctly. She wrote the correct spelling above each word. Which words did Sally misspell? How should each one be spelled?

Find the other editing marks Sally used. What does each one mean? Why did Sally change the order of her sentences?

Practice

A. Copy Sally's paragraph correctly.

Apply

B. Look at the how-to paragraph you wrote in Lesson 9. Did you make any spelling mistakes?

Are your sentences in order? Does each sentence begin with a capital letter? Edit your paragraph. Then write it again.

MECHANICS PRACTICE

Writing Paragraphs

- Indent the first line of a paragraph.
- Use a period at the end of a statement or command.
- Use a question mark at the end of a question.
- Use an exclamation point at the end of an exclamation.

Write each paragraph correctly.

1. Have you ever made a bird feeder It is an easy thing to do First you must have an empty milk carton Cut a flap in the front Fold the flap down to make a perch Then fill the carton with birdseed Tie a string to it, and hang it from a branch
2. Was there ever a worse storm Thunder crashed, and lightning flashed The trees bowed down to touch the ground The wind blew so wildly We all hid behind the curtains
3. Do you know how to give a dog a bath Fill the tub with warm water It should not be too hot Lift the dog into the tub Soap it with dog shampoo Then rinse it carefully Watch out The dog will shake water all over you if you are not careful

LITERATURE

Lesson 11: Understanding Describing Words in Poetry

A poet must choose words carefully. Poems use a few words to tell a lot. Many poems describe things. What kinds of words might a poet use to describe things?

Think and Discuss

Read this poem by Charlotte Zolotow.

The wind I love the best
comes gently after rain
smelling of spring and growing things
brushing the world with feathery wings
while everything glistens, and everything sings
in the spring wind
after the rain.

Charlotte Zolotow

What does this wind smell like? What does it feel like?

Now read a different kind of poem about wind.

Over the wintry
forest, winds howl in a rage
with no leaves to blow.

Soseki

This poem paints a picture of a certain kind of wind. Everyone has heard a wind howl. This poet has thought of a reason for the wind to howl. What is the reason?

Some poets use interesting nouns, verbs, and adjectives to describe things. Other poets put words together in unusual ways. They give the reader a new way of looking at things.

Practice

A. Read this poem. Answer the questions below.

Flowers are happy in summer.
In autumn they die and are blown away.
    Dry and withered,
Their petals dance on the wind
Like little brown butterflies.

Langston Hughes

1. List two adjectives that describe the petals in autumn.
2. How can flowers look happy? Describe what happy flowers would look like.
3. Draw a picture to go with the poem. Try to picture what the poet saw.

Apply

B. **4.** Think about what rain means to you. List some adjectives or interesting words that describe rain. Use the words to write a short poem. You might use the poem by Soseki as an example.

Lesson 12: Understanding Comparisons in Poetry

Poets often use words in unusual ways. They often describe something by comparing it to something else. They may compare two things that do not seem alike—a train and a dragon, for example. How might a train be like a dragon?

Think and Discuss

The words *like* and *as* are often used to compare two things. Read this poem. Think about the two things that are being compared.

The Park

I'm glad that I
    Live near a park
For in the winter
    After dark
The park lights shine
    As bright and still
As dandelions
    On a hill.

James S. Tippett

What two things are being compared in this poem? How are they alike?

Practice

A. Read the poem on page 179. Answer the questions that follow.

In a high wind the
leaves don't
fall but fly
straight out of the
tree like birds

A. R. Ammons

1. What two things are compared in this poem?
2. How are the two things alike?

Apply

B. Finish these comparisons with interesting words.

3. as cold as a ______
4. as big as a ______
5. as fast as a ______
6. as strong as a ______

A BOOK TO READ

Title: **High on a Hill: A Book of Chinese Riddles**
Author: Ed Young
Publisher: William Collins Publishers

After work was done, some Chinese families would gather together to tell stories and enjoy jokes or riddles. The author of this book was born in China. His family help him collect these favorite riddles. Read this one.

They love to work, although they're small,
And never, ever shirk at all;
They're gathering food, for winter's coming
And, as they work, just hear them humming!

5 UNIT TEST

Adjectives pages 154–155

One word in each sentence is an adjective. Write the letter of the word that is an adjective.

1. Tall buildings towered over the street.
   a b c
2. Noisy cars and trucks jammed the avenues.
   a b c
3. People went to work in fast trains.
   a b c
4. We strolled along the crowded sidewalks.
   a b c
5. Two officers were directing traffic.
   a b c

Kinds of Adjectives pages 156–157

Copy the sentences. Underline the adjectives. Then tell what each adjective tells about the noun it describes. Write *size, number, feel, taste,* or *sound.*

6. The hot soup burned Lorraine's tongue.
7. From my room we heard the whistling teapot.
8. Allen boiled five eggs on the stove.
9. Nancy helped by shelling the sweet peas.
10. Her two cousins bustled around the kitchen.
11. I sat on the high stool and watched.
12. A pot fell to the floor with a loud crash.

Articles pages 158–159

Copy the sentences. Underline the articles.

13. The giraffe has a neck that is quite long.
14. An okapi has a neck that is shorter.
15. The giraffe reaches the leaves of tall trees with its long tongue.
16. The giraffe is an animal from Africa.
17. It may share a watering hole with an elephant.

Comparisons with er and est pages 160–161

Choose the correct answer. Write the sentences.

18. This obstacle course is (harder, hardest) than last year's.
19. This rope is (thicker, thickest) than my wrist.
20. We ran on the (colder, coldest) day this year.
21. Dotty's time was the (faster, fastest) of the three.

Comparisons with More and Most pages 162–163

Choose the correct answer. Write the sentences.

22. Annette is the (more, most) musical person in her family.
23. This is the (more, most) important concert of the year.
24. The teachers are (more, most) excited than the students.
25. This was the (more, most) enjoyable evening I've spent in a long time.

Synonyms and Antonyms pages 166–167

Read each pair of words. Write whether they are synonyms or antonyms.

1. speak, talk
2. inside, outside
3. whisper, shout
4. ill, sick
5. narrow, wide
6. smooth, creamy
7. tall, short
8. happy, sad
9. above, over
10. many, few

Homophones pages 168–169

Choose the correct answer. Write the sentences.

11. Mr. Sims has his horse up for (sail, sale).
12. He (knows, nose) he will find her a good home.
13. Her long (main, mane) is the same color as her (tail, tale).
14. Hasn't she (one, won) first prize at many state (fairs, fares)?
15. (Some, Sum) people are (knot, not) able to ride a horse as well trained as this one.

Descriptive Paragraphs pages 170–171

1. Describe a place on another planet or a monster who lives there. Use at least five adjectives in your paragraph.

Writing and Editing How-to Paragraphs pages 172–175

2. Write a paragraph that tells how to do something. Use words such as *first, next,* and *last* to make your directions easy to follow. Edit your paragraph to be sure the steps are in the right order. Here are some ideas for your paragraph:

   How to Plan a Birthday Party
   How to Make a Wonderful Snack
   How to Do a Somersault
   How to Get From My House to School
   How to Tie a Knot
   How to Edit a Paragraph

Describing Words in Poetry pages 176–177

Copy the poems. Underline the adjectives.

1. soft furry rabbit
hopping through the frozen field
under silver stars

2. small yellow flower
peering up from muddy ground
in the early spring

3. little brown pony
standing by the leafless tree
under stormy skies

4. one yellow leaf
spiraled from the dying branch
to the frosty ground

5. seven black geese
honked their way across the sky
tossed by chilly winds

6. one silver dewdrop
hovered on the blade of grass
like a shiny dime
then it dropped a glowing tear
on the earth's soft cheek

Comparisons in Poetry pages 178–179

Copy the comparisons below. Use this list of animals to complete the comparisons. Each line contains a rhyme. When the lines are put together, they make a poem.

seal	hare	cat	snail
whale	eel	bear	bat

7. as hungry as a ____, as fast as a ____;
8. as blind as a ____, as quiet as a ____;
9. as skinny as an ____, as smart as a ____;
10. as big as a ____, as slow as a ____.

6
U.S. MAIL
811635
P81163

LANGUAGE
Learning About Nouns and Pronouns

STUDY SKILLS
Learning About Word Meaning

COMPOSITION
Writing Social Notes and Letters

LITERATURE
Reading Poetry

Cal sent Ms. Bly a letter. He invited her to visit his city. Have you ever sent a letter? To whom did you send it? Did you receive an answer? Look at the pictures on page 184. How did Cal's letter get to Ms. Bly? What answer do you think she may send?

Letters are like visits from close friends. You can use letters to keep in touch with people who are far away. Best of all, letters can be saved to be read over and over again.

In this unit you will learn how to write letters to friends. You will learn about different kinds of letters. You will also learn how to put words together to form new words. You will see how poets use special words to make their poems fun to read.

LANGUAGE

Lesson 1: Using Pronouns in Place of Nouns

Li wrote some sentences about the town parade. Read her sentences.

1. Ms. Karr helped Ed plan a parade.
2. Ms. Karr showed Ed what to do.
3. Ed thanked Ms. Karr.

Which nouns appear in all three sentences?

Think and Discuss

Li thought of a way to make her sentences more interesting. She did not repeat the nouns each time. She rewrote sentences 2 and 3. Read her new sentences.

4. She showed him what to do.
5. He thanked her.

Look at sentences 2 and 4. Which words did Li use to replace the nouns? These words are called **pronouns.** Pronouns take the place of nouns.

Which pronouns took the place of nouns in sentence 5? *Ed* was the subject of sentence 3. *He* is the subject of sentence 5. What pronoun follows the action verb *thanked* in sentence 5?

These pronouns are used in the subject of a sentence: *I, we, you, he, she, it,* and *they.*

These pronouns follow action verbs: *me, us, you, him, her, it,* and *them.*

- A **pronoun** is a word that takes the place of one or more nouns.

Practice

A. Copy each sentence. Underline the pronoun.

1. They will play the drums.
2. She will twirl a baton.
3. Murray called us.
4. Jan wants me to play the cymbals.
5. I think the parade will be wonderful.

B. Read each pair of sentences. Write the pronoun from the second sentence of each pair. Then write the noun from the first sentence that each pronoun replaces.

6. The parade is coming. It is noisy.
7. The children are ready. They are dressed up.
8. The audience sees Chris. People watch her.
9. Chris leads the band. She wears a tall hat.
10. People applaud the band. People wave at it.

Apply

C. 11.–15. Write two sentences with pronouns in the subject. Write three sentences with pronouns that follow action verbs.

Lesson 2: Understanding Singular and Plural Pronouns

Read the sentence pairs below.

1. Ned waits for the doctor.
2. He sits in the waiting room.

3. Many children are in the waiting room.
4. They play and talk.

Think and Discuss

What is the noun in the subject part of sentence 1? Is it singular or plural? What pronoun takes its place in sentence 2? This is a singular pronoun.

What noun is in the subject part of sentence 3? Does it name one person or more than one person? What pronoun takes its place in sentence 4? This is a plural pronoun.

The chart below names singular and plural pronouns.

Pronouns in the Subject		**Pronouns That Follow Action Verbs**	
Singular	*Plural*	*Singular*	*Plural*
I	we	me	us
you	you	you	you
he, she, it	they	him, her, it	them

- A **singular pronoun** names one person, place, or thing.
- A **plural pronoun** names more than one person, place, or thing.

Practice

A. Copy each sentence. Underline the pronoun. Tell whether each is *singular* or *plural.*

1. Dr. Marsh looks at him.
2. She asks Ned some questions.
3. They walk into the office.
4. A nurse shows them an X-ray.
5. Ned finds it very interesting.

B. Copy the second sentence in each pair. Use a singular or plural pronoun to replace the underlined word(s).

6. Dr. Marsh looks at Sue. She weighs ______.
7. Ned follows the nurse. ______ walks quickly.
8. Ned and the nurse enter an office. ______ must fill out some forms.
9. One nurse is named Ms. Jacobs. Ned helps ______ fill out the papers.
10. The X-rays will be ready tomorrow. Ned can see ______ then.

Apply

C. 11.–15. Write two sentences that use singular pronouns. Write three sentences that use plural pronouns.

A Challenge

Which pronoun looks the same whether it is singular or plural? Write some sentences that use this pronoun in the subject. Write some that use it after action verbs.

Lesson 3: Using Pronouns as Subjects

The people in the picture are having an apple-picking contest. Each team works together to fill the baskets. Words in sentences must work together too. The subject works with the verb.

Think and Discuss

Most present time verbs agree with singular subjects by adding *s*. That is true whether the subject is a noun or a pronoun. Read these sentences.

1. He picks apples.
2. She lifts the basket.
3. We eat apples.
4. They taste good.

Which sentences have singular subjects? What endings do the verbs in those sentences have? Verbs that agree with plural subjects do not add any endings.

The pronoun *I* does not fit this rule. Read this sentence.

5. I help Roger fill his basket.

I is a singular pronoun, but the verb that agrees with the subject *I* is *help*. It does not add the *s* ending.

Think of a present time verb to complete each sentence.

6. He ______ the basket of apples away.
7. We ______ some apples off the ground.
8. I ______ a bright red apple.

Practice

A. Choose the verb in ( ) that agrees with each subject. Write the sentences.

1. We (like, likes) to pick apples.
2. He (drive, drives) to the orchard each fall.
3. They (follow, follows) him there.
4. She (take, takes) a basket.
5. I (climb, climbs) the apple tree.

B. Choose the correct pronoun in ( ) to agree with each verb. Write the sentences.

6. (He, We) make a pie with the apples.
7. (They, She) mixes the crust.
8. Then (he, I) rolls it out.
9. (It, They) stays on the table.
10. (She, We) cut the apples.
11. Then (he, I) add cinnamon.
12. (They, He) take turns stirring.
13. (It, They) smell wonderful.
14. (She, We) pours the filling into the crust.
15. After that (it, we) wait for the pie to bake.

Apply

C. 16.–20. Write five sentences. Use the pronouns *she, I, it, we,* and *they* as your subjects.

Lesson 4: Using I and Me

Whenever you talk about yourself, you use the pronouns *I* and *me.* Bruce wrote some sentences about himself. Read them.

1. I started a new business.
2. Now people pay me for my work.
3. Sonia and I water house plants.
4. Ms. Kay left Sonia and me four plants to water.

Think and Discuss

In sentence 1 Bruce used the word *I* to name himself. *I* is always used in the subject of a sentence. How did Bruce name himself in sentence 2? Is that pronoun in the subject or does it follow an action verb?

Look at sentences 3 and 4. When Bruce talks about Sonia and himself, whom does he name first?

You may have noticed something special about the pronoun *I.* It is always written with a capital letter.

- The word *I* is always used in the subject part of a sentence. The word *me* follows an action verb.
- Always capitalize the word *I.*

Practice

A. 1.–5. Listen as your teacher reads some sentences. Write each sentence as it is read.

B. Use *I* or *me* in each sentence. Write the sentences.

6. ______ washed my first car today.
7. It took ______ two hours to do the job.
8. First ______ sprayed the car with water.
9. Somehow the hose sprayed ______ too.
10. That job tired ______ out.

C. Use the words *Bruce and I* or *Bruce and me* in each sentence. Write the sentences.

11. ______ found another way to earn money.
12. First ______ put up a sign.
13. People asked ______ about the sign.
14. They brought their dogs to ______.
15. ______ walked the dogs each day.

D. These sentences are incorrect. Look at the rules on page 192 and write them correctly.

16. Sonia and me cleaned the garage.
17. Dad paid Sonia and I for our work.
18. Sonia and me felt happy.
19. Then Dad drove I and Sonia downtown.
20. Me and Sonia went shopping.

Apply

E. 21.–25. Write five sentences about working with a friend. Use the words *I* and *me* correctly in your sentences.

Lesson 5: Understanding Possessive Nouns

Read these sentences.

1. The hammer that belongs to the boy is in the toolbox.
2. The saw that belongs to the girl is there.

Who owns the hammer? Who owns the saw?

Think and Discuss

Sentences 1 and 2 tell about ownership, or **possession.** They can be written another way. Read these sentences.

3. The boy's hammer is in the toolbox.
4. The girl's saw is there.

The words *boy's* and *girl's* are **possessive nouns.** Most singular possessive nouns are formed by adding an **apostrophe** and *s* to the singular noun.

- A **possessive noun** shows ownership.
- Add an apostrophe and an *s* to singular nouns to show possession.

Practice

A. Change the noun in ( ) to a possessive form. Write the sentences.

1. The ______ suitcase is on the airplane. (man)
2. ______ guitar is on top of the pile. (Rita)

3. They are unloading ______ trunk. (Mr. Hawley)
4. Grab ______ brown bags. (George)
5. ______ camera case is lost. (Mindy)

B. Make these sentences show possession in a different way. Write the sentences.

6. That is the pencil that belongs to Azami.
7. The art books that belong to Sara are here.
8. Sara and Azami are in the class of that teacher.
9. The easel that belongs to Seth is gone.
10. He must use the desk of Jim Lone Eagle.

Apply

C. Use possessive forms of the nouns below in your own sentences.

11. tree **12.** flower **13.** gardener **14.** bug **15.** Jan

HOW OUR LANGUAGE GROWS

Native Americans have lived here for thousands of years. They are the first Americans. Many of our words come from them.

Native Americans named the state of Ohio. It comes from a word that means "beautiful waters." Our word *tomato* comes from the Native American word *tomatl.* Can you guess our word for Native American *chocolatl*?

1. Here are some Native American names for animals. Can you tell what we call those animals now?
   coyotl musquash chitmunk
2. *Moose, caribou,* and *raccoon* were Algonquian words. Use a dictionary to find what they once meant.

Lesson 6: Understanding Plural Possessive Nouns

Read these sentences.

1. The bike that belongs to my brother is blue.
2. The car that belongs to my brothers is red.

Who owns the blue bike? Who owns the red car?

Think and Discuss

The red car in sentence 2 is owned by more than one person. *Brothers* is a plural noun. Sentences 1 and 2 must show possession in different ways. Read the sentences below.

3. My brother's bike is blue.
4. My brothers' car is red.

Which object is owned by more than one person? *Brothers'* is a **plural possessive noun.**

Most plural nouns end in *s* or *es.* These nouns show possession by adding an apostrophe after the *s.*

Read these sentences.

5. My mother's bike has a flat tire.
6. My sisters' skateboard is cracked.

Which object belongs to more than one person? How can you tell?

- Add an apostrophe to plural nouns that end in *s* to show possession.

Practice

A. Copy each sentence. Underline the possessive noun. If the noun is a singular possessive noun, write *singular.* If it is a plural possessive noun, write *plural.*

1. This is John's bicycle.
2. The girls' skates are in the closet.
3. Kari will have to wear Nancy's skates.
4. They will skate in the Smiths' parking lot.
5. John will drive them there in his sisters' car.

B. Change the plural noun in ( ) to a possessive form. Write the sentences.

6. This is the ______ house. (Hudsons)
7. The ______ bedroom is upstairs. (boys)
8. Their ______ rooms are nearby. (sisters)
9. The ______ room has a small porch. (parents)
10. The ______ house is next door. (Jensens)

C. Make these sentences show possession in a different way. Write the sentences.

11. The hair of the clown is red.
12. That is the dog that belongs to the clowns.
13. The ball that belongs to the dog is small.
14. Here are the tickets that belong to the boys.
15. The trailer that belongs to the acrobats is blue.

Apply

D. Write five sentences. Use possessive forms of these nouns.

16. cats **17.** uncles **18.** bees **19.** foxes **20.** flies

LANGUAGE REVIEW

Pronouns in Place of Nouns pages 186–187

Write the sentences. Draw one line under each pronoun in the subject. Draw two lines under each pronoun in the predicate.

1. After school I showed them the dollhouse.
2. They liked it very much.
3. He bought me a china doll in Europe.
4. You amaze us with this doll collection.
5. We gave a book about dolls to her.

Singular and Plural Pronouns pages 188–189

Copy each sentence. Underline the pronoun. Tell whether each is *singular* or *plural.*

6. Charlotte gave them the recipe.
7. It explained how to make fancy pancakes.
8. They are made with blueberries.
9. Paula invited me to breakfast.
10. We ate more pancakes than ever before.

Pronouns as Subjects pages 190–191

Choose the correct answer in ( ). Write the sentences.

11. (We, He) follow Missy and Allen.
12. (She, They) pretend not to see us.
13. (I, She) come after you on the class list.
14. (It, They) goes in alphabetical order.
15. (He, They) look at the list to make sure.

Using I and Me pages 192–193

Choose the correct answer in ( ). Write sentences 16–20.

16. (I, me) climbed the oak tree with Carlos.
17. Kim showed (I, me) how to climb.
18. (Carlos and I, Carlos and me) are building a treehouse.
19. Dad gave (me and Carlos, Carlos and me) some boards.
20. Now (I and Carlos, Carlos and me, Carlos and I) must nail the boards together.

Possessive Nouns pages 194–195

Make these word groups show possession in a different way. Use possessive nouns.

21. the cat that belongs to Sue
22. the bell that belongs to the cat
23. the dog that belongs to that boy
24. the leash that belongs to the dog
25. the box turtle that belongs to that small girl

Plural Possessive Nouns pages 196–197

Make these word groups show possession in a different way. Use possessive nouns.

26. the shirts that belong to the boys
27. the shoes that belong to the girls
28. the houses that belong to the families
29. the uniforms that belong to the players
30. the whistles that belong to the captains

Applying Pronouns

Use a pronoun in place of each item below. Then write the pronouns in complete sentences.

31. Mr. Sanchez
32. Sarah
33. Alice and Jane
34. the school
35. baseball players

STUDY SKILLS

Lesson 7: Building Compound Words

The underlined words in these sentences are made of two smaller words. Name the words.

1. Springtime is a wonderful season.
2. Go for a walk in the countryside.

Think and Discuss

Some words are made up of two smaller words. The new word is a **compound word.** *Spring* and *time* make *springtime. Country* and *side* make *countryside.*

Read these sentences. What compound words do you find?

3. Have you ever seen a groundhog?
4. It sleeps underground all winter.
5. In spring the sunlight warms its home.

Which two smaller words make up each compound word in sentences 3–5? These smaller words may help you understand the meaning of the compound word. What does *raindrop* mean? What is a *honeybee?*

Practice

A. Which word in each pair is a compound word? Write it. Then write the two smaller words that form each compound word.

1. cats, catbird
2. sunny, sunfish
3. housefly, houses
4. popping, popcorn
5. outing, outside
6. barnyard, barns
7. sailed, sailboat
8. snowball, snowy
9. toads, toadstool
10. rainiest, raincoat

Apply

B. Think of compound words that begin with these smaller words. Use each compound word in a sentence.

11. sun **12.** rose **13.** butter **14.** after **15.** fire

To Memorize

There was an old lady of France,
Who taught little ducklings to dance;
When she said, "Tick-a-tack!"
They only said, "Quack!"
Which grieved that old lady of France.

Edward Lear

This kind of poem is called a *limerick*. Do you think it is funny? Why?

Lesson 8: Building Words with Prefixes

Ana wrote some sentences about vegetables. Read her sentences.

1. I <u>like</u> cucumbers.
2. I <u>dislike</u> tomatoes.

Which vegetable would Ana rather eat?

Think and Discuss

You can change a word's meaning by adding letters to it. *Like* is a **base word.** No special ending or beginning has been added to it. When *dis* is added to *like,* it changes the meaning of the base word. *Dis* is a **prefix.** It means "not." What does *dislike* mean? Now read these sentences.

3. It is <u>polite</u> to eat the food you are served.
4. It is <u>impolite</u> to refuse to eat.

Which underlined word above has a prefix? This prefix also means *not.* What is the base word?

Read this chart. Think about how each prefix changes the meaning of the base word.

Prefix	Meaning	Example
dis	not	disagree
im	not	impossible
re	again	redo
re	back	rebound
un	not	unlucky
un	opposite of	unwrap

- A **prefix** is a letter or group of letters added to the beginning of a base word. A prefix changes the meaning of a word.

Practice

A. Copy the sentences. Underline the word in each sentence that has a prefix.

1. Our phone was disconnected.
2. I waited impatiently for a worker to come.
3. I asked the worker whether the phone could be reconnected today.
4. She said that it seemed unlikely.
5. She will try to rejoin the wires tomorrow.
6. Now we are unable to use the phone.

B. Choose a word from each sentence that could be used as a base word. Add the prefix in ( ) to the base word. Write the sentences.

7. I will heat this soup for dinner. (re)
8. This stove is safe. (un)
9. It is possible to cook this soup. (im)
10. I will have to cover the pot. (un)
11. I really like cooking on this stove. (dis)

Apply

C. Add a prefix to each word below. Check your words in the dictionary. Then use each new word in a sentence of your own.

12. proper **13.** pay **14.** write **15.** trust **16.** ripe

Lesson 9: Building Words with Suffixes

Read these sentences.

1. The worker must be careful.
2. If he is careless, the breakable glass cracks.

The underlined words have special endings added to base words. What are the base words?

Think and Discuss

A prefix is added to the beginning of a base word. Special endings can also be added to base words. An ending of this kind is called a **suffix.**

Look at sentences 1 and 2. What suffix was added to the base word *work?* What suffix was added to the base word *break?* What two suffixes were added to the base word *care?* Does *careful* have the same meaning as *careless?* Now read this chart.

Suffix	Meaning	Example
able	able to be	wearable
er	one who	builder
ful	full of	hopeful
ible	able to be	flexible
less	without	harmless
or	one who	visitor

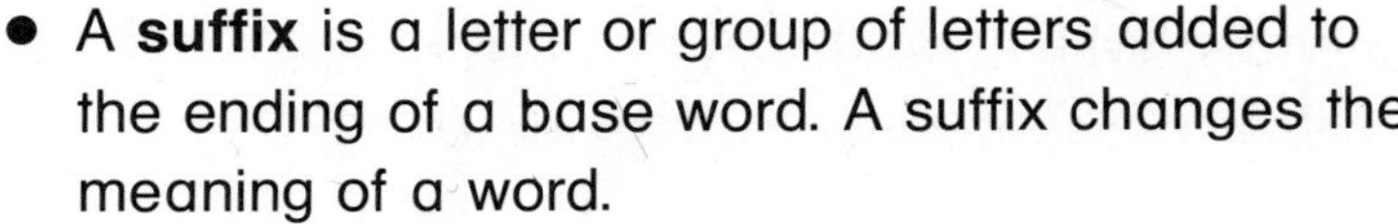

- A **suffix** is a letter or group of letters added to the ending of a base word. A suffix changes the meaning of a word.

Practice

A. Copy the sentences. Underline the word in each sentence that has a suffix.

1. Meg's new dog is very playful.
2. It seems to have boundless energy.
3. It greets her at the door with a joyful bark.
4. Meg hopes that the dog is trainable.
5. She wants to find a teacher for the dog.

B. Write the word from each sentence that has a suffix. Then write the meaning of the word.

6. The boat's flexible sails flap in the breeze.
7. They are covered with colorful designs.
8. A good sailor can sail the boat alone.
9. The boat moves through the powerful surf.
10. It rocks on the restless waves.

C. Change the words in (   ) to a single word with a suffix. Write the sentences.

11. This story seems (without meaning) to me.
12. A (person who reads) would be confused.
13. I prefer stories that are more (able to be read).
14. I like stories that are (full of truth).
15. A (person who writes) should write clearly.

Apply

D. Add a suffix to each word below. Check your words in the dictionary. Then use each new word in a sentence of your own.

16. sing **17.** predict **18.** tear **19.** edit **20.** reverse

COMPOSITION

Lesson 10: Writing a Friendly Letter

Linda wrote this letter to her friend, Rosa.

Heading
13 Apple Street
Milton, Vermont 05468
December 6, 19--
Greeting
Dear Rosa,
Body
We had a big snowstorm yesterday. I went sledding on the hill near my house. What have you been doing? Write soon and tell me.
Closing
Your friend,
Signature
Linda

Think and Discuss

This letter has five parts. Name them.

The **heading** of a letter contains the letter writer's address and the date. Linda's street address is on the first line. How does the name of Linda's street begin? Street names are proper nouns. The name of Linda's town and state are on the second line. The date is on the third line. A comma comes between the city and the state. Where else is a comma used here?

The **greeting** says hello to the person who receives the letter. The first word begins with a capital letter. A comma follows the greeting.

The **body** of a letter tells the message. It is in the form of a paragraph. The first line is indented.

The **closing** is at the end of a letter. The first word is capitalized. A comma follows the closing.

The **signature** is the written name of the person who wrote the letter. Who signed this letter?

- Use a comma in an address between the city and the state.
- Use a comma between the day and the year in a date.
- Begin each important word in the names of streets and their abbreviations with a capital letter.

Practice

A. Write these parts of a letter correctly. Finish the body of the letter. Put capital letters and commas where they belong.

34 grand ave.
dayton Ohio 45419
november 18 19--

dear perry,
your friend
julio

I am sorry to hear that you are sick. *(Finish the paragraph by telling Perry some news to cheer him up.)*

Apply

B. Pretend you are Rosa, the girl who received Linda's letter. Write a letter to Linda.

Lesson 11: Addressing an Envelope

Don was waiting for a letter from his cousin, Luke Dawson. This morning he found this envelope in the mailbox.

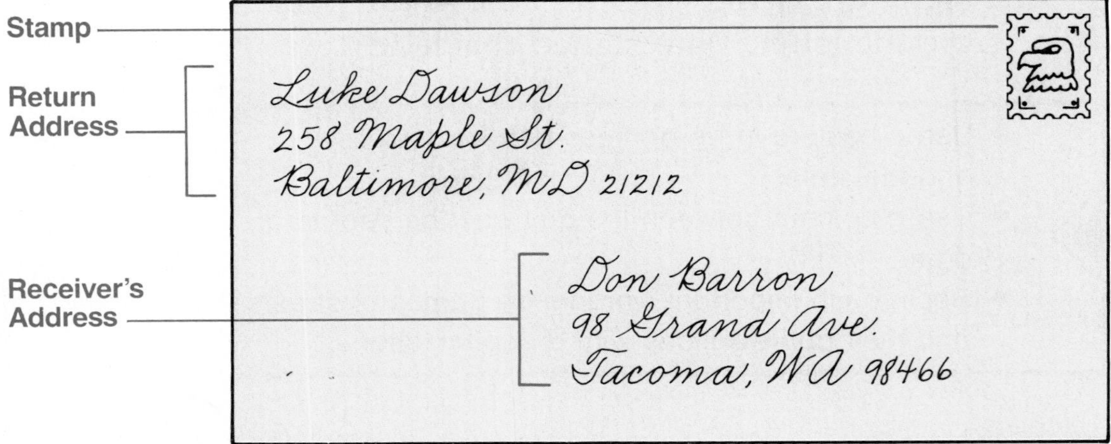

Stamp
Return Address
Receiver's Address
Luke Dawson
258 Maple St.
Baltimore, MD 21212
Don Barron
98 Grand Ave.
Tacoma, WA 98466

Think and Discuss

Don looked in the upper left corner for the **return address.** The return address is the name and address of the person who wrote the letter. Is this letter from cousin Luke?

The address in the middle of the envelope is the **receiver's address.** It shows the name and address of the person receiving the letter. Who is receiving this letter?

Look at the street names in the addresses. Luke used abbreviations for the street names. A period comes after each street abbreviation.

Here are some common street abbreviations.

Avenue — Ave. Drive — Dr.
Road — Rd. Street — St.

Look at the last line of the receiver's address. The name of the city is listed first. A comma follows it. The postal abbreviation for the name of the state comes next. It contains two capital letters and no period. Look at the chart of state names and abbreviations. In what state does Don live?

The ZIP code is placed after the name of the state. The ZIP code is an important five-number code. It is used by the post office to sort mail quickly. What is Luke's ZIP code?

States:

Alabama	AL
Alaska	AK
Arizona	AZ
Arkansas	AR
California	CA
Colorado	CO
Connecticut	CT
Delaware	DE
District of Columbia	DC
Florida	FL
Georgia	GA
Hawaii	HI
Idaho	ID
Illinois	IL
Indiana	IN
Iowa	IA
Kansas	KS
Kentucky	KY
Louisiana	LA
Maine	ME
Maryland	MD
Massachusetts	MA
Michigan	MI
Minnesota	MN
Mississippi	MS
Missouri	MO
Montana	MT
Nebraska	NB
Nevada	NV
New Hampshire	NH
New Jersey	NJ
New Mexico	NM
New York	NY
North Carolina	NC
North Dakota	ND
Ohio	OH
Oklahoma	OK
Oregon	OR
Pennsylvania	PA
Rhode Island	RI
South Carolina	SC
South Dakota	SD
Tennessee	TN
Texas	TX
Utah	UT
Vermont	VT
Virginia	VA
Washington	WA
West Virginia	WV
Wisconsin	WI
Wyoming	WY

Practice

A. Write each address correctly. Add capital letters and commas. Use abbreviations for the underlined words.

1. patricia brennan
160 state Street
ada, Kansas 67414

2. yoluta bold
90 pike Avenue
canton Ohio 44711

3. stuart mann
23 newton Road
denver, Colorado 80233

4. sharon goldstein
456 amity Drive
bath Maine 04530

Apply

B. 5. Fold a piece of paper in half. Pretend it is an envelope. Write your own name and address as the return address on the envelope. Make up a receiver's address.

Lesson 12: Writing an Invitation

Read the letter Michael wrote to his parents.

92 Hicks Drive
Waco, Texas 76704
March 11, 19--

Dear Mom and Dad,

On March 20 our class will present the play Cinderella. It will start at 11:30 a.m. in room 6 at our school. It will end at 1:00 p.m. Please come to see it.

With love,
Michael

Think and Discuss

This kind of letter is called an **invitation.** It has five parts. Michael's invitation tells these things. Answer the questions.

1. Who is invited?
2. What is happening?
3. When is it?
4. Where is it?

Michael used abbreviations to show what time the play will begin and end. A.M. is an abbreviation meaning *in the morning.* P.M. means *in the afternoon or evening*. Periods are used in these abbreviations.

Look at the mark (:) Michael used to write the time. It is called a **colon.** The colon separates the hour and the minutes. At what time will the play begin? Suppose the play began at three in the afternoon. How would you write the abbreviation?

> **How to Write an Invitation**
>
> 1. **Tell who is invited.**
> 2. **Tell what the invitation is for.**
> 3. **Tell when to come and when the event will end.**
> 4. **Tell where it is.**

Practice

A. Write the abbreviations for these times.

1. two o'clock in the afternoon
2. seven thirty in the morning
3. ten o'clock in the morning
4. four thirty in the afternoon
5. eight o'clock in the evening

Apply

B. 6. Pretend you are writing an invitation to a party. Include this information.

Who: your friend Diane
What: a birthday party
When: April 4, from three to five o'clock in the afternoon
Where: at your house

Lesson 13: Writing a Thank You Note

Adam received a birthday gift in the mail. It was a football from his Uncle Stan. The next day Adam wrote his uncle this letter.

424 Dryden Road
Ithaca, New York 14850
September 1, 19--

Dear Uncle Stan,

Thank you for the football you sent me. Robin and I kick it back and forth in the yard every day. I hope you come to see us soon. Then you and I can play football.

Love,
Adam

Think and Discuss

The kind of letter Adam wrote is called a **thank you note.** A thank you note is a short letter. It has the same five parts as any friendly letter. Name the parts. Where are commas used?

A thank you note should tell why you are thanking the person. You can thank people for gifts or for good times. How did Adam say he was using his gift?

How to Write a Thank You Note

1. Tell what you are thanking the person for.
2. If you have been a guest at someone's house, tell why you enjoyed yourself.
3. If you received a gift, say how you are using it.

Practice

A. Copy this thank you note on your paper. Make up a heading, a greeting, and a closing.

____
____
____

____

I really had fun at your party yesterday. The water races were exciting. Thank you for inviting me.

____
Terry

Apply

B. Think of someone who has done something nice for you. Then write a real thank you note to that person. Follow the rules on this page.

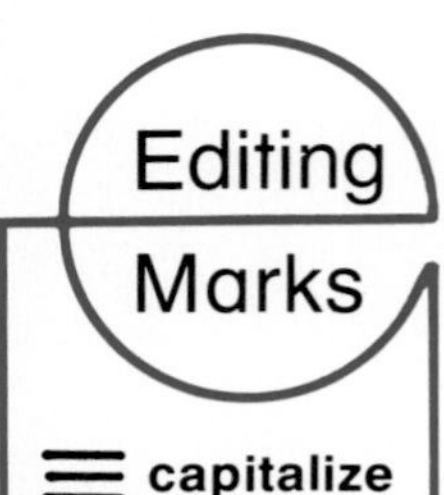

- capitalize
- make a period
- add something
- add a comma
- add quotation marks
- take something away
- spell correctly
- indent the paragraph
- make a lowercase letter
- transpose

Lesson 14: Editing a Thank You Note

Lisa received a birthday gift from John. Lisa wrote John a thank you note. Before she sent the letter, she edited it.

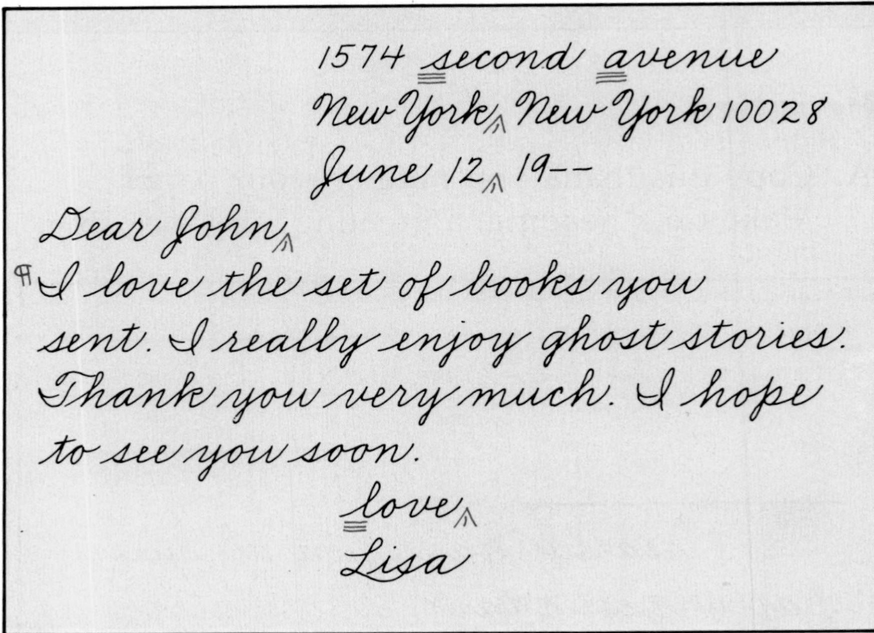

1574 second avenue
New York New York 10028
June 12 19--

Dear John

I love the set of books you sent. I really enjoy ghost stories. Thank you very much. I hope to see you soon.

love
Lisa

Think and Discuss

Lisa did not write the body of her letter in paragraph form. This editing mark ¶ tells Lisa to indent her paragraph.

Lisa used some other marks to make changes. Where did she add commas? Where did she make capital letters?

Practice

A. Rewrite Lisa's letter correctly.

Apply

B. Look at the thank you note you wrote in Lesson 13. Did you indent your paragraph? Are your commas in place? Edit the note and write it again.

MECHANICS PRACTICE

Writing Times, Names, and Addresses

- Use a colon between the hour and the minute in the time of day.
- Use a period after an abbreviation.
- Begin proper nouns with a capital letter.
- Use a comma in an address between the city and the state.

A. Write these times using abbreviations.

1. one thirty in the morning
2. three o'clock in the afternoon
3. five thirty in the afternoon
4. eight o'clock in the morning

B. Write these addresses correctly. Use abbreviations for the underlined words.

5. john michaels
217 west <u>street</u>
woodstock NY 12498
6. tao chin
18 valley <u>road</u>
charlotte VT 05445
7. maria cruz
9 pacific <u>avenue</u>
la jolla CA 92037
8. jenny chung
42 mountain <u>drive</u>
cody WY 82414

LITERATURE

Lesson 15: Understanding Rhythm and Rhyme in Poetry

It is great fun to read poetry aloud. Listen as this poem is read aloud. Listen for the sound of the words.

The Frog

Be kínd and ténder tó the Fróg,
    And do not call him names,
As 'Slimy skin,' or 'polly-wog,'
    Or likewise 'Ugly James,'
Or 'Gap-a-grin,' or 'Toad-gone-wrong,'
    Or 'Bill Bandy-knees':
The Frog is justly sensitive
    To epithets like these.
No animal will more repay
    A treatment kind and fair;
At least so lonely people say
Who keep a frog (and, by the way,
    They are extremely rare).

Hilaire Belloc

Think and Discuss

Rhythm is a beat to which you can clap your hands. The rhythm in line 1 is shown with this mark ′. The mark shows you which words have a strong beat. How many strong beats does that line have? Clap the beats as you read it aloud.

Many poets make the lines in their poems rhyme. When lines of poetry have the same last sounds, the lines rhyme. Look at the first four lines of the poem. Which lines rhyme?

Practice

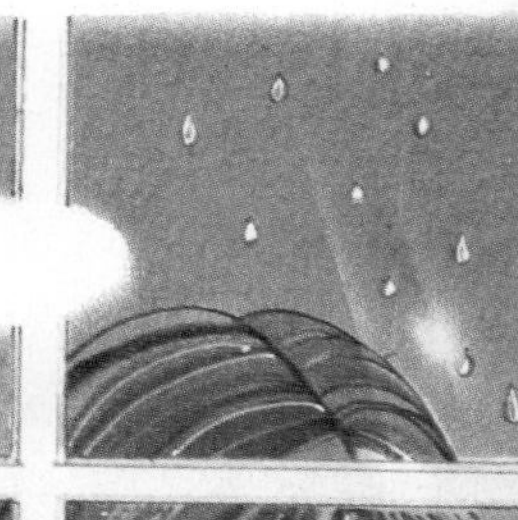

A. Use the poem below to answer the questions.

> The rain was like a little mouse,
> quiet, small, and gray.
> It pattered all around the house
> and then it went away.
>
> *Elizabeth Coatsworth*

1. How many strong beats does line 1 have?
2. Which lines in the poem rhyme?
3. Pick the line below that rhymes with line 1 in the poem above.

   The fish was in a great big bowl.
   The dog and Andy scared a grouse.

4. Pick the line below that has the same number of strong beats as line 1 in the poem above.

   A tree was near the house.
   A cat can be your dearest friend.

Apply

B. 5. Use this line as the first line of your own four-line poem. Make at least two lines rhyme.

> A giant man rode down the hill . . .

Lesson 16: Understanding Sound Words in Poetry

Rhyming words have the same ending sounds. Poets may also use words with the same beginning sounds. Read this poem.

Galoshes

Susie's galoshes
Make splishes and sploshes
And slooshes and sloshes,
As Susie steps slowly
Along in the slush.
They stamp and they tramp
On the ice and concrete,
They get stuck in the muck and the mud;
But Susie likes much best to hear
The slippery slush
As it slooshes and sloshes,
And splishes and sploshes,
All round her galoshes!

Rhoda W. Bacmeister

Think and Discuss

What beginning sound is repeated over and over in "Galoshes"? Do any lines rhyme?

The poet used special sound words. Words such as *splishes* and *sploshes* make sounds like boots splashing in puddles. What other sound words are in the poem? The poet used these sound words to help readers imagine Susie splashing.

Practice

A. Write the lines that have words with the same beginning sounds.

1. I rode a red rooster on the road to the river.
2. The chickens clucked and ran away.
3. One hundred horses hurried by.
4. I walked with Willie to the wishing well.
5. The collie followed us on the narrow path.

B. Write two things that could make each sound.

6. clack **7.** whirr **8.** zoom **9.** ding **10.** bam

Apply

C. 11.–15. Copy this poem and add sound words. Then write a fourth line that rhymes with line 2.

My bat hit the ball with a ______,
And the ball hit the ground with a ______.
With a ______ and a ______ I slid into the base . . .

A BOOK TO READ

Title: **The Blue Horse and Other Night Poems**
Author: Siv Cedering Fox
Publisher: Clarion Books, Ticknor & Fields

How would you describe a dream? What makes nighttime special? Each of these poems by Swedish poet Siv Cedering Fox is about sleeping, dreaming, or waking up. Donald Carrick drew the dreamlike pictures.

6 UNIT TEST

Pronouns pages 186–187

One word in each sentence is a pronoun. Write the letter of the word that is a pronoun.

1. I like to take trips on passenger trains.
   a b c
2. Have you ever eaten dinner in a dining car?
   a b c
3. A family on the train joined us for dinner.
   a b c
4. They were traveling from Boston to Chicago.
   a b c
5. Once we had a room in a sleeping car.
   a b c

Singular and Plural Pronouns pages 188–189

Copy the sentences. Underline the pronouns. After each sentence write whether the pronoun is singular or plural.

6. Uncle Al gave us tickets to a baseball game.
7. Doesn't he go to most of the home games?
8. Mom and I sat right behind third base.
9. It was an exciting game with four home runs.
10. The other team hit all four of them!

Pronouns as Subjects pages 190–191

Choose the correct answer. Write the sentences.

11. (I, She) know how to make yeast bread.
12. (She, They) teaches me how to knead dough.
13. At first (they, it) feels warm and sticky.

14. (He, They) watch me pound it on a table.
15. (We, He) eat the bread with homemade jam.

I and Me pages 192–193

Choose the correct answer. Write the sentences.

16. Grandmother and (I, me) collect fall leaves.
17. She pastes leaves in a book for (I, me).
18. She and (I, me) take long walks in the woods.
19. Sometimes she takes pictures of (I, me).
20. (I, Me) know she enjoys being with (I, me).

Possessive Nouns pages 194–195

Write a possessive noun for each group of words.

21. the coins of the girl
22. the marbles of Kim
23. the chair of the man
24. the toy of the child
25. the cup of the baby
26. the paints of Sal

Plural Possessive Nouns pages 196–197

Write a possessive noun for each group of words.

27. the hands of the boys
28. the nest of the birds
29. the noses of the clowns
30. the eyes of the babies

Compounds pages 200–201

Make compound words from these words. Use them to complete the sentences.

table	beach	sea	sword	life
guard	fish	cloth	shells	ball

1. I caught a small ______ with my fishing line.
2. Mother looked for unbroken ______ in the sand.
3. The ______ blew her whistle at swimmers.
4. We spread a ______ on the sand for lunch.
5. After lunch we played with a big red ______.

Prefixes pages 202–203

Copy each word. Circle the prefix.

6. improper	**7.** dislike	**8.** refinish
9. rejoin	**10.** unlucky	**11.** distaste
12. impossible	**13.** distrust	**14.** unsure

Suffixes pages 204–205

Copy each word. Circle the suffix.

15. enjoyable	**16.** helpful	**17.** colorless
18. farmer	**19.** sailor	**20.** drinkable
21. peaceful	**22.** banker	**23.** hairless

Friendly Letters pages 206–207

1. Rewrite this friendly letter correctly.

44 Austin Place
Laurelton, Pennsylvania 17835
January 2, 19- -

Dear Laura
I can hardly wait for school to start again! I have a part in a play we are giving for the other third-grade classes. I wish you could come to see it. Please write to me soon!

Your friend
Amanda

Addressing an Envelope pages 208–209

2. Use a ruler to draw an envelope on your paper. Use your address as the return address. Address the envelope to:

Miss Adrienne Alonzo 4 Newcombe Rd.
Los Angeles, CA 90034

Invitations pages 210–211

3. Choose one of the events below. Write an invitation, inviting your friend to the event.

a skating party	a picnic lunch
a class play	a neighborhood fair
a canoe trip	an overnight hike

Writing and Editing a Thank You Note pages 212–215

4. Pretend you have just received a present from someone you know. Plan and write a thank you note. Edit it for correct form and for capital letters and punctuation.

Rhythm and Rhyme in Poetry pages 216–217

Read the poem. Then answer the questions.

The Owl and the Pussy-Cat went to sea
    In a beautiful pea-green boat;
They took some honey, and plenty of money
    Wrapped up in a five-pound note.

Edward Lear

1. How many strong beats does line 2 have?
2. Write two pairs of words that rhyme.

Sound Words in Poetry pages 218–219

Read the poem. Then answer the questions.

Wham! Bam! The building fell
With a creak and a crumbling crunch
A doorway stood in a pile of dust
And the workers all went to lunch.

3. List four sound words from this poem.
4. Write three words that begin with the same sound.

MAINTENANCE and REVIEW

Parts of a Sentence pages 10–11

Copy the sentences. Draw one line under the subjects. Draw two lines under the predicates.

1. The family went camping in the forest.
2. They drove through Lexington, Kentucky.
3. The campground overlooked a beautiful lake.
4. They planned to stay in the woods until Friday.
5. Dr. Zarkoff set up the largest of the three tents.

Common and Proper Nouns pages 46–47

6.–15. Find ten nouns in the sentences above. Write them. Tell whether each one is a common noun or a proper noun.

Past Time Verbs pages 82–83 and 86–89

Write the past time form of each verb below.

16. study	**17.** play	**18.** show
19. dance	**20.** trip	**21.** gather

Topic Sentence and Keeping to the Topic pages 118–119 and 124–125

Write the paragraph. Leave out the sentence that does not keep to the topic. Underline the topic sentence.

22. Ants are very strong. They can carry heavy things. Some ants are red. I saw an ant carrying a grape five times its size.

Adjectives and Articles pages 154–159

Copy the sentences. Circle the describing adjectives. Underline the articles.

23. Lisa danced in a lovely ballet.
24. She wore an orange tutu and white tights.
25. Her partner was a tall boy from the class.
26. He did a high jump and many long leaps.
27. The audience gave a loud cheer.

Comparisons pages 160–163

Choose the correct answer in ( ). Write the sentences.

28. This is the (more interesting, most interesting) book I know.
29. It is (longer, longest) than that other book.
30. Luckily, I am a (faster, fastest) reader than you are.
31. You will find this book (more exciting, most exciting) than the one you are reading now.

Pronouns pages 186–187

Copy the sentences. Underline the pronouns.

32. Cy Redbird gave me a pet.
33. It is a small bird.
34. I will take care of it.
35. I thanked him for the gift.

I and Me pages 192–193

Choose the correct pronoun in ( ). Write the sentences.

36. (I, Me) discovered a secret place in the woods.
37. On Sunday (I, me) found an old hollow tree.
38. The hole in the tree is big enough for Juan and (I, me).
39. (Juan and I, Juan and me) can meet at the old tree.
40. Juan will thank (I, me) for showing it to him.

Possessive Nouns pages 194–197

Write possessive nouns to take the place of each word group.

41. the puppy of Nori
42. the ball of the boys
43. the keys of Mother
44. the barks of the dog
45. the nest of the birds

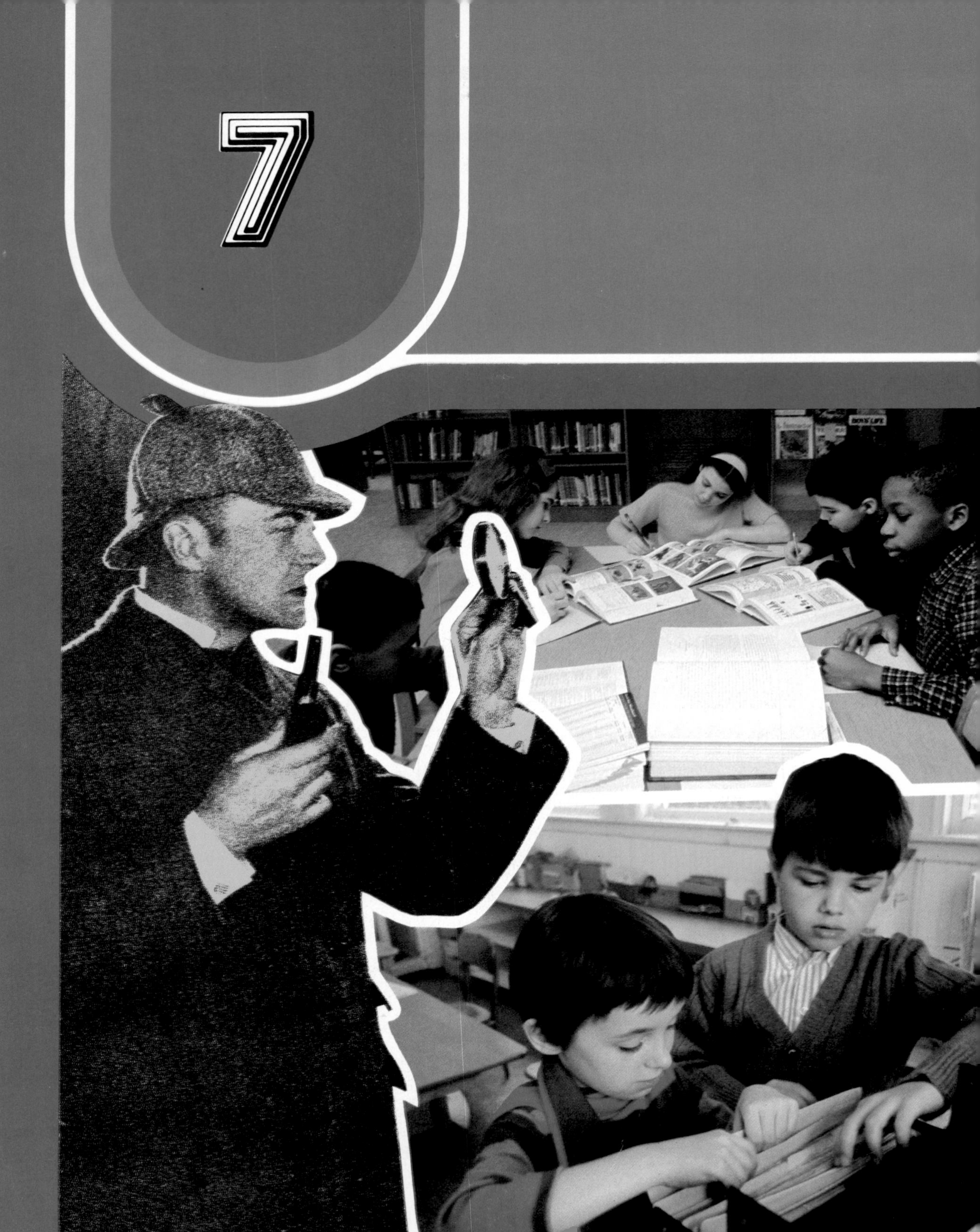
7

LANGUAGE
Learning More About Verbs

STUDY SKILLS
Finding and Organizing Information

COMPOSITION
Writing a Report

LITERATURE
Reading an Article

What does a detective do? A detective hunts for information about something. A good detective knows where to look for clues. Then he or she decides how all the information fits together. Who are some famous detectives you know?

Look at the pictures on page 226. All these people are detectives. They are finding the information they need to answer their questions. Which of them could be you? The students in the pictures are hunting for clues. They may use the information they find to write a report.

In this unit you will learn to be a detective. You will use books, notes, and magazines in your search. Can you guess what kind of "mysteries" you will solve?

LANGUAGE

Lesson 1: Using Present and Past Time Verbs

Read these sentences.

1. The Hopi people lived and worked here 800 years ago.
2. Some Hopi families live and work in the city now.

Which sentence tells about present time? Which tells about past time?

Think and Discuss

In Unit 3 you learned about two kinds of verbs. Present time verbs tell about action that is happening now. Past time verbs tell about action in the past.

Most verbs add *ed* to show past time. Some verbs drop their final *e* and add *ed*. Some double their final letter and add *ed*. How do verbs that end in *y* show past time?

Make these sentences show past time.

3. Two girls carry handmade dolls.
4. They dress the dolls in colorful clothes.

Make these sentences show present time.

5. The girls raised these sheep themselves.
6. The sheep cropped the grass short.

Practice

A. Copy the sentences. Underline the verbs. Tell whether each verb shows *present* or *past time.*

1. The Pueblo people live in Arizona and New Mexico.
2. Pueblo villages consisted of stone buildings.
3. The buildings look like apartment houses.
4. Desert sands surround the towns.
5. Pueblo people designed beautiful pottery.

B. These sentences should tell about past time. Rewrite the sentences. Make the verbs tell about past time.

6. Spanish explorers explore New Mexico.
7. They look for gold in the area.
8. Many Spanish explorers stay in New Mexico.
9. Traders open the Santa Fe Trail.
10. Stagecoaches travel along the trail.

C. Add a verb to each sentence. Write the sentences.

11. The Ramóns ______ in Santa Fe, New Mexico.
12. Long ago, the family ______ in a Pueblo village.
13. Mr. Ramón ______ the village last year.
14. He ______ there on a bus last summer.
15. Now the Ramóns ______ him questions about the trip.

Apply

D. 16.–20. Write five sentences about this picture. Make two sentences show past time. Make three sentences show present time.

Lesson 2: Using Forms of Be

Have is one verb that does not add *ed* to show past time. Here is another verb with special past time forms. Read these sentences.

1. The boy is in the water.
2. The boy was on the diving board.

Which sentence tells about present time? Which tells about past time?

Think and Discuss

The verb *be* has many different forms. Look at these sentences.

3. I am a diver.
4. I was a diver.
5. She is a swimmer.
6. She was a swimmer.
7. They are lifeguards.
8. They were lifeguards.

Sentences 3, 5, and 7 show present time. Sentences 4, 6, and 8 show past time. Name the pronouns and the verb that goes with each one.

These forms of *be* do not show action. They link, or join, subjects to words in the predicates. These verbs are called **linking verbs.**

Read the chart below.

Verb	Present	Past	Past with *Have, Has,* or *Had*
be	am, is, are	was, were	been

What form of *be* is used with the helping verb *have* to show past time?

Forms of *be* can be helping verbs too. They can be used with other verbs that end in *ing*. Read these sentences.

9. Joe is diving into the water.
10. The girls were swimming in the deep end.

Which verbs are the helping verbs?

- A **linking verb** connects the subject with words in the predicate.

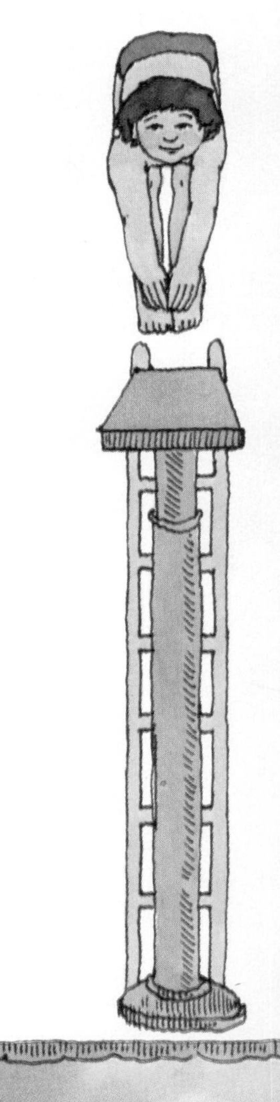

Practice

A. Choose the correct verb. Write the sentences.

1. Molly (was, were) sleeping in the sun.
2. Now she (is, am) ready to swim again.
3. They (is, are) splashing her.
4. They (been, have been) swimming already.
5. I (is, am, are) getting wet too.

B. Copy each sentence. Underline the forms of *be*. Then tell whether they are used as *helping verbs* or *linking verbs*.

6. The pool is very large.
7. My friends are watching me swim.
8. I am having a great time.
9. We were playing together before.
10. The water was too cold for them.

Apply

C. 11.–15. Write five sentences about a summer sport. Use five different forms of *be*.

Lesson 3: Using Irregular Verbs

The sentences below use forms of the verb *ring*.

1. The telephones ring.
2. The phones rang all day yesterday.
3. The phones have rung each day for a week.

Which sentences show past time actions?

Think and Discuss

Sentence 1 tells about present time. Is the subject of the sentence singular or plural?

Sentences 2 and 3 tell about past time. Which form of *ring* is used with a helping verb?

The chart below shows different forms of the verbs *begin, ring,* and *sing*.

Verb	Present	Past	Past with *Have, Has,* or *Had*
begin	begin(s)	began	begun
ring	ring(s)	rang	rung
sing	sing(s)	sang	sung

Each verb changes one letter to show past time. Which letter changes? How does that letter change to form past with *have*?

Practice

A. Copy each sentence. Underline all the verbs. Then tell whether each one shows *present time, past time,* or *past time with have.*

1. The phones ring with calls about the concert.
2. Two rock groups sing in the concert hall.

3. The concert has begun already.
4. It began at 8:30.
5. One group sang from 8:30 until 9:30.

B. Write the sentences. Change the underlined verb to the form shown in ( ).

6. The alarm clock <u>rings</u>. (past)
7. I <u>begin</u> to wake up. (past)
8. I <u>sang</u> in the shower. (present)
9. My brothers <u>begin</u> breakfast. (past with *have*)
10. The school bells <u>ring</u>. (past with *have*)

Apply

C. Use these verb forms in sentences of your own.

11. rang **12.** have sung **13.** begin
14. sang **15.** has begun

HOW OUR LANGUAGE GROWS

People in England speak English, just as you do. Sometimes they use words differently from the way you use them. In England, for example, children go *on holiday*. You would call it *taking a vacation*. English children put their suitcases in the *boot* of the car. You put yours in the *trunk*. These words mean the same things.

The words below do not mean the same thing in England as they do here. Look in a dictionary. Find out what each word means in England.

1. bobby **2.** biscuit **3.** lift **4.** stone

Lesson 4: Understanding Contractions with Not

Read these sentences.

1. This police officer is directing traffic.
2. That police officer is not directing traffic.

What are the helping verbs in sentences 1 and 2?

Think and Discuss

The word *not* is often used with verbs. Read these sentences.

3. The driver is not happy.
4. The officer has not stopped the other cars.

Which sentence uses an action verb and a helping verb? Which uses a linking verb?

Now read these sentences.

5. The driver isn't happy.
6. The officer hasn't stopped the other cars.

Isn't and *hasn't* are **contractions.** They are short ways of saying *is not* and *has not.* An **apostrophe** takes the place of one or more letters that are dropped when a contraction is formed. Which letter is replaced by apostrophes in *isn't* and *hasn't*?

Here is a list of some common contractions.

is + not = isn't	was + not = wasn't
are + not = aren't	were + not = weren't
have + not = haven't	had + not = hadn't
has + not = hasn't	

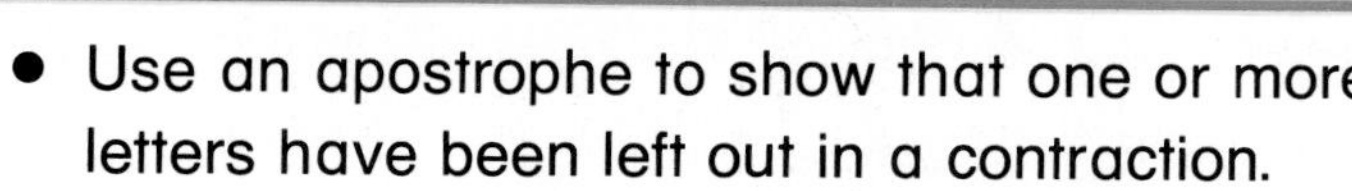

- Use an apostrophe to show that one or more letters have been left out in a contraction.

Practice

A. **1.–5.** Listen to your teacher read sentences. Write them as they are read.

B. Copy the sentences. Underline the contractions. Write the two words from which each is made.

6. The driver hadn't seen the stop sign.
7. He wasn't driving very fast.
8. The other cars weren't breaking the rules.
9. The officers haven't stopped them.
10. They aren't talking to the other drivers.

C. Use a contraction in place of the underlined words. Write the sentences.

11. Traffic rules <u>are not</u> hard to follow.
12. The other drivers <u>were not</u> having any trouble.
13. That driver <u>was not</u> paying attention.
14. He <u>had not</u> stopped at the corner.
15. He <u>has not</u> been stopped by the police before.
16. He <u>is not</u> very pleased with himself.
17. The officers <u>are not</u> pleased with him either.
18. They <u>have not</u> finished writing a ticket.
19. Now the driver's record <u>is not</u> perfect.
20. It <u>is not</u> smart to break traffic rules.

Apply

D. **21.–25.** Write five sentences about safety rules. Use five different contractions.

Lesson 5: Understanding Other Contractions

Kathy wrote to Jenny about an interesting park. Read the sentences she wrote.

1. I am going to visit Everglades National Park.
2. I'm riding on a train to Florida.

Which word uses an apostrophe?

Think and Discuss

Kathy used a contraction in sentence 2. *I'm* is short for the words *I am.* What letter does the apostrophe replace?

Pronouns are often used with forms of the verb *be.* The pronoun and verb can be put together in a contraction. Read these sentences.

3. My parents and I will go there together.
4. They're excited about the trip.
5. We're going to see alligators.

Which words are contractions? Which contraction is short for the words *they are*? Which is short for the words *we are*?

Look back at sentences 3 and 4. Notice the words *there* and *they're.* These words sound alike. They are homophones. It is easy to confuse them.

Look at sentence 5. Suppose Kathy had forgotten to put the apostrophe in *we're.* What word would she have written? *We're* and *were* mean different things. Always remember to use the apostrophe when you write a contraction.

Look at this list of contractions. They are all made up of pronouns and present time forms of *be*.

I + am = I'm		we + are = we're
you + are = you're		
he + is = he's		
she + is = she's		they + are = they're
it + is = it's		

Practice

A. Copy the sentences. Underline the contractions. Then write the two words from which each contraction is made.

1. I'm taking a boat trip with my father.
2. He's snapping pictures of the palm trees.
3. Now we're looking for interesting birds.
4. They're hard to find among the leaves.
5. I know you're going to love our pictures.

B. Use a contraction in place of the underlined words. Write the sentences.

6. Now we are hiking with our guide.
7. She is pointing out a strange plant.
8. She tells us that it is a mangrove tree.
9. I hope you are home when I return.
10. I must tell you all the wonderful things I am learning.

Apply

C. 11.–15. Write five sentences about a park you like. Use five different contractions from the list in this lesson.

LANGUAGE REVIEW

Present Time and Past Time Verbs pages 228–229

Write the sentences. Underline the verbs. Tell whether the verbs show *past time* or *present time.*

1. Ali plays the same record every day.
2. She received the record for her birthday.
3. She listens to the story of "Peter and the Wolf."
4. In the story, the wolf chased after the duck.
5. Peter carried the wolf to a Russian zoo.

Forms of Be pages 230–231

Choose the correct verb in ( ). Write the sentences.

6. Salad (is, are) my favorite food.
7. We (is, are) making some now.
8. I (am, been) slicing peppers and onions.
9. The bowl (were, was) sitting on the counter.
10. Salads (was, have been) my favorite food for years.

Irregular Verbs pages 232–233

Make the underlined verbs show past time. Write the sentences correctly.

11. Music class begins at 3:15 P.M. each day.
12. First we sing a few simple tunes.
13. Then we begin to learn some new songs.
14. Joe sings a solo, and then I sing one.
15. A bell rings at the end of class, and we begin to prepare to leave.

Contractions with <u>Not</u> pages 234–235

Change the underlined words into contractions. Write the sentences. Remember to use an apostrophe.

16. Diana <u>has not</u> packed her suitcase yet.
17. She <u>is not</u> ready to leave.
18. We <u>were not</u> planning to carry so much luggage.
19. We <u>had not</u> realized that the weather would be so warm.
20. We <u>have not</u> needed any of our winter clothes.

Other Contractions pages 236–237

Change the underlined words into contractions. Write the sentences.

21. <u>We are</u> planting tulip bulbs in the garden.
22. Trina raked the dirt, and <u>she is</u> very muddy now.
23. <u>I am</u> trying to decide which end of this bulb is which.
24. <u>It is</u> very hard to tell.
25. We plant tulips in the fall, and <u>they are</u> going to bloom in the spring.

Applying More Verbs

Use these verbs and contractions in complete sentences.

26. have discovered
27. aren't climbing
28. hasn't jumped
29. have begun
30. am running
31. has sung
32. has fished
33. wasn't eating
34. isn't ringing
35. haven't tried

STUDY SKILLS

Lesson 6: Using an Encyclopedia

The students in Ms. Vander's class are writing a book. Each pair of students must choose a city in the United States. They will write reports about the city they choose. The reports will be put together in a book for the whole class.

Vicki and Naldo decided to write about Seattle, Washington. They looked at this set of books.

Think and Discuss

An **encyclopedia** is a good place to find information. Encyclopedias are usually sets of books. Each book is called a **volume.** The volumes list information in alphabetical order. There are letters on the side or spine of each volume. The letters guide you to the topics in that volume.

Look at the volumes in the picture. Information on *Denver* would be in volume 5. Volume 5 has information on things that begin with the letter *D.* Where would information on *Albany* be found?

Suppose you need information about a person. Look under the first letter of the person's last name. In which volume would you find information about *George Clark*?

Practice

A. Look at the volumes in the picture on page 240. Write the number of the volume that includes these topics.

1. Gold
2. Alaska
3. Mars
4. Texas
5. Honolulu
6. Weather
7. Radio
8. Owls
9. Utah
10. Wyoming
11. Squash
12. Eleanor Roosevelt

Apply

B. Think of a city about which you would like to write. Use an encyclopedia in your library. Answer these questions.

13. How many volumes are in this encyclopedia?
14. Which volume has information on things that begin with the letter *T*?
15. In which volume would you find information on the city you chose?

A Challenge

Write the one word from each group of words that you would use to look up these topics in the encyclopedia.

1. trees of the world
2. different kinds of dogs
3. how tigers get food
4. people in France

Lesson 7: Taking Notes

Vicki and Naldo are working on their report. Vicki wrote some questions about Seattle. The report will answer these questions.

Where is Seattle?
How did Seattle become a big city?
What jobs do people have in Seattle?

Where can Naldo find answers to these questions?

Think and Discuss

Naldo found this article in the encyclopedia.

Seattle is an important city. It is in western Washington. It lies between Puget Sound and Lake Washington. Many people work in Seattle's ship and airplane factories. Other people work in lumber mills.

Seattle was first settled in 1851. It was a small lumber town for many years. In 1884 a railroad was built. Seattle began to grow. Gold was found in Alaska in 1897. Many people came to Seattle on their way to Alaska. A canal was built in 1917, and Seattle became a large port. Today, Seattle is a busy city with almost a half-million people.

Naldo must take notes for the report. First he writes the title and volume number of the encyclopedia. Then he writes the page number where he found the information. Read the notes he took to answer the first question. Did Naldo copy the information exactly?

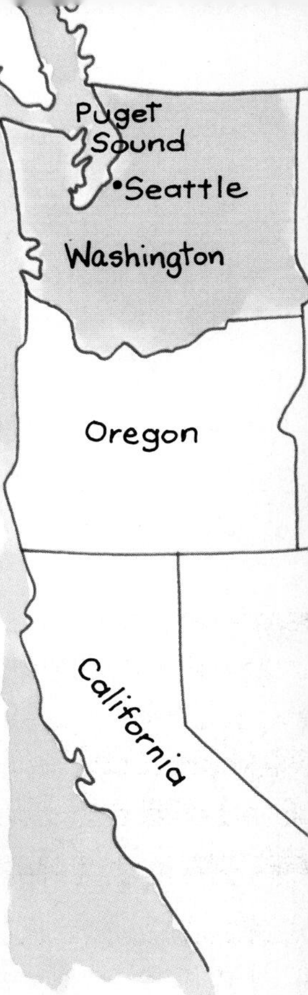

> *Where is Seattle?*
> *in the western part of Washington*
> *near Lake Washington and Puget Sound*

How to Take Notes

1. **List the title of the book, the author, and the page numbers. If you use an encyclopedia, list the volume number.**
2. **Write only the facts you need for your report.**
3. **Write the information in your own words.**
4. **Write sentences or short groups of words.**

Practice

A. Pretend you are answering the question: What jobs do people have in Seattle? Write the notes you would use from the list below.

1. Settlers arrived in 1851.
2. lumber workers
3. work in ship factories
4. work with airplanes
5. gold found in Alaska

Apply

B. 6. Write three questions about the city you chose in Lesson 6. Find an encyclopedia or a book. Take notes on your questions.

Lesson 8: Making an Outline

Vicki decided to write her part of the report on how Seattle became a big city. She looked at Naldo's notes on the question.

How did Seattle become a big city?
first settlers in 1851
small lumber town at first
now 481 thousand people
gold in Alaska in 1897-- many people arrived in Seattle
railroad in 1884
canal (1917) makes Seattle bigger port

Vicki must put these notes in order. Her report must be in an order that makes sense.

Think and Discuss

Vicki put her information into an **outline.** She chose three main topics to discuss in her report. Main topics are shown by roman numerals I, II, and III. A period follows each numeral. What are Vicki's main topics? What is her title?

How Seattle Became a Big City
I. *A small lumber town*
II. *A railroad and a Gold Rush help Seattle grow*
III. *A busy port city*

How to Make an Outline

1. **Write a title. The title tells the subject of your report.**
2. **Write main topics. Use a roman numeral and a period. Begin each main topic with a capital letter.**

Practice

A. Write these main topics in outline form. Give the outline a title.

Columbus sets sail from Spain
three ships cross the Atlantic
Columbus lands in San Salvador

Apply

B. Read the notes you took in Lesson 7. Choose one question to outline. Think of three main topics. Follow the rules to make an outline.

To Memorize

America is a tune. It must be
sung together.

Gerald Stanley Lee

What does the author mean when he says, "It must be sung together"?

COMPOSITION

Lesson 9: Writing a Report

Read Vicki's report.

How Seattle Became a Big City

Seattle began as a small lumber town in 1851. It remained a small town for many years.

Two things happened in the late 1800's to help Seattle grow. First a railroad was built in 1884. This linked Seattle to other towns in the West. Then gold was discovered in Alaska. Many people passed through Seattle on their way to find gold. Seattle began to grow.

Today Seattle is a busy port city. A canal that was built in 1917 helped the port grow. Now ships come to Seattle from all over the world.

Think and Discuss

What is the title of Vicki's report? How many paragraphs are in her report? She wrote one paragraph for each main topic in her outline. Each paragraph has a topic sentence. Find the topic sentence in paragraph 2.

Look back at Lesson 8. Does each paragraph of Vicki's report follow her outline?

How to Write a Report

1. **Use the title from your outline.**
2. **Write a paragraph for each main topic in your outline.**
3. **Write a topic sentence from each main topic. Use your notes to write details.**
4. **Indent the first line of each paragraph.**

Practice

A. Here are the steps Vicki and Naldo took to write their reports on Seattle. Write the steps in the correct order.

1. Take notes on the questions.
2. Choose a topic.
3. Write the report from the outline.
4. Find a book or encyclopedia on the topic.
5. Write questions about the topic.
6. Put the notes in order in an outline.

Apply

B. 7. Use your outline from Lesson 8 and your notes from Lesson 7. Write a report about the city you chose. Follow the rules given in this lesson.

Lesson 10: Editing a Report

Naldo has finished his part of the report. Now he will edit the report. He will correct any mistakes. Read this paragraph from Naldo's report.

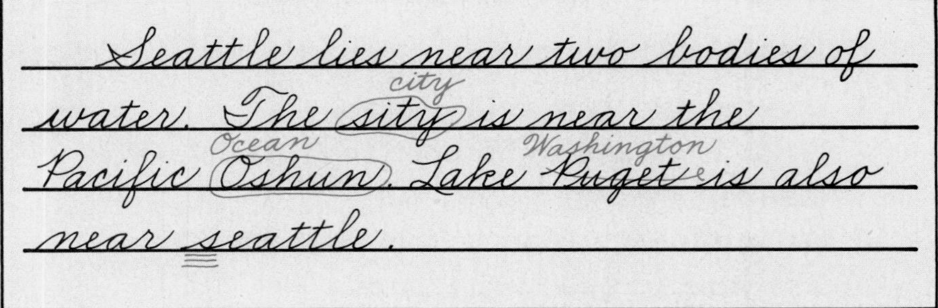
Seattle lies near two bodies of
water. The sity (city) is near the
Pacific Oshun (Ocean). Lake Puget (Washington) is also
near seattle.

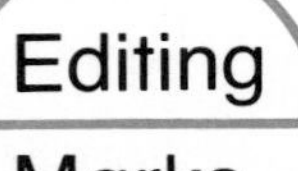

Editing Marks

- capitalize
- make a period
- add something
- add a comma
- add quotation marks
- take something away
- spell correctly
- indent the paragraph
- make a lowercase letter
- transpose

Think and Discuss

Naldo made some spelling mistakes. He circled the words he spelled wrong. How should those words be spelled?

Naldo checked his report by looking back at his notes. He found that he had made a mistake. The lake near Seattle is named Lake Washington. How did Naldo correct this mistake? What other mistake did Naldo make?

Practice

A. Rewrite Naldo's paragraph correctly.

Apply

B. Look at the report you wrote in Lesson 9. Did you spell each word correctly? Compare your report to your notes. Is your information correct? Edit your report and rewrite it.

MECHANICS PRACTICE

Using Apostrophes

- Use an apostrophe (') to show that one or more letters have been left out in a contraction.
- Add an apostrophe and an *s* to singular nouns to show possession.
- Add an apostrophe to plural nouns that end in *s* to show possession.

Write these sentences correctly. Add apostrophes.

1. Jacobs lawn needs mowing.
2. Im going to mow our lawn.
3. Mrs. Harveys lawn is a mess.
4. Mrs. Harveys plum tree is blooming.
5. She hasnt raked the leaves yet.
6. Dads rake is in the garage.
7. Its a very good rake for raking leaves.
8. Im going to call my friends.
9. Theyre going to help me rake my lawn.
10. Then were going to rake Mrs. Harveys leaves.
11. Shes going to be happy that were helping her.
12. We havent raked Mrs. Harveys leaves before.
13. I havent used Dads rake before, either.
14. Dads old rake wasnt as good as this one.
15. The handle wasnt made very well.
16. Im glad that this rake is better.
17. Its easy to rake with Dads new rake.
18. The teeth arent bent out of shape.
19. The teeth of the old rake werent good.
20. It isnt going to be hard to rake Mrs. Harveys lawn.

LITERATURE

Lesson 11: Reading a Magazine Article

Do you have a favorite magazine? Some magazines have stories about people. Some magazines tell about animals. Magazines may have games and puzzles to do. Some show things you can make.

Think and Discuss

Many magazines have **articles** for you to read. An article is a nonfiction piece of writing. Articles tell facts about many different topics. Different magazines have different kinds of articles.

Read this magazine article. It is from a magazine called *Owl*.

Odd Splash Facts

by Paul Brock

Humans aren't the only ones who can float on their backs, do the butterfly stroke, or even snorkel. Read about other animal swimmers in this article. We have chosen these mammals not because they are champions—after all, who could beat the whale?—but because each does something unusual in the water. Think about them the next time you take a dip. . . .

Sea Otter. The sea otter is so much at home in the water that when it's time for a nap it floats on its back in a bed of seaweed. A tired baby simply climbs up onto its mother's chest and is gently rocked to sleep.

Elephant. If you were on a river boat and an elephant crossed the river, you might not notice it pass by. How can you miss a mammal of this size in the water? It's easy. The elephant uses its trunk as a snorkel. Usually all that shows on the surface is the top of its head and the tip of its trunk.

Fruit Bat. Most bats would be miserable in the water. The fruit bat has a waterproof fur coat. It does the "bat version" of the butterfly stroke. It uses its strong wings to scoop along in a very elegant manner.

What is the title of this article? Does this article tell a story or give facts?

Now read this article. It is from a nature magazine called *Ranger Rick.*

Baby Bird Dos and Don'ts

by Eva Bell

What should *you* do—or not do—when you see a baby bird on the ground?

If the bird is naked or has a few feathers and a little fuzz, and if it can't walk or hop, it's a *nestling.* A nestling out of its nest is in trouble. DO pick it up and warm it in your hands. Then look for the nest—one nearby with birds of the same kind and age inside — and gently set the baby bird back in it. If you can't find or reach the nest, DO adopt the bird.

If the nest has fallen out of a tree or bush, try to put it back and fasten it so it will stay put. DON'T climb a tree or use a ladder by yourself. Get an adult to help you. If the parent birds don't come back in an hour or so, you have a baby bird to raise.

If the bird has feathers, a short tail, and can walk, hop, or fly a little, it's a *fledgling*. It has probably left the nest on its own but still is being fed by its parents. DON'T rescue a fledgling unless you are sure it is hurt, sick, an orphan, or in danger.

If you're sure the baby bird is sick or hurt, DO take it home right away. If the bird is healthy but seems to be in danger from cats or dogs, DO put it in a bush or on a low tree limb where its parents can find it. Watch the bird from a distance for two to three hours. If the bird's parents don't show up to feed or protect it, go ahead and adopt it.

If you adopt a bird, DO find out how to care for it right away. Call your local animal shelter, nature center, or Audubon chapter. Also, call your game warden or wildlife officer for permission to raise the bird. It's against the law to keep most wild birds as pets.

Remember: Adopt a baby bird *only* if it really needs your help.

Practice

A. Answer these questions in complete sentences.

1. What is the title of the second article?
2. Is that article fiction or nonfiction?
3. Write two facts from the first article.
4. Write two facts from the second article.

Apply

B. 5. Pretend you are a magazine writer. Write a nonfiction article about one of these subjects. You may use the encyclopedia if you wish.

football   cats   Thanksgiving   the moon

A BOOK TO READ

Title: **An Oak Tree Dies and a Journey Begins**
Author: Louanne Norris and Howard E. Smith, Jr.
Publisher: Crown Publishers

The old oak tree in this book is uprooted in a storm. It becomes a home for growing mushrooms. Raccoons nap in the dead tree.

Later, heavy rains wash the tree out to sea. There it becomes a resting place for sea birds. Seaweed and barnacles attach to the tree. Children use it as a boat.

Even after the tree washes up on the sand, it is still useful. The pictures in this book will show you more uses for an old tree than you ever imagined.

7 UNIT TEST

Present Time and Past Time Verbs pages 228–229

Write the letter of the verb that shows past time.

1. William _____ the leaves into a large pile.
   a. raking **b.** rakes **c.** raked
2. Charlie _____ the lawn early this morning.
   a. watered **b.** waters **c.** watering
3. Heidi _____ tiny shoots under the leaves.
   a. discover **b.** discovered **c.** discovers
4. Mother _____ a flowerbed for spring planting.
   a. prepares **b.** preparing **c.** prepared
5. We _____ dead branches from all the trees.
   a. remove **b.** removed **c.** removing

Forms of Be pages 230–231

Copy the sentences. Choose the correct verb in ( ).

6. I (am, are) the son of a forest ranger in Montana.
7. My father (is, am) also a wildlife scientist.
8. One night the moonlight (were, was) very bright.
9. Some raccoons (was, were) watching us from the yard.
10. The mother (were, was) cleaning the babies with her tongue.
11. The babies (were, was) about two months old.
12. They (are, am) coming toward us in single file.
13. I (are, am) leaving some table scraps for them.
14. One baby (am, is) eating more food than the others.
15. Now we (are, is) the proud owners of a baby raccoon!

Irregular Verbs pages 232–233

Choose the correct answer. Write the sentences.

16. Mrs. Fromm's parakeet (sung, sings) to her.
17. She has (began, begun) to sing to him too!
18. He (rang, rung) a small bell with his beak.
19. He has (rang, rung) it when his food dish is empty.
20. Parakeets (ring, rung) their bells when they are bored.
21. The bird (sang, sung) to himself in the mirror.
22. I (began, begun) taking care of the parakeet.
23. My job had (began, begun) last Wednesday.
24. Sometimes you (begin, begun) to think they are human.
25. We have (sang, sung) a song about parakeets in school.

Contractions with Not pages 234–235

Make contractions from these words. Use each contraction in a sentence.

26. is not
27. were not
28. had not
29. have not
30. are not
31. was not

Other Contractions pages 236–237

Write the sentences. Change the underlined words to contractions.

32. She is taking their class to Washington, D.C.
33. I am looking forward to the trip myself.
34. It is a wonderful chance to see the capital.
35. Do you know when they are leaving?
36. We are going to the bus station at one o'clock.
37. I told Jack that he is welcome to join us.
38. He thinks it is going to be exciting.
39. You are coming with the class, aren't you?
40. I hope we are all ready on time.

The Encyclopedia pages 240–241

Look at this set of encyclopedias. Write the number of the volume you would use to find information about each topic.

1. Groundhog Day
2. Zuñi Indians
3. Margaret Mead
4. astronomy
5. porpoise
6. Canada
7. Babe Ruth
8. Colorado
9. Nepal
10. sea lion

Taking Notes pages 242–243

11. Read and take notes on the paragraph.

    A gecko is a small, scaly lizard that lives in warm climates. It is named for the sound it makes at night. A gecko has thousands of tiny hooks on each of its toe pads. With them the gecko can walk up and down walls and windows. This helps it to catch insects for food.

Outlining pages 244–245

12. Put these main topics in outline form. Give the outline a title.

    the Statue of Liberty is built
    the Statue of Liberty is important to people

Writing and Editing a Report pages 246–248

Write a two-paragraph report. Use the outline you wrote about the Statue of Liberty. Add information from the notes below. Edit your report. Be sure all your facts are correct.

How was the Statue of Liberty built?
designed by Frédéric Bartholdi
built in France
parts were shipped to America
set up again in New York
Why is the statue important?
means freedom to people around the world
welcomes people to America from other lands

Magazine Articles pages 250–253

Read this short magazine article. Answer the questions that follow. Write complete sentences.

Do you know the history of April Fools' Day? Until 1564 April 1 was the first day of the new year. Then the king of France decided to use a new calendar. New Year's Day was changed from April 1 to January 1. People who still celebrated New Year's the old way, on April 1, were called April Fools.

1. Does this article tell a story or give facts?
2. Is this article fiction or nonfiction?
3. Write one fact you learned about April Fools' Day.
4. Look at these titles of magazine articles. Choose the best title for this article.

   An April Fools' Trick
   Facts About April Fools' Day

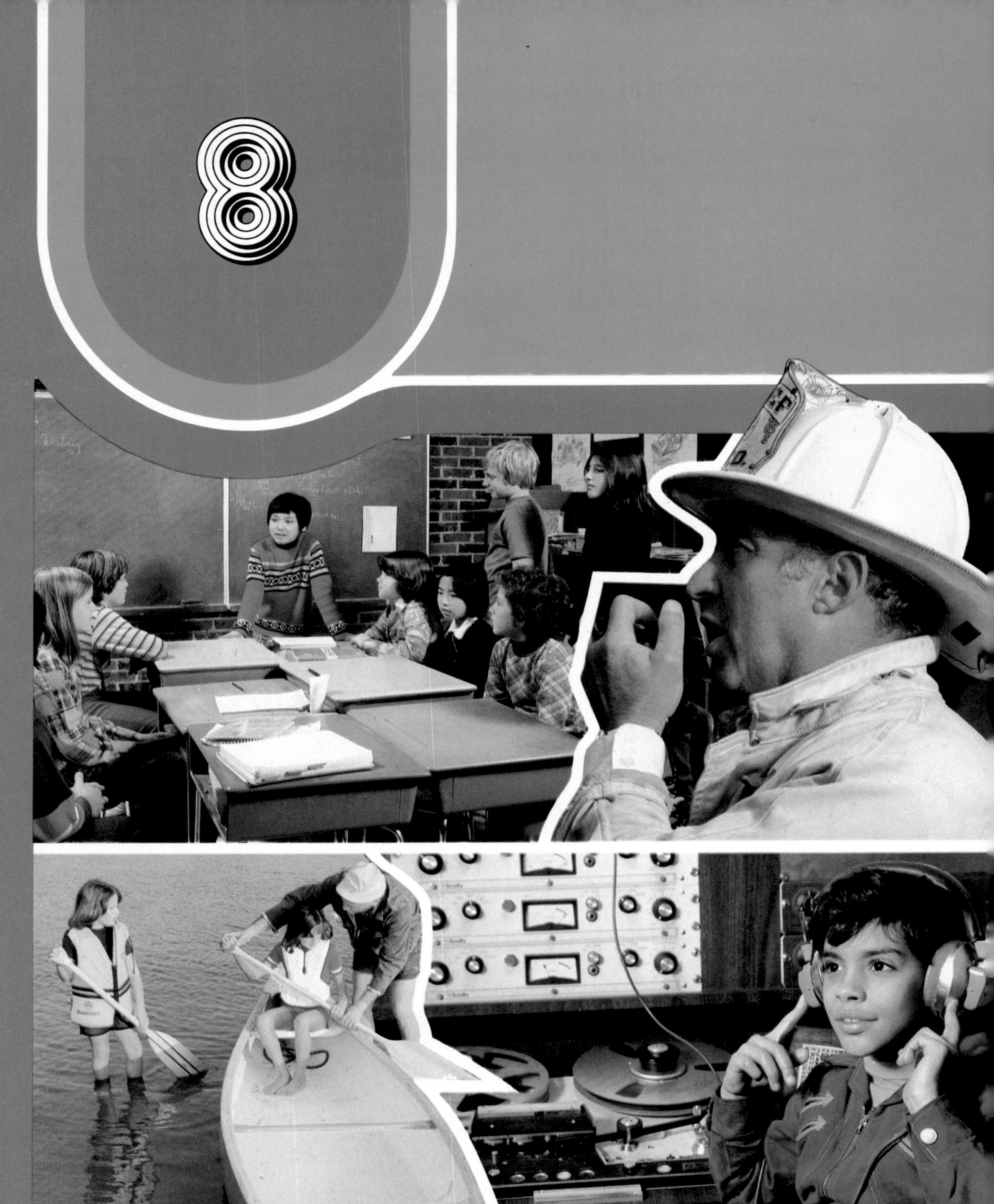

LANGUAGE
Listening and Speaking

STUDY SKILLS
Getting Information

COMPOSITION
Writing a Book Report

LITERATURE
Reading a Play

Close your eyes for a minute and listen. What do you hear? Is it windy or rainy outside? Can you hear other students on the playground or in the hall? What can you listen to inside your own body?

Look at the pictures on page 258. Who is speaking? Who is listening? Find the picture where listening carefully could save someone's life. Think of another time when listening might be especially important.

This unit is about two important skills: listening and speaking. They are skills you use every day. You use them at home, at school, and with your friends.

LANGUAGE

Lesson 1: Making Introductions

Morris taught his little sister, Mitzi, how to shake hands. Now Morris is going to see just how well she learned her lesson. Morris is going to introduce Mitzi to his friend Calvin. Read what he says.

1. "Calvin, I'd like you to meet my sister, Mitzi. Mitzi just had her fourth birthday."

Mitzi shakes hands with Calvin. Read what Calvin says.

2. "Well, Mitzi, it's very nice to meet you. My brother is just your age."

Think and Discuss

Shaking hands is something we often do when we meet someone new. We also make an introduction. When you introduce people, say their names. Try to say something about the people you are introducing. This makes it easier for them to talk to each other. What did Morris say to make the introduction? What did Calvin say? Morris told Calvin a little about Mitzi. What did he say?

When you introduce two people, say the older person's name first. This is the polite thing to do.

Practice

A. Read the introductions below. Write the introductions that are best. Remember that an introduction should make it easy for people to talk to each other.

1. a. Mom, this is my gym partner, Alexis. She's going to teach me how to do flips.
b. Mom, this is my friend.

2. a. Grandpa, meet the Craig family.
b. Grandpa Joe, please meet our new neighbors, the Craigs. They just moved here all the way from British Columbia.

3. a. Mrs. Phillips, I would like to introduce Dr. Sloan. He is the chief doctor at our hospital.
b. Mrs. Phillips, this is Dr. Sloan.

4. a. Sasha, this is Joe. He will be in fourth grade next year.
b. Sasha, meet Joe.

5. a. Amy, this is Mrs. Jones. Amy is my sister.
b. Mrs. Jones, I would like you to meet my sister, Amy.

Apply

B. 6. Choose a partner in the class. Talk to your partner for a few minutes about his or her interests. Ask your partner what he or she likes best. Then take turns introducing your partner to your teacher. Be sure to add some interesting extra information about the person being introduced.

Lesson 2: Taking Messages

Today is Betsy Bubb's birthday. Her good friend Sally is calling to say, "Happy Birthday!" Betsy is not home. Read the message her father left for her.

Sunday, 2:00 P.M.
For Betsy:
Sally called. She wanted to wish you a happy birthday. You may call her at 273-9203.
Dad

Think and Discuss

For whom is the message? On what day and at what time did Sally call? It is important to write this information.

Why did Sally call? Betsy's father wrote the message. He wrote Sally's telephone number. Now Betsy can call Sally.

How to Take Telephone Messages

1. **Write the time and date of the call.**
2. **Write the name of the person called.**
3. **Write the name of the person calling.**
4. **Write the message.**
5. **Write your name.**

Practice

A. Read the conversations. Write messages on your paper. Use today's date and time.

1. This is Vic Dahl calling from the clock shop. Please tell your father that his clock will be ready tomorrow afternoon at 4:00 P.M.
2. This is Kay Kim, Mary's swimming coach. Tell her we will practice tomorrow at 3:00 P.M.
3. This is Tala Deere, Ken's teacher. Please tell your mother that Ken fell on the playground. I am taking him to Dr. Volk's office.

Apply

B. 4. Choose a partner. Have a make-believe telephone conversation in front of the class. The caller should make up a message. The message taker must write the message on the chalkboard.

HOW OUR LANGUAGE GROWS

The words *telephone* and *television* have something in common. They begin the same way. *Tele* comes from a Greek word that means "far away." *Phone* means "sound." A telephone lets you hear sounds that are far away. *Vision* means "sight." A television lets you see things that are far away.

1. *Graph* means "writing." What does a *telegraph* do?
2. Use the dictionary. Find the meanings of these words: *telescope, telephoto, telemeter.*

Lesson 3: Giving and Getting Directions

Tia is going to visit her friends, the Neill twins. Both girls gave Tia directions to their apartment building. Read the directions they gave below.

Greta's Directions

Go to the drugstore. I think it's on your street somewhere. When you find Olive Street, you'll see our apartment building. Knock on our door.

Jill's Directions

1. Go out your door and turn right.
2. Walk past the drugstore and the pet shop.
3. When you come to Olive Street, turn left.
4. Walk to 36 Olive. We live in apartment 607.

Think and Discuss

Which directions are clearer? Which directions would you choose to use?

Try to give clear directions. You must tell the steps in order. You must tell all the important details.

Be careful when you listen to directions. You must listen to every word. You must listen for all the details.

Your teacher is going to read a set of directions. Close your book. Take out a sheet of paper. Listen carefully.

Now look at your paper. Did you write only your first name? Is your age in the bottom left corner?

Practice

A. Annie had a special game at her birthday party. Her father set up an obstacle course. Look at the picture. Write directions in order for the children to follow. They may go over, under, around, and through things.

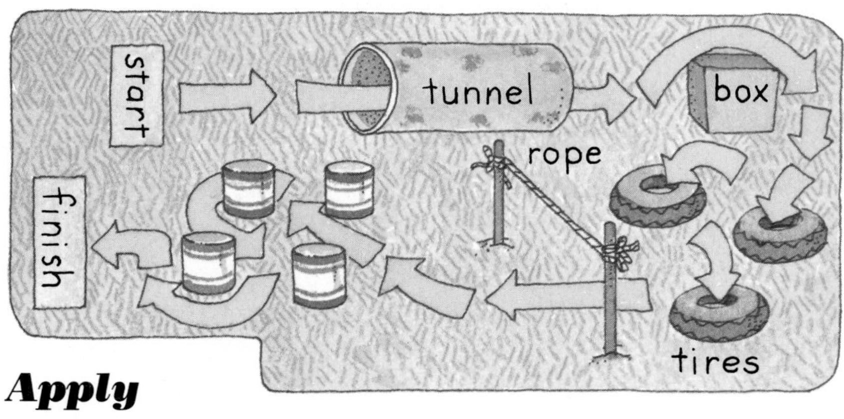

Apply

B. Choose a partner. Write five directions for your partner to follow.

Example: Fold a sheet of paper in half.

Then take turns. Read your directions to your partner. See if your partner can follow them. Listen as your partner reads his or her directions. Try to follow them.

A Challenge

Write directions. Tell someone how to go from your classroom to one of these places. Write the steps in order.

the gym	the main office
the playground	the drinking fountain

Lesson 4: Thinking About What You Hear

It is World Series time. Big Bill James and Smokey Reed are announcing the baseball game. Read what they say.

Big Bill: Here we are at WDMT in Dayton. The Dayton Dragons are playing the Sacramento Majors. There is no score yet at the top of the second inning. The Dragons are on the field. The Majors' first batter is Clem Orozco. I'm Big Bill James with the play-by-play. . . .

Smokey: I'm Smokey Reed standing by. This should be an exciting inning. It's a beautiful day for a ball game.

Think and Discuss

A **statement of fact** gives information that can be proved or checked. A **statement of opinion** tells what someone thinks or how someone feels.

Which announcer states the facts? What are some of the facts? Which announcer states opinions? What is one of his opinions?

Practice

A. Read these statements carefully. Then close your book. Copy the sentences as your teacher reads them. Then label each one *fact* or *opinion.*

1. You haven't been to a baseball game before.

2. I'm sure that you will enjoy it.
3. What an exciting time we're having!
4. It's a perfect day for a ball game.
5. He's selling drinks, and she's selling peanuts.

B. Read what each announcer says. Then write *fact* for each statement of fact. Write *opinion* for each statement of opinion.

6. Maxie Meraldo has three balls and two strikes.
7. I think he seems to be nervous.
8. He just smacked his shoes with his bat.
9. I'd say the fans are going wild.
10. Here's the pitch. It's a home run!
11. It was a beauty!
12. The Sacramento Majors are ahead 1–0.
13. This is turning into an exciting afternoon.
14. Sparky Little is up to bat.
15. The Dragons are going to have to watch out.
16. What a terrible pitch!
17. Sparky did not swing at it.
18. The pitcher just threw again.
19. Sparky should have tried to hit that one.
20. Sparky is a truly great ball player.
21. He hit more home runs than any other player.

Apply

C. **22.–25.** Choose one of the subjects below. Write two facts and two opinions on that subject.

Kickball	Weather	Gym Class
Your Hair	Flowers	Your Lunch

LANGUAGE REVIEW

Introductions pages 260–261

Copy the introductions. Circle the names of the two people being introduced. Underline the extra information being given about one of the people.

1. Miss Lee, I'd like you to meet Ira Fallon. He helped to build the new playground.
2. Marylou, this is Jerome Norbert. He is my cousin from North Carolina.
3. Dr. Barstow, I'd like to introduce you to Ann. She also wants to be a doctor when she grows up.
4. Vincent Loree, this is Morgan Lasser. Did you know that Morgan went to your summer camp?
5. Mother, I want you to meet Parker O'Day. He knows one of our neighbors.

Taking Messages pages 262–263

6. Write a message for the conversation below. Use today's date and time.

Miranda: Hello.
Mrs. Eli: Hello. This is Mrs. Eli. May I speak to Mrs. Zwick?
Miranda: I'm sorry, but my mother is not here. May I take a message for her?
Mrs. Eli: Yes. Please tell your mother that I can give you flute lessons either Wednesday at 4:00 or Saturday at 2:00. I'd like her to call me this week to tell me which is better. My number is 778-4610.

Giving and Getting Directions pages 264–265

7. Winema is lost in the forest. Look at the picture. Write directions that will help Winema get home.

Thinking About What You Hear pages 266–267

Write the sentence from each pair that states a fact.

8. Scientists found Dandee peanut butter lowest in sugar. You will love its taste!
9. PURRRRR cat food will make your cat purr. It is made from beef, chicken, and fish.
10. The Bumper Car is an exciting new toy. It is made of unbreakable plastic.
11. When you wear Tootsies, it feels as if you're walking on air. These shoes are made of foam.
12. Smelz perfume costs less than Whiff or Spring. Smelz will have everyone talking!

Applying Listening and Speaking

13.–15. Introduce yourself to the class. State one fact and two opinions about yourself.

STUDY SKILLS

Lesson 5: Following Test Directions

Julia is taking a test. Here is the first question and her answer.

1. Which word means *sofa*? Circle the answer.
   lamp   light   <u>couch</u>

Did Julia follow the directions?

Think and Discuss

Where have you seen these words?

Fill in the circle . . .
Draw a line under . . .
Circle the word . . .
Put an X next to . . .
Circle the letter . . .

These are test directions. To do well on tests, you must know the answers. You must also follow the directions carefully. Read them. Be sure you know what to do.

Practice

A. Look at each test direction. Which student has followed the directions correctly? Write the name of the student.

Test Direction 1: Fill in the circle next to the word that is the opposite of *high.*

Mary		**John**		**Susie**	
●	high	○	high	○	high
○	often	○	often	○	often
○	low	●	low	○	(low)

Test Direction 2: Put an X next to the verb.

Mary		**John**		**Susie**	
at	____	at	____	at	____
me	____	me	X	me	____
soak	X	soak	____	soak	✓

Test Direction 3: Draw a line under the prefix.

Mary	**John**	**Susie**
returned	returned	returned

Apply

B. Copy this test answer form. Then follow the directions below.

4.		not		inside		under
5.	○	dry	○	ill	○	soaked
6.		twelve		eleven		nine
7.		sneeze		big		sunny
8.	**a.**	white	**b.**	bear	**c.**	train

4. Circle the compound word.
5. Fill in the circle next to the word that means *wet.*
6. Underline the number that follows ten.
7. Put an X beside the word that describes a giant.
8. Circle the letter of the color word.

Lesson 6: Using a Map

Cindy is going on a trip. She will travel by train from Centerville to Jamestown. She wants to know what she will see along the way. She looks at this map.

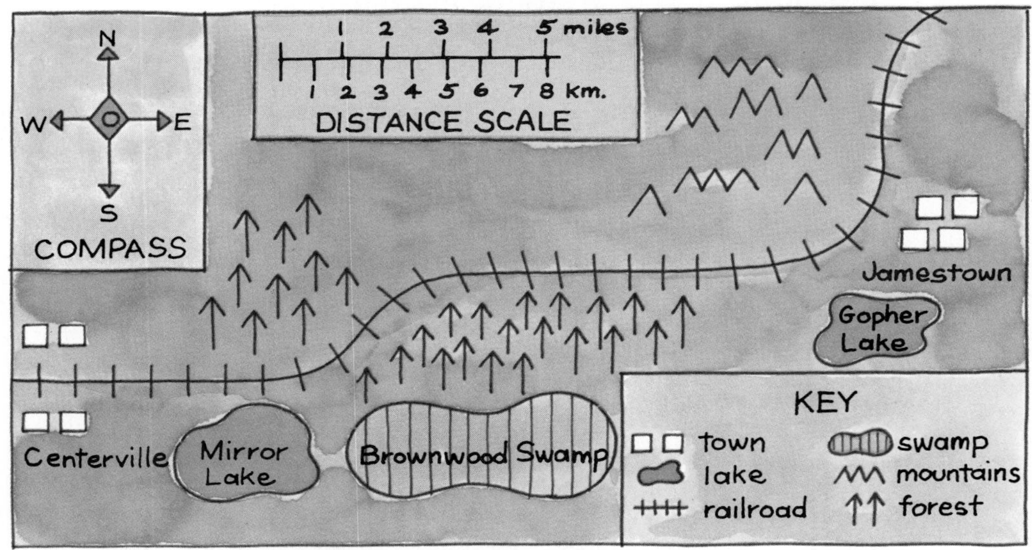

Think and Discuss

This map shows many places. It has a **key** at the bottom. A key uses symbols to explain what is shown on the map. This symbol ++++ stands for a railroad. Which symbol means a lake? A map key may also be called a **legend.**

This map also has a **direction symbol,** or **compass.** This shows which way *n*orth, *s*outh, *e*ast and *w*est are on the map. In which direction will Cindy travel to go from Centerville to Jamestown?

The **distance scale** shows the distance on the map in miles and kilometers. Cindy can use the distance scale to find out how far she will travel.

Practice

A. Use the map on page 272 to answer these questions.

1. What does this symbol mean: ?
2. Is the swamp north of the mountains?
3. Is Centerville west of Mirror Lake?
4. What is the symbol that means *forest*?
5. In what direction would you go to travel from the swamp to Mirror Lake?
6. Is Gopher Lake more than 5 miles (8 kilometers) long?
7. Is Gopher Lake east of Jamestown?
8. In what direction would you go to travel from Mirror Lake to Gopher Lake?
9. What is just south of the big forest?
10. What is just north of the big forest?

B. 11. Help Cindy plan her trip. Write down what she will see along the railroad from Centerville to Jamestown. Tell about it in order.

Apply

C. 12. Draw a map of your classroom. Include all the most interesting things you see. Remember that a map is not the same as a picture. Make a key for your map. Use your own symbols. You do not need a direction symbol or a distance scale.

Lesson 7: Using a Telephone Directory

Stefan wants his Aunt Lola to go to the movies with him. He does not know her telephone number. He will look for the number in the telephone book.

Think and Discuss

The telephone book lists names, addresses, and telephone numbers. The names are listed in alphabetical order, last name first. Aunt Lola's last name is Martinez. Under what letter in the telephone book should Stefan look?

Read this page from a telephone book.

Lyons–Moore

Lyons, Dr. Jerome	4 May Rd.	**222-5223**
Maas, Eli	23 Hoyt St.	**422-8756**
Mann, Susan	523 Lee Rd.	**422-9977**
Martinez, Lola	14 May Rd.	**222-4344**
May, Lianne	44 East Ave.	**343-5665**
Meek, John	8 High St.	**322-4644**
Mendel, Sal	49 Hoyt St.	**432-9988**
Mirez, Julia	62 High St.	**444-2225**
Moek, Stu	23 East Ave.	**889-0028**
Moore, Kay	72 West Rd.	**432-8790**

The words at the top of the page are guide words. They tell Stefan that *Lyons* is the first name listed on this page. *Moore* is the last name listed. Does *Martinez* come between *Lyons* and *Moore* in alphabetical order? *Martinez* must be listed on this page.

Find the listing for *Lola Martinez.* Next to her name you will see her address and telephone number. What is Aunt Lola's address? What is her telephone number?

Practice

A. Look at these guide words from the telephone book. List the names from the group below that you would find on that page.

Yang–Zack

1. Yurman	**2.** Young	**3.** Zizzo
4. Yaffey	**5.** Yardley	**6.** Zigler
7. Ward	**8.** Zollen	**9.** Zack

B. Look at the telephone book page on page 274. Answer these questions in complete sentences.

10. What is Lianne May's telephone number?
11. What is Stu Moek's address?
12. What is Susan Mann's telephone number?
13. What is Julia Mirez's address?
14. Who lives at 49 Hoyt Street?
15. Who lives at 72 West Road?
16. Who has this telephone number: 222-5223?
17. Who is listed right after Julia Mirez?
18. Who is listed just before Sal Mendel?
19. Which two people live on May Road?
20. What is Mr. Meek's first name?

Apply

C. 21.–25. Make your own telephone book page. Make up five names, addresses, and telephone numbers. List the names, last name first, in alphabetical order. Add the addresses and telephone numbers.

COMPOSITION

Lesson 8: Writing Titles

The name of a book is called its **title.** Stories, poems, and television shows have titles too. Read these sentences.

1. I read a book called <u>Catch a Cricket</u>.
2. I read a story called "The Three Bears."
3. I read a poem called "The Gnu Family."
4. I watched a show called "The Muppet Show."

What was the title of the story?

Think and Discuss

Most of the words in titles begin with capital letters. The first and last words of titles always begin with capital letters. Look at the title in sentence 1. Which word does not begin with a capital letter? Small words such as *a, an, the,* and *and* do not need capital letters if they come in the middle of a title.

Titles of books are always underlined. Which title is underlined in the sentences above?

Titles of stories, poems, and television shows are written in a different way. Look at the marks around the titles. They are called **quotation marks.** One quotation mark is put at the beginning of the title. The other goes after the title.

- Use a capital letter to begin the first, last, and all important words in the title of a book, story, poem, or television show.
- Underline the title of a book.
- Use quotation marks (“) before and after the title of a story, poem, or television show.

Practice

A. Write these sentences correctly.

1. The title of this poem is eletelephony.
2. This story is called the three little pigs.
3. I read a book called rascal.
4. I like the television show called the waltons.
5. The title of this book is becky and the bear.

Apply

B. 6.–10. Write five sentences about a book or show you like. Write the title correctly.

To Memorize

Arithmetic is numbers you squeeze from your
head to your
hand to your pencil to your paper till you
get the answer.

Carl Sandburg

This is Carl Sandburg's idea of arithmetic. What is yours? Choose a subject such as spelling, and give your notion of what it is.

Lesson 9: Writing a Book Report

Sharing books is fun. You may have friends who enjoy the same books you do. You can tell them about books you like.

Think and Discuss

A book report is a good way to share a book you enjoyed. Perhaps your friends will want to read the book too. Read this book report by Leroy Leonard.

Title My Father's Dragon

Author Ruth Stiles Gannett

About the Book How do you rescue a dragon? That is what Elmer Elevator sets out to do in this book. He packs many things to take on his trip to rescue the dragon. Some wild animals are holding the dragon prisoner. Elmer has to outwit them all!

Opinion My favorite part is when Elmer tricks the rhinoceros. I love this funny book.

Who wrote the book about which Leroy wrote? What is the book's title? Leroy told a few things about the book. He also gave his opinion about the book. He told about the part he liked best.

How to Write a Book Report

1. **Write the title of the book.**
2. **Tell the author's name.**
3. **Tell what the book is about. Give details.**
4. **Tell your opinion of the book.**

Practice

A. Write this book report in order. Use the form on page 278.

by John Shearer

The best part is Billy Jo and Susie at work in their crime fighting lab. I really enjoyed this book.

The Case of the Sneaker Snatcher

Billy Jo Jive is the private eye on the block. He and his partner, Susie Sunset, help Sneakers Jones. Someone has taken Sneakers' lucky basketball shoes, and a big game is coming up.

Apply

B. Write a book report about a book you have just read. The book could be fiction or nonfiction. Tell about the book. Did you like it? Give your opinion. Write the title of the book correctly. Use the form shown on page 278.

Editing Marks

- capitalize
- make a period
- add something
- add a comma
- add quotation marks
- take something away
- spell correctly
- indent the paragraph
- make a lowercase letter
- transpose

Lesson 10: Editing a Book Report

Read Anita's edited book report.

Title *Whispers and Other Poems*

Author *Myra Cohn Livingston*

About the Book *This is a book of short poems. There are poems about people There are poems about animals in the zoo. Each poem has a picture to go with it*

Opinion *I enjoyed reading these poems. They are easy to read. My favorite poem is called i know a place.*

Think and Discuss

Anita used this mark to add quotation marks. Where did she add quotation marks? Why did she need them?

Anita used two other editing marks. Where did she add periods? Which words did she capitalize? Why did she add capital letters to those words?

Practice

A. Rewrite Anita's report correctly.

Apply

B. Look at the book report you wrote in Lesson 9. Did you write the title correctly? Did you use end marks? Edit your book report. Then copy it over correctly.

MECHANICS PRACTICE

Writing Titles

- Use a capital letter to begin the first, last, and all important words in the title of a book, story, poem, or television show.
- Underline the title of a book.
- Use quotation marks (") before and after the title of a story, poem, or television show.

Write these sentences correctly. Add capital letters. Be sure to use the correct marks. Write the titles correctly.

1. One story I like very much is called cinderella.
2. I read it in a book called famous fairy tales.
3. Michael Bond wrote a book called Paddington Bear.
4. My brother watches Sesame Street on television.
5. In class I read a poem called the four friends.
6. The title of that television special was a charlie brown thanksgiving.
7. Have you read the book called the tailypo?
8. I read a poem by Karla Kuskin called me.
9. the pickety fence is another poem I like.
10. This book is called king of the cats.

Lesson 11: Giving a Book Talk

Leroy Leonard wrote a book report on *My Father's Dragon*. Leroy's teacher asked him to talk about the book in class. Leroy had to prepare to speak in front of his class.

Think and Discuss

Leroy took notes on his book report. He put the notes on note cards. Read his note cards.

1.

<u>My Father's Dragon</u>
Ruth Stiles Gannett

2.

Elmer Elevator goes to rescue a dragon.
The dragon is held prisoner by wild animals.
Elmer must outwit the animals.

3.

This book is funny.
I like the part where Elmer tricks the rhinoceros.
You will enjoy this book.

What information is on Leroy's first card? How does he know which card to use first, second, and third? Leroy kept his sentences simple. He will not read his cards. He will use them as helpers when he gives his report.

When you write information on note cards, number each card in order. Write short simple sentences. Write only the important points you wish to cover.

How to Give a Book Talk

1. **Stand up straight. Look at your audience.**
2. **Speak clearly and slowly.**
3. **Give the title and the author of the book.**
4. **Say what the book is about.**
5. **Tell an interesting part of the book.**

Practice

A. Read these sentences about giving a book talk. Label them *true* or *false.*

1. You must read the book aloud.
2. You should stand up straight.
3. You must tell how the book ends.
4. You can write important points on cards.
5. You should tell the title of the book.

Apply

B. 6. Make note cards from the book report you wrote in Lesson 9. Then give a talk to your class. Follow the rules in this lesson.

LITERATURE

Lesson 12: Reading a Play

There are many ways to tell a story. One way is to act it out. A play is a story that is acted out. The conversations between the characters tell the story.

Think and Discuss

The people who act and speak in a play are the characters. Every play also has a setting. The setting is the place where the play happens.

As you read a play, pay attention to the words in (   ). These are the **stage directions.** They tell how the characters should act and move. They tell when characters should come onto the stage or move off the stage. Stage directions help you understand what is happening in the play.

Listen as your class reads this play. Think about what you hear. Follow along in your book.

The Six Wise Travelers

by Sally Jarvis

Players: **Six Travelers and a Boy**

(Six wise travelers have come to the edge of a river.)

First Traveler: Oh, look, friends. We have come to a river. How will we get across?

Second Traveler: I see a boy with a boat. We will ask him to take us.

Third Traveler: Boy! Boy! Will you take us across the river in your boat?

Boy: There are too many of you for my little boat.

Fourth Traveler: Silly boy! We are wiser than you. Let us use your boat.

Boy: Very well, but I will not go with you.

Fifth Traveler: Let us go, travelers! *(They put the boat in the river.)*

Sixth Traveler: Ready? Everybody in! *(The six wise travelers climb into the boat. The boat sinks.)*

First Traveler: Swim! Swim! Get to land! *(The six travelers swim to the land.)*

Second Traveler: Now I will count us to see that we are all here. *(He touches each traveler on the head as he counts.)* One, two, three, four, five. *(He does not count himself.)* Oh! Oh! One of us is missing!

Third Traveler: Silly! You are counting wrong. Let me do it. *(He touches each traveler on the hand as he counts. He counts two hands for each traveler.)* One, two, three, four, five, six, seven, eight, nine, ten. Why, there are ten of us! That is why the boat sank!

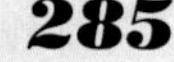

Fourth Traveler: Oh, you silly person. You counted two hands for each traveler. Let me do it. *(She touches each traveler on the back as she counts.)* One, two, three, four, five. *(She does not count herself.)* You are right! One traveler is missing! We will have to find him.

Fifth Traveler: *(She sees the boy.)* Boy! Go and find the missing traveler!

Sixth Traveler: We will give you a bag of gold if you find him.

Boy: Very well. Let me count you all first. One, two, three, four, five, six. *(Of course he counts them all.)* You are all here. I have found the missing traveler!

All Six Travelers: What a good boy! Here is your gold. When you grow up, maybe you will be as wise as we are! *(The six travelers jump into the river and swim to the other side.)*

A play can be about real people and places. It can be about make-believe people and places. Do you think this play is real or make-believe?

This play has many characters. Who are the characters?

You learn where the play takes place at the very beginning. What is the setting of this play?

Practice

A. Answer these questions in complete sentences.

1. Which character speaks first in this play?
2. What is the stage direction that goes with the Fifth Traveler's first line?

B. Finish the sentences with words from the box.

character	play	setting	stage direction

3. The boy is a ______ in this play.
4. A story that is acted out is called a ______.
5. A ______ tells how characters should move.
6. The ______ is the place where the play happens.

Apply

C. 7. Choose a partner from your class. Think of a good story to act out. Write it as a play. Your play should have two characters. You and your classmate can act out the play.

A BOOK TO READ

Title: **My Friend the Monster**
Author: Clyde Robert Bulla
Publisher: Thomas Y. Crowell

Sad Prince Hal had a hard life. His parents thought he was too ordinary. His life changed when he met Humbert, the gentle monster. He helped to rescue Humbert from his cage. Humbert took Hal to the monsters' world. Hal was afraid, but he went along. He was surprised to find that the monsters were afraid of him too. The ordinary prince was not so ordinary in the world of the monsters. Read this tale of the prince and his monster friend.

Making Introductions pages 260–261

Write the letter of the sentence that tells what is wrong with each introduction.

1. Janet Marshall, I'd like you to meet Ann Weiss.
   - **a.** Speaker did not say the older person's name first.
   - **b.** Speaker did not tell two names.
   - **c.** Speaker did not tell extra information.
2. Mother, this is my best friend from school. She wants me to teach her how to play chess.
   - **a.** Speaker did not say the older person's name first.
   - **b.** Speaker did not tell two names.
   - **c.** Speaker did not tell extra information.
3. Lisa Hartwell, I'd like to introduce Dr. Wong. Lisa's father is a doctor too!
   - **a.** Speaker did not say the older person's name first.
   - **b.** Speaker did not tell two names.
   - **c.** Speaker did not tell extra information.

Taking Messages pages 262–263

Take a message about this telephone conversation. Use today's date and time.

4. Hello, Peter, this is Aunt Barbara. May I leave a message for your mother? Tell her to meet me at the Press Club for lunch. I have a table for one o'clock. Please ask her to bring two books and the photographs I gave her. By the way, how are you doing? I hope that school and hockey practice are going well.

Directions pages 264–265

5. Help the bear find his honey. Write the directions he must follow. Put them in order.

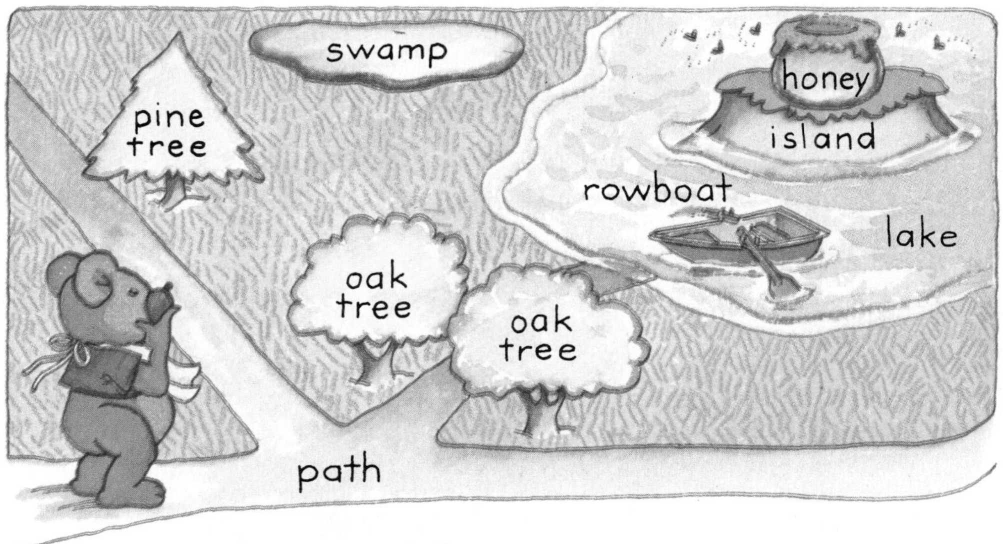

Thinking About What You Hear pages 266–267

Write the sentence from each pair that states a fact.

6. Ye Olde Chicken is the best money can buy. These birds are fed a special diet.
7. Tower of Power vitamins will make you the strongest person on the block. They contain ten vitamins and minerals.
8. Whizzz rollerskates make skating a breeze. Their wheels are made of extra-heavy plastic.
9. Mrs. Mudd's shampoo is an excellent product. You can buy it at many drugstores.
10. Sure-Fine Hotel is the biggest in town. You'll love our room service.
11. The Rambling Rotors are the best singers in the nation. Their concert is Saturday at 8:00 P.M.
12. Pan-fakes taste even better than real pancakes. They cost less than most pancake mixes.

Test Directions pages 270–271

Read each test direction. Which student followed the directions correctly? Write the student's name.

Test Direction 1: Circle the letter of the pronoun.

Juan		Kim		Nan	
a.	ran	**a.**	ran	**a.**	ran
b.	blue	**b.**	blue	**b.**	blue
c.	it	**c.**	it	**c.**	it

Test Direction 2: Fill in the circle of the word that rhymes with *fast.*

Juan	Kim	Nan
○ first	● first	○ first
● last	○ last	○ last
○ fat	○ fat	○ fat

Using Maps pages 272–273

Look at the map. Answer the questions.

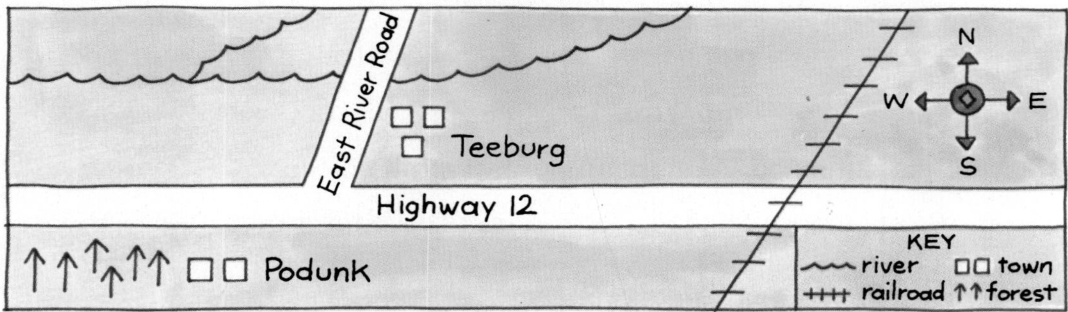

3. Does a railroad cross Highway 12?
4. Is Teeburg north of the river?
5. What is just west of Podunk?

The Telephone Directory pages 274–275

Study the guide words from a page of the telephone book. List only the names you would find on that page.

Limburger–Liu

6. Livingston
7. Little
8. Lincoln
9. Libby
10. Lipkin
11. Liao

12. Ling	**13.** Lillet	**14.** Luck
15. Lisle	**16.** Lopez	**17.** Liu
18. Linnett	**19.** Lionel	**20.** Lirrell

Titles pages 276–277

Write these titles correctly.

1. doug meets the nutcracker (a book)
2. sleet storm (a poem)
3. it's the great pumpkin, charlie brown (a television show)
4. the pearl and the ghost (a book)
5. puss in boots (a story)

Writing and Editing a Book Report pages 278–280

6. Write a book report about a book you have read. Tell what happens. Give your opinion. Edit your book report. Be sure to write titles correctly.

Giving a Book Talk pages 282–283

Write the rules from this list you must follow to give a book talk.

7. Use note cards that are numbered in order.
8. Write every word of the report on your cards.
9. Speak clearly and slowly.

A Play pages 284–287

Answer these questions. Write complete sentences.

1. What are the people in a play called?
2. Which sentence below could tell about the setting of a play?

   a. *(A small girl enters, crying loudly.)*
   b. The scene is a dark forest in winter.
   c. Wolf: What is wrong, my child?

3. What is one thing that makes a play different from a story?
4. What are stage directions?

MAINTENANCE and REVIEW

Parts of a Sentence pages 10–11

Copy the sentences. Draw one line under the subjects. Draw two lines under the predicates.

1. Maria and her brothers went skating.
2. They took a bus to a nearby town.
3. Pedro laced up his new black skates.
4. The smooth sidewalks were filled with skaters.
5. One excellent skater was doing fancy turns.

Singular and Plural Nouns pages 40–41

6.–15. Find ten nouns in the sentences above. Write them. Tell whether each noun is singular or plural.

Past Time Verbs pages 82–83 and 86–89

Write the past time form of each verb below.

16. marry **17.** prance **18.** cook
19. pound **20.** hop **21.** try

Topic Sentence and Keeping to the Topic pages 118–119 and 124–125

Rewrite the paragraph. Leave out the sentence that does not keep to the topic. Underline the topic sentence.

22. There are many kinds of birds called jays. The blue jay is common. Sparrows are common too. The Canada jay is gray.

Adjectives pages 154–155

Copy the sentences. Circle the adjectives. Underline the noun that is described by each adjective.

23. Kate has a new jacket. **24.** The jacket is yellow.
25. It has thin stripes. **26.** Kate is pleased with it.

Pronouns pages 186–187

Write the two pronouns from each sentence. Tell whether each is found in the subject or the predicate.

27. Tama and I borrowed bikes from them.
28. We rode them far into the countryside.
29. She had packed giant lunches for us.
30. I found an apple and gave it to Tama.
31. She followed me on the bike to the pond.

Forms of Be pages 230–231

Copy the sentences. Underline the forms of the verb *be.* Tell whether each is used as a helping verb or a linking verb.

32. I am in Ms. Lambert's third-grade class.
33. Paige is a new girl in our classroom.
34. She is learning the names of her classmates.
35. At first, Paige was in a different class.
36. We are glad that she came to our class instead.
37. I know that Paige and I are going to like each other.

Contractions pages 234–237

Write contractions to take the place of these words.

38. has not **39.** was not **40.** she is
41. had not **42.** it is **43.** I am
44. they are **45.** were not **46.** we are

Introductions pages 260–261

Copy the introductions that are best.

47. Dr. Milo, this is Ima Sakurai. She goes to school in Etna.
48. Dr. Milo, I would like you to meet Ima Sakurai.
49. Trudy Forrester, meet my good friend Ana Morales.
50. Trudy Forrester, I'd like to introduce Ana Morales. Ana has a pet turtle too!

REVIEW HANDBOOK

GRAMMAR

Sentences

sentence
- A **sentence** is a group of words that states a complete thought. Every sentence begins with a capital letter. *(page 3)*

statement
- A **statement** tells something. It ends with a period (**.**). *(page 4)*

  I cut my finger.

question
- A **question** asks something. It ends with a question mark (**?**). *(page 4)*

  Did you tell the secret?

command
- A **command** gives an order or a direction. It ends with a period (**.**). *(page 6)*

  Go home.

exclamation
- An **exclamation** shows strong feeling. It ends with an exclamation mark (**!**). *(page 8)*

  What a great beach this is!

Practice

Write only the groups that are sentences. Add capital letters and end punctuation. Then tell what kind of sentence the word group is.

1. as we walked
2. will you sing
3. take this to Mr. Po
4. in the night
5. blowing the horn
6. i left early
7. what a day it was
8. erase that letter

Subjects and Predicates

GRAMMAR

- The **subject** of the sentence is the part about which something is being said. *(page 11)* **subject**

  The truck is here. Sally sees it.

- The **predicate** is all the words that tell something about the subject. *(page 11)* **predicate**

  The truck stopped. It is parked on Baker Street.

Practice

A. Write each sentence. Draw one line under the subject of each.

1. Sophia raced down the hill.
2. Her friend ran after her.
3. The dog ran after the girls.
4. The ice cream truck was on Jay Street.
5. Sophia reached the bottom of the hill.
6. Her money dropped out of her pocket.
7. Both girls looked for the money.

B. Write each sentence. Draw two lines under the predicate of each.

8. Tony loves ice cream.
9. He likes chocolate best.
10. Tony made a chocolate ice cream cone.
11. He wanted to save it to eat in the park.
12. The day was very hot.
13. Tony walked and walked.
14. The ice cream dripped.

Nouns

noun
- A **noun** is a word that names a person, place, or thing. *(page 38)*

common noun
- A **common noun** names any person, place, or thing. It begins with a small letter. *(page 47)*

  picture apple coat foot

proper noun
- A **proper noun** names a special person, place, or thing. A proper noun begins with a capital letter. *(page 47)*

  Mrs. Takara California Halloween

possessive noun
- A **possessive noun** shows ownership. *(page 194)*

  dog's collar man's coat boys' gym

Practice

A. Copy the sentences. Underline each common noun. Circle each proper noun.

1. Meet my two dogs.
2. One dog is brown.
3. This dog is a poodle.
4. Here is its dish.
5. Its name is Clyde.
6. I like that name.
7. My hound is friendly.
8. It loves people.
9. Once we went to a fair.
10. Uncle Dan came too.

B. Copy the sentences. Circle each possessive noun.

11. This is my mother's work table.
12. Here is my brother's aquarium.
13. Under the table is Clyde's bed.
14. Charlie's bed is in the kitchen.
15. The note told me to fill the dogs' dishes.

Singular and Plural Nouns

- A **singular noun** names one person, place, or thing. *(page 41)*
- A **plural noun** names more than one person, place, or thing. *(page 41)*
- To form the plural of most nouns, add *s. (page 41)*
- To form the plural of nouns ending in *s, x, ch,* or *sh,* add *es. (page 42)*

bus—buses box—boxes

- To form the plural of nouns ending with a consonant and *y,* change the *y* to *i* and add *es. (page 44)*

berry—berries fairy—fairies

singular nouns

plural nouns

Practice

A. Tell whether each noun is singular or plural.

1. tree **2.** berry **3.** melon **4.** glass
5. houses **6.** octopus **7.** friends **8.** cat
9. bees **10.** truck **11.** cows **12.** toys

B. Write the plural form of each word.

13. puppy **14.** pencil **15.** wish **16.** fox
17. orange **18.** patch **19.** pass **20.** knee
21. plum **22.** peach **23.** boat **24.** fly

C. Write sentences of your own. Use the plural forms of these nouns.

25. beach **26.** box **27.** sky
28. blueberry **29.** dish **30.** kitten

Verbs

action verb

- An **action verb** is a word that shows an action. It is found in the predicate of a sentence. *(page 80)*

eat scratch dash call

linking verb

- A **linking verb** connects the subject with words in the predicate. It tells what the subject *is* or *is like.* The following forms of *be* are often used as linking verbs. *(page 231)*

am is are was were

helping verb

- A **helping verb** helps the main verb tell about an action. The following words are often used as helping verbs. *(page 91)*

am is are was were
have has had

Practice

A. Copy the verb from each sentence. Next to the verb write *action verb* or *linking verb* to tell the kind.

1. Miriam sleds by.
2. She is a good sledder.
3. She speeds along.
4. We are cold.
5. Miriam stops.
6. She slips in the snow.

B. Copy each sentence. Draw two lines under the verbs. Then circle each helping verb.

7. We are sledding.
8. Jon has waited for us.
9. Bill is going first.
10. I am getting colder.
11. Flakes were flying.
12. She has lost a glove.

Verb Tenses

- **Present time verbs** tell about actions that are happening now. *(page 82)*

present time

The party starts. She wins a prize.
Children laugh and play.

- **Past time verbs** tell about actions in the past. *(page 82)*

past time

Abby walked quickly. Her dog trotted.
The dog hurried. Abby chased him.

Practice

Copy each sentence. Use the verb in ( ). Make it tell about the time shown in ( ).

1. Lois ______ with a baby. (help, present)
2. She ______ it when it cries. (hush, present)
3. The baby ______ yesterday. (cry, past)
4. Lois ______ around and made funny faces. (skip, past)
5. At last the baby ______. (smile, past)
6. Lois ______ the baby's bottle. (prepare, present)
7. She ______ milk on the stove. (warm, present)
8. The baby ______ for an hour. (nap, past)
9. Lois ______ a television show. (watch, past)
10. Then the baby ______. (howl, past)
11. Lois ______ into the room. (hurry, past)
12. The baby ______ the bottle. (grab, past)
13. Now Lois ______ the baby up. (lift, present)
14. The baby ______ happily. (gurgle, present)

Irregular Verbs

irregular verbs

- **Irregular verbs** are verbs that do not add *ed* to show past time. Some of these verbs are on the chart. *(pages 92 and 232)*

Verb	**Present**	**Past**	**Past with *Have, Has,* or *Had***
come	come(s)	came	come
go	go(es)	went	gone
run	run(s)	ran	run
ring	ring(s)	rang	rung
sing	sing(s)	sang	sung
begin	begin(s)	began	begun

Practice

A. Use the correct present time form of the verb in ( ). Write the sentences.

1. Jan often ______ to school with me. (go)
2. Sometimes other friends ______ too. (come)
3. The school day ______ at 9:00 A.M. (begin)
4. One student ______ up to the bell tower. (run)
5. The student ______ the big brass bell. (ring)

B. Use the correct past time form of the verb in ( ). Write the sentences.

6. Yesterday the doorbell ______. (ring)
7. Father ______ to answer it. (go)
8. Two people ______ into the house. (come)
9. We had ______ dinner already. (begin)
10. When I saw the men, I ______ to smile. (begin)

Adjectives

- An **adjective** is a word that describes a noun. *(page 154)* **adjective**

  We drink hot cocoa.

- Add *er* to most one-syllable adjectives when they are used to compare two things. *(page 161)*

  My nose is longer than yours.

- Add *est* to most one-syllable adjectives when they are used to compare more than two things. *(page 161)*

  My nose is the longest in our family.

- Use *more* with many adjectives of two syllables. Use *more* with adjectives of three or more syllables. *More* is used to compare two things. *(page 162)*

  This flower is more beautiful than mine.

- Use *most* with many adjectives of two syllables. Use *most* with adjectives of three or more syllables. *Most* is used to compare more than two things. *(page 162)*

  This is the most beautiful flower I see.

- *A, an,* and *the* are adjectives called **articles.** *(page 158)* **article**

  A bird and an egg are in the nest.

Practice

Underline the adjectives and articles.

1. We spent the beautiful day outside.
2. Three friends went on an outing.
3. We hiked up a mountain under the blue sky.
4. The mountain was higher than a hill.

Pronouns

pronoun

- A **pronoun** is a word used in place of one or more nouns. *(page 187)*
- These pronouns are used in the subject of a sentence. *(page 186)*

I	we
you	
he, she, it	they

- These pronouns follow action verbs. *(page 187)*

me	us
you	
him, her, it	them

Practice

A. Copy the sentences. Use a pronoun in place of the underlined word or words.

1. Ryan went swimming in the pond.
2. Carol went too.
3. Then Mike, Jesse, and Maria came along.
4. Mark and I decided to go to the pond.
5. Soon the pond was filled with people.

B. Use the correct pronouns. Write the sentences.

6. Carol splashed (me, I).
7. (He, Him) dove off a rock.
8. The sun warmed (they, them).
9. After a while (we, us) felt cold and tired.
10. Ryan walked with (we, us) down the path.

Paragraph

- A **paragraph** is a group of sentences that tell about one main idea. *(page 116)*
- The **topic sentence** tells the main idea of the paragraph. *(page 118)*
- The first line of a paragraph is indented. *(page 116)*

paragraph

topic sentence

Practice

A. Read the groups of sentences below. Decide which sentence in each paragraph is the topic sentence. Write it on your paper.

1. Harbor seals are usually a dark color. Often they have dark brown spots on them. They have very dark eyes.

2. These seals are most at home in the water. There they can swim fast, roll, and jump. On land these animals are clumsy and slow.

B. Copy the paragraphs. Leave out the sentences that do not belong.

3. There are five harbor seals at our zoo. Two are babies. There are monkeys too. Three of the seals are adults. Fish swim in the tank. All five seals live together.

4. The baby seals are playful. They swoop and slide on the ramp. Dolphins play too. The seals nip each other and splash. The zookeeper feeds the fish.

Friendly Letters

113 Seacord Road
New Rochelle, New York 10804
April 5, 19--

Dear Tracy,
Guess what? We are really moving to your town. I can't wait to see you. We will move on June 15.

Sincerely,
Bess

- The **friendly letter** and most notes such as **invitations** and **thank you notes** have five parts. *(pages 206–207)*

heading
- The **heading** contains the letter writer's address and the date. A comma is used between the name of the city and the state and between the day and the year.

greeting
- The **greeting** welcomes the person who receives the letter. The greeting begins with a capital letter. The greeting is followed by a comma.

body
- The **body** of the letter contains the message.

closing
- The **closing** is the end of the letter. The first word is capitalized. A comma follows the closing.

signature
- The **signature** is the written name of the person who wrote the letter.

Practice

Write a friendly letter to a relative or friend. Tell the person about something that you did.

Envelope

Myra Kasin
17 Fulton Avenue
Mt. Vernon, NY 10522

Billy Randall
44 High Street
Denver, CO 80220

- An addressed envelope has two parts. *(page 208)*
- The **return address** is the name and address of the person who wrote the letter. The return address is in the upper left-hand corner of the envelope. *(page 208)*
- The **receiver's name and address** are written in the middle of the envelope. Postal abbreviations of states' names are written with two capital letters and no periods. Use the ZIP code in all addresses. *(page 208)*

return address

receiver's name and address

Practice

Draw a sample envelope on your paper. Address the envelope correctly. Use this information.

To:	mr. allan chester 210 West End ave new york 10022 NY	From:	José Casa 340 Central Ave. Fort Myers FL 33901

Editing Marks

- ≡ capitalize
- ⊙ make a period
- ∧ add something
- ∧ with comma: add a comma
- ∨ with quotation marks: add quotation marks
- take something away
- ◯ spell correctly
- ¶ indent the paragraph
- / make a lowercase letter
- ∿ tr transpose

Editing

- It is important to review your work after you write. Use editing marks to show the changes you want to make to improve your writing. *(page 26)*

Editing Checklist

1. Did I express a complete thought in each sentence?
2. Did I write a good topic sentence for each paragraph?
3. Did I write detail sentences that support the main idea?
4. Did I write detail sentences that keep to the topic?
5. Did I begin each sentence with a capital letter?
6. Did I end each sentence with the correct end mark?
7. Did I use other punctuation marks correctly?
8. Did I indent the first line of each paragraph?
9. Did I spell correctly?
10. Did I write neatly?

Practice

Rewrite this paragraph correctly.

read story
I red a poem called Seven at One
Blow. Carlos gave it to me and i
loved it It is about a little
pictures tr
Tailor. The pitchers wonderful are.

Names and Titles of People and I

- Begin the name of a person with a capital letter. *(page 49)* **person's name**

  Douglas Dunn   Marsha Billings

- Begin titles of a person such as *Ms., Mrs., Mr.,* and *Dr.* with a capital letter. *(page 49)* **titles of people**
- Capitalize initials that take the place of names. *(page 49)*

  Dorothy J. Arthur   Jackie E. Smith

- Always capitalize the word *I.* *(page 67)* **I**

Names of Places

- Begin each important word of the name of a town, city, state, and country with a capital letter. *(page 52)* **place names**
- Begin each important word in the names of streets and their abbreviations with a capital letter. *(page 207)*

  Enfield, New York   Green St.

Practice

A. Rewrite these words correctly.

1. dr. frank arnold   **2.** j. r. adams
3. jackson, mississippi   **4.** united states

B. Rewrite these sentences correctly.

5. mr. thomas and his family traveled by car.
6. One day they stopped in phoenix, arizona.
7. There they visited louis radson.
8. In omaha, stephanie thomas met jane cree.

Names of Days, Months, and Holidays

days

- Begin the name of a day of the week or its abbreviation with a capital letter. *(page 50)*

  Saturday Sat. Thursday Thurs.

months

- Begin the name of a month or its abbreviation with a capital letter. *(page 50)*

  December Dec. August Aug.

holidays

- Begin each important word in the name of a holiday with a capital letter. *(page 50)*

  Washington's Birthday Halloween

Names of Books, Stories, Poems, and Television Shows

titles

- Use a capital letter to begin the first, last, and all important words in the title of a book, story, poem, or television show. *(page 277)*

  Language for Daily Use

Practice

Write these proper nouns and titles correctly.

1. monday
2. november
3. "spring rain"
4. arbor day
5. the long winter
6. february
7. "the brady bunch"
8. groundhog day
9. wednesday
10. "under the tree"

The Period

- Use a period (.) at the end of a statement or command. *(pages 4 and 6)* **to end sentences**

    I see you. Go away.

- Use a period (.) after an abbreviation. *(page 49)* **in abbreviations**

    Wed. Ave. A.M. Dr.

- Use a period (.) after a numeral in the main topic of an outline. *(page 245)* **in outlines**

    I. United States II. Mexico

The Comma

- Use a comma (,) between the city and the state. *(page 207)* **in addresses**

    Baton Rouge, Louisiana Albany, New York

- Use a comma (,) before the word *and* when two sentences are joined together. *(page 22)* **in compound sentences**

    We went to Joe's, and we stayed until noon.

- Use a comma (,) between the day and the year. *(page 207)* **in dates**

    January 1, 1916

- Use a comma (,) after the greeting in a friendly letter and after the closing of any letter. *(page 207)* **in greetings and closings**

    Dear Sara, Sincerely,

Practice

Write these items correctly.

1. March 3 1979 **2.** Dear Ms Perez
3. Creek Rd **4.** Miami Florida

Question Mark

in questions

- Use a question mark (**?**) at the end of a question. *(page 4)*

Did they stay long?

Exclamation Point

in exclamations

- Use an exclamation point (**!**) at the end of an exclamation. *(page 8)*

What a cute baby she is!

Quotation Marks and Underlines

in titles

- Use quotation marks (" ") before and after the title of a story, poem, or television show. *(page 277)*
- Underline the title of a book. *(page 277)*

"Sesame Street"   Encyclopedia Brown

Apostrophes and Colons

in contractions

- Use an apostrophe (') to show that one or more letters have been left out in a contraction. *(page 235)*

in possession

- Add an apostrophe (') and an *s* to singular nouns to show possession. *(page 194)*
- Add an apostrophe (') to plural nouns that end in *s* to show possession. *(page 196)*

he's   Fran's toy   the boys' bikes

in time

- Use a colon (**:**) between the hour and the minute in the time of day. *(page 211)*

4:00   6:00   11:00

Troublesome Words

- The word *I* is always used in the subject part of a sentence. The word *me* follows an action verb. *(page 192)* **I, me**

  I made pancakes.
  He gave me some pancakes.

- Some words sound alike but are spelled differently. Be sure to use these words correctly. *(pages 168 and 237)*

  You're going to lose your pet gerbil. **your, you're**
  It's running out of its cage. **its, it's**
  The two mice are going to escape too. **to, too, two**

Practice

A. Write the sentences correctly.

1. Arent you going to the library at 330
2. I havent read the book Secret of the Andes.
3. What a great book
4. I walked over to Graces house at 400.
5. Were going to watch Electric Company on television.

B. Choose the correct word. Write the sentences.

6. (I, me) said good-by to them.
7. They walked (to, two) the airplane.
8. (There, They're) very excited.
9. This is (there, their) third trip.
10. (It's, Its) the longest flight they have taken.

MORE PRACTICE

UNIT 1

Sentences pages 2–3

Write the word groups that are complete sentences. Begin them in the right way.

1. Jan has a new bicycle.
2. with ten speeds.
3. she goes for long rides.
4. she takes a picnic lunch.
5. eats in the nearby woods.

Four Kinds of Sentences pages 4–9

Copy the sentences. End them correctly. Then write what kind of sentence each one is. Write *statement, question, exclamation,* or *command.*

1. Akiko is going horseback riding
2. Lift her onto the horse
3. The horse is very large
4. Can she reach the stirrups
5. She is on the horse
6. Help, the horse is bucking
7. How do you stop this animal
8. What a wild ride she is having
9. Now it is slowing down
10. Help Akiko to get down

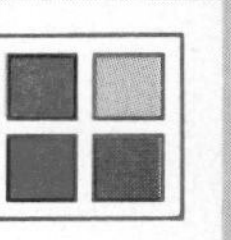

Parts of a Sentence pages 10–11

Copy each sentence. Draw one line under each subject. Draw two lines under each predicate.

1. Kathy went out in a rowboat.
2. She rowed out on the lake.
3. Some dark clouds moved across the sky.
4. A strong wind blew.
5. The rowboat moved toward land.

Changing Word Order in Sentences pages 14–15

Change these questions into statements. The underlined words will help you.

1. <u>Have</u> <u>you</u> seen this movie before?
2. <u>Will</u> <u>Bo</u> go to see it with me?
3. <u>Could</u> <u>it</u> be the best movie of the year?
4. <u>Does</u> <u>Winema</u> like adventure films?
5. <u>Can</u> <u>Mother</u> drive us to the theater?

The Library pages 20–21

Where would you find each of these books in the library? Write *fiction, nonfiction,* or *biography.*

1. a book about learning to write poetry
2. a book about a talking butterfly
3. a book about a fish with legs
4. a book about Pocahontas
5. a book called *Facts About Sailing*

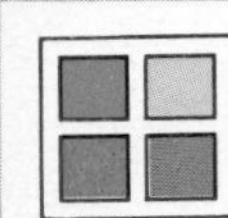

Sentence Combining with <u>and</u> pages 22–23

Combine each pair of sentences with the word *and.* Put a comma (,) in the correct place.

1. Maria bought some seeds. She bought a rake.
2. Maria raked the soil. She planted the seeds.
3. Soon vegetables grew. Flowers bloomed.
4. Maria harvested the vegetables. She used some of the flowers for decorations.
5. The family ate vegetables all winter. Maria planted again in the spring.

Editing Sentences pages 26–27

1.–5. Write five sentences on one of the following subjects. Edit your sentences for capital letters and end marks.

My Science Class A Huge Meal Fishing

Mechanics Practice page 27

Rewrite these sentences correctly. Use capital letters where they belong. Put commas (,) in where needed. Add end marks.

1. Randy was visiting her uncle's farm and she wanted to milk a cow
2. she picked up a bucket and she pulled a stool over to the cow
3. why is the cow mooing
4. the cow kicked out and Randy jumped
5. it is not easy to milk a cow

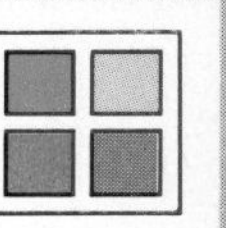

A Story pages 28–31

Read the story. Then answer the questions.

Anna knew there was a unicorn in Bellewood Forest. Most people don't believe in unicorns, but Anna was stubborn. She knew it was there.

One day, Anna was picking berries in the forest. Soon she fell asleep under a tree.

A noise woke her. She looked up to see a silver horse with a graceful horn. She stared at it, and it turned and ran off. Anna never told anyone about the unicorn. She remembered its beauty and grace for the rest of her life.

1. Who is the main character in the story?
2. What is the setting of the story?

UNIT 2

Singular and Plural Nouns pages 40–41

Copy the sentences. Underline the nouns. Then tell whether they are singular or plural.

1. The dog ran fast.
2. The cats ran faster.
3. A boy chased them.
4. The gates were closed.
5. The chase ended.
6. The animals were tired.
7. They took a nap.
8. Raindrops began to fall.
9. The puppy barked.
10. Two girls came outside.
11. One girl laughed.
12. The cats were wet.
13. The beagle ran in.
14. The door slammed shut.

Plural Nouns pages 42–45

Change these singular nouns to plurals.

1. address
2. dictionary
3. watch
4. wish
5. canary
6. box
7. dress
8. country
9. bush
10. match

Common and Proper Nouns pages 46–47

Copy the sentences. Underline the common nouns. Circle the proper nouns.

1. Daniel lives in the town of Plymouth.
2. Settlers came to that small town in Massachusetts.
3. Their leader was John Bradford.
4. The first Thanksgiving was celebrated in the town where Daniel lives now.
5. Daniel and his family still celebrate that holiday.

Names and Abbreviations pages 48–51

Write these words correctly. Then write the abbreviations for the titles, names of days, and names of months.

1. mister lopez
2. friday
3. february
4. doctor lee
5. wednesday
6. september
7. sharon gold
8. sunday
9. january
10. miss weber

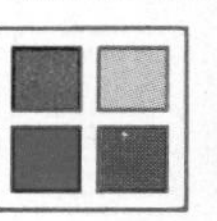

Names of Places pages 52–53

Write these sentences correctly. Add capital letters.

1. solana beach is a small town in california.
2. We drove across the united states of america.
3. We also visited parts of canada and mexico.
4. Our trip began in providence, rhode island.
5. It ended in del mar, a small town near la jolla.

Alphabetical Order pages 56–57

Put these groups of words in alphabetical order.

1.	lush	lake	lurk	love	luck
2.	tree	trip	track	toad	terrible
3.	dog	down	dawn	dare	dig
4.	snail	snore	sail	sad	stare
5.	catch	car	cab	core	cry

Guide Words and Entry Words pages 58–61

Look at the dictionary guide words and entry word. Then answer the questions.

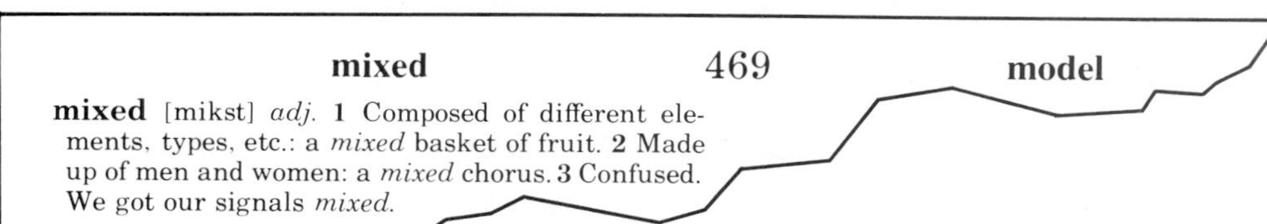

mixed 469 **model**

mixed [mikst] *adj.* 1 Composed of different elements, types, etc.: a *mixed* basket of fruit. 2 Made up of men and women: a *mixed* chorus. 3 Confused. We got our signals *mixed.*

1. Would the word *mob* be found on page 469?
2. What entry word is shown?
3. What word would be the last entry on this page?
4. What is the respelling of the entry word?

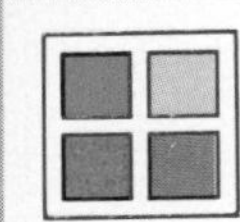

Combining Subjects pages 62–63

Combine the subjects in these pairs of sentences. Use the word *and*. Write the new sentences.

1. Anna went to the lake. Bill went to the lake.
2. The bikes were there. The boats were there.
3. Mrs. Volk packed lunches. Mr. Hansen packed lunches.
4. The lunches fit into the bike baskets. The life jackets fit into the bike baskets.
5. Their family waved. Their friends waved.

Sentences About People pages 64–65

1.–5. Write five sentences about people you know. Be sure to use capital letters correctly.

Editing Sentences pages 66–67

Rewrite these edited sentences correctly.

1. I am on a baseball Team.
2. Our Coach is mrs. andrews.
3. jan and I used to play very badly.
4. then we began to work out every Day.
5. now we can beat the team from endor.
6. we have the best Team in the county.
7. mrs. andrews is very pleased.
8. mr. jones from the newspaper took our pictures.

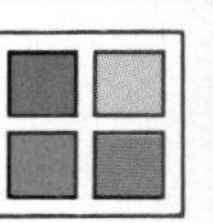

Mechanics Practice page 67

Rewrite these sentences. Be sure to use capital letters and periods (.) where needed.

1. mrs johnson decided to become a doctor.
2. She went to school in new york City.
3. mr johnson worked while his wife went to school.
4. When she finished, she became dr johnson.
5. My family and i visit her office.

Biography pages 68–71

Write *true* if the statement is true. Write *false* if it is not true.

1. A biography could be about an elf.
2. Biographies can be about famous people.
3. A biography tells only about a person's adult life.
4. Biographies can be written about Presidents.
5. The facts in a biography are made up.

UNIT 3

Verbs pages 80–81

Copy the sentences. Underline the verbs.

1. My uncle went to flying school.
2. He learned many things about planes.
3. He flew to places in the United States.
4. I travel in a plane sometimes.
5. My uncle flies the plane.

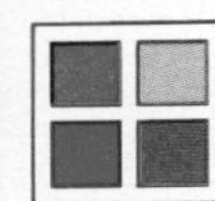

Present Time and Past Time pages 82–83

Rewrite these sentences. Change the present time verbs to past time.

1. Ellen enjoys her new fishing rod.
2. She fishes with it.
3. She hooks many fish.
4. She shows them to her family.
5. She and her family cook fish for dinner.

Subject-Verb Agreement pages 84–85

Choose the correct verb in ( ). Write the sentences.

1. Joe (see, sees) a truck.
2. The ice cream truck (arrive, arrives).
3. His friends (run, runs) to their houses.
4. The boys (find, finds) some money.
5. The vendor (sell, sells) them ice cream.

Past Time Verbs pages 86–89

Write the past time forms of these verbs.

1. laugh
2. cry
3. kick
4. sniff
5. jump
6. try
7. turn
8. learn
9. dry
10. slap
11. trip
12. sigh
13. spell
14. reply
15. ask
16. skip
17. hope
18. pry
19. invent
20. use

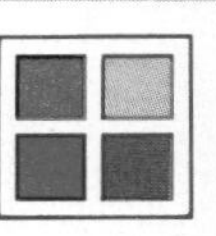

Irregular Verbs pages 92–93

Change the underlined verbs to the forms shown in ( ). Write the sentences.

1. Miguel comes to the track meet. (past)
2. He comes for the big race. (past with *had*)
3. He runs as soon as the starter gun went off. (past)
4. Down the track he goes! (past)
5. He runs faster than anyone else. (past)

The Right Meaning pages 96–97

Read the dictionary entry. Then write the number of the definition that fits the underlined word in each sentence below.

flute [flo͞ot] *n., v.* **flut·ed, flut·ing** **1** *n.* A musical wind instrument having a high, clear pitch and made in the shape of a narrow tube. A flute is played by blowing across a mouthpiece at one end and by opening and closing holes along its length with the fingers or with keys. **2** *v.* To play on the flute. **3** *v.* To make flutelike sounds by whistling or singing. **4** *n.* In buildings, one of the rounded grooves cut from the top to the bottom of a column. **5** *n.* A small ruffle or pleat in cloth. **6** *v.* To make flutes in (columns or cloth).

Flute

1. She wore a fluted skirt.
2. The courthouse has fluted columns.
3. Paco plays the flute in the school band.

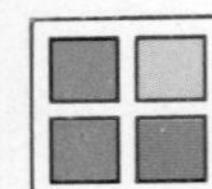

Homographs pages 98–99

Which entry word fits the sentence? Write *fly*[1] or *fly*[2].

> **fly**[1] [flī] *v.* **flew,** *for def.* 7 **flied, flown,** *for def.* 7 **flied, fly·ing,** *n., pl.* **flies** **1** *v.* To move through the air on wings, as birds or insects. **2** *v.* To move or travel through the air in an aircraft. **3** *v.* To cause to fly in the air: to *fly* a kite. **4** *v.* To move very fast: Summer *flies* by. **5** *v.* To wave or flutter in the air, as a flag. **6** *v.* To run away; flee: to *fly* for one's life. **7** *v.* In baseball, to bat the ball high over the field. **8** *n.* A baseball batted high over the field.
> **fly**[2] [flī] *n., pl.* **flies** **1** One of a large group of small, two-winged insects, especially the housefly. **2** Any of several other flying insects, as the dragonfly, May fly, etc. **3** A fishhook to which bits of colored cloth or feathers are tied so that it looks like an insect.

1. I hit a fly ball to left field.
2. The flags fly on Flag Day.
3. A fly landed on my hand.
4. I attached a fly to my fishing pole.
5. The runners fly down the path.

Combining Predicates pages 100–101

Combine the predicates in these pairs of sentences. Use the word *and*. Rewrite each sentence pair as one sentence.

1. Kim runs in races. Kim jumps over poles.
2. Jesse plays basketball. Jesse skates.
3. Kim's coach trains her. Kim's coach watches her run.
4. Jesse stretches his legs. Jesse bends his body.
5. Kim dances. Kim exercises in the gym.

Editing Sentences pages 104–105

Rewrite these edited sentences correctly.

1. Miguel ^trudged walked to school slowly.
2. He ^noticed saw some friends and stopped to talk.
3. Is the class having a test today?
4. Miguel could ^not remember.
5. He went to ^study look at his English book.

Mechanics Practice page 105

Rewrite these words and abbreviations correctly.

1. february **2.** friday
3. wednesday **4.** thurs., jan 14

A Story pages 106–109

Read the story. Then answer the questions.

There once was a dreadful beast named Grendel. He lived in a cave with his mother. Grendel and his mother went to the king's house every night. They captured people and took them back to their cave.

The king's bravest knight fought the beasts. Grendel's mother tried to protect her son. At last the knight won. The two beasts were defeated once and for all.

1. List two settings from the story.
2. Tell the story's plot in your own words.

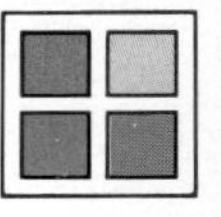

UNIT 4

Main Ideas and Details pages 116–117 and 120–121

Read the paragraph below. Then read the numbered word groups. Write down whether each word group is a *main idea* or a *detail.*

In the Middle Ages, boys worked hard to learn to be knights. A boy would be made a squire first. He would serve a knight and take care of the knight's horse. He had to learn to use a sword. He had to obey orders and grow strong. Then if he were brave in battle, he might be knighted by the king.

1. taking care of horses
2. learning to be a knight
3. becoming a squire
4. using a sword
5. bravery in battle

Topic Sentences and Keeping to the Topic
pages 118–119 and 124–125

Read the paragraph below. Then rewrite it. Leave out the sentences that do not keep to the topic. Underline the topic sentence.

Lola studies to be a scientist. She studies science in school. She studies ballet too. In her spare time, she looks at bugs and plants. Then she reads about them. She also likes reading mysteries. She plans to enter the science fair next year.

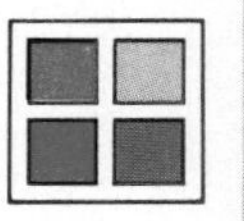

Sentence Order in Paragraphs pages 122–123

Put these sentences in the correct order. Write them in paragraph form.

1. Second you should mix the ingredients together.
2. After the pans go in the oven, make the frosting.
3. When baking a cake, you should first light the oven.
4. Pour the mix into greased pans, and put them in the oven.
5. When the cake is done, frost it and eat it!

Main Idea pages 128–129

Read this paragraph. Then choose the title that best states the main idea.

> A peanut grows in a very strange manner. It first grows like a normal plant. A flower blooms at the top. Then the flower dies, and a pod forms. The plant bends until the pod touches the ground. The pod is pushed under the earth. A peanut forms from this pod. The peanut continues to grow beneath the earth.

1. The Flower of the Peanut Plant
2. The Normal Peanut
3. A Peanut Has Two Roots
4. The Strange Growth of the Peanut
5. How to Make Peanut Butter

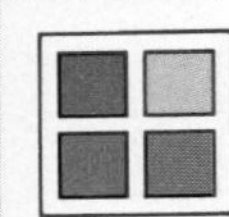

Choosing and Limiting the Topic pages 130–131

Write the topic in each pair that would work better as a paragraph topic.

1. Boats of the World
   Our New Rowboat
2. Training Dogs
   Giving Rover a Bath
3. Electing Our Mayor
   American Presidents
4. Sports in New York
   My First Home Run

Story Beginnings and Stories in Order pages 132–135

Read these paragraphs. They tell part of a story, but they are not in order. Rewrite them in order. Label them *beginning* and *main part.*

The class worked very hard. They mixed sticky clay and found wire. They put the bones together with the wire and the clay.

Ms. Carson asked the class to decide on a science project. The whole school was having a science fair. Ms. Carson wanted the third grade to have the best project at the fair.

Larry said that the class should build a cow. He was only joking, but Ms. Carson thought it was a wonderful idea. She asked farmers and animal doctors for cow bones. Each student was given a set of bones to link together.

Story Endings pages 136–137

Make up an ending for the story above. Tell what you think happened to the characters. Make your ending believable. Write it neatly on your own sheet of paper.

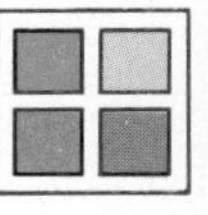

Editing a Story pages 140–141

Read this story. Then rewrite it correctly.

Tomas loved to dance and he loved his ballet class. He had never seen a ballet on stage.

One day mrs. hill brought two dancers to class. The class clapped and cheered. The dancers danced for the class. Tomas had finally seen real live dancers.

Mechanics Practice page 141

Rewrite this paragraph correctly.

David is learning to be an acrobat. he is taking a special gym class. the balance beam is his favorite part of class. david has very good balance. he will enter a contest for acrobats.

A Fable pages 142–145

Read these statements about fables. Then write whether each statement is *true* or *false.*

1. A fable is about a famous person.
2. The characters in fables may be animals.
3. A fable teaches a lesson.
4. A fable is a true story.
5. Most fables have morals at the end.

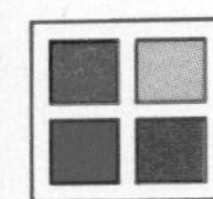

UNIT 5

Adjectives pages 154–155

Copy these sentences. Circle the describing adjective in each sentence. Underline the noun that is described by the adjective.

1. Jeremy keeps a large turtle as a pet.
2. The turtle has a green shell.
3. It can draw its scaly feet into its shell.
4. It likes to eat fresh strawberries.
5. Jeremy enjoys his strange pet.

Kinds of Adjectives pages 156–157

Rewrite these sentences. Add an adjective to each sentence. The word in ( ) tells you what kind of adjective to use.

1. Annette's cat had a ______ litter. (size)
2. There were five ______ kittens. (feel)
3. The cat's box was full of ______ kittens. (size)
4. Annette heard the ______ kittens. (sound)
5. She counted ______ little cats. (number)

Articles pages 158–159

Copy these sentences. Underline the articles.

1. I went on a trip.
2. We went to the nation's capital.
3. We saw the White House.
4. We visited a senator and a congresswoman.
5. The senator gave me an autograph.

Comparisons with <u>er</u> and <u>est</u> pages 160–161

Choose the correct adjective in ( ). Write the sentences.

1. Tracy is a (great, greatest) kickball player.
2. She is in a (higher, highest) grade than I am.
3. She is the (faster, fastest) runner in the class.
4. The team that gets her is the (strong, strongest) team of all.
5. They are glad to have (quicker, quick) Tracy on the team.
6. She may be the (shorter, shortest) player on the team, but she is the best.

Comparisons with <u>More</u> and <u>Most</u>

pages 162–163

Write these sentences. Finish each one with *more* or *most*.

1. Jim Running Bear is the ______ intelligent boy I know.
2. His homework is always ______ accurate than mine.
3. He paints the ______ beautiful pictures I've ever seen.
4. He does ______ imaginative science experiments than I do.
5. He is also the ______ polite boy in the class.
6. I think he is ______ interesting than a famous movie star.

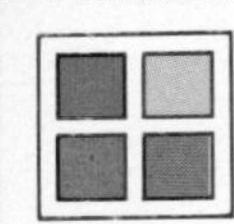

Synonyms and Antonyms pages 166–167

Here are two groups of words. For numbers 1–5, match the words with their synonyms. For numbers 6–10, match the words with their antonyms.

1. shout	**a.** leap
2. jump	**b.** stair
3. cry	**c.** grin
4. step	**d.** weep
5. smile	**e.** yell
6. sit	**f.** lose
7. large	**g.** enemy
8. asleep	**h.** stand
9. win	**i.** awake
10. friend	**j.** small

Homophones pages 168–169

Pick the right word in ( ). Write the sentences.

1. My horse has (too, two) white feet.
2. She has a white mane (to, too).
3. (There, Their) is a beautiful animal.
4. She comes (to, two) me when I call.
5. She shakes her pretty (main, mane).

A Descriptive Paragraph pages 170–171

Write a descriptive paragraph on one of the subjects listed. Use descriptive adjectives and interesting verbs.

Spring in My Town　　A Thunderstorm

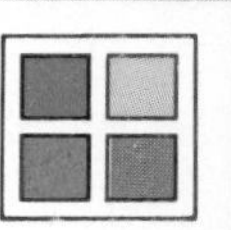

A How-to Paragraph pages 172–175

Write a how-to paragraph on one of the subjects listed. Then edit it. Be sure that the sentences are in order.

How to Paint a Fence
How to Set a Table
How to Make Ice Cubes

Mechanics Practice page 175

Rewrite this paragraph correctly. Use correct end marks.

There are many ways to save energy. One way is to turn off the lights in a room that is not being used Another way is to keep the thermostat set low in the winter If you do these things, you will save energy and money

Describing Words in Poetry pages 176–177

Copy this poem. Underline the adjectives.

Once upon a summer day,
When my best friend had gone away,
I took my bike and pedaled down
The dusty road that leads to town.

Comparisons in Poetry pages 178–179

Fill in the blanks with the words you think fit best. Then use each comparison in a sentence.

1. as hot as a ______
2. falling like a ______
3. tremble like a ______
4. as thin as a ______

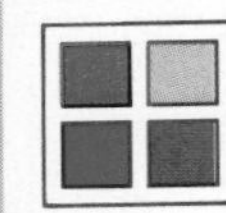

UNIT 6

Pronouns pages 186–187

Copy these sentences. Underline the pronouns.

1. James and I went to the boat race.
2. We went close to the water to watch the racers.
3. They were readying the boats.
4. James went to the pier's edge and stood on it.
5. He fell in the water, and people laughed at us.

Singular and Plural Pronouns pages 188–189

Copy these sentences. Underline the pronouns. Tell whether the pronouns are plural or singular.

1. Becky asked us to go on a picnic.
2. She packed a lunch.
3. It was filled with good food.
4. We drove out to the woods.
5. Becky made sure I ate every bite.

Pronouns as Subjects pages 190–191

Choose the correct pronoun in ( ). Write the sentences.

1. (He, We) joins the Hunger Walk every year with hundreds of other people.
2. (They, He) walks a little more than twenty miles.
3. (He, I) go on the Hunger Walk each year too.
4. (It, We) raise a lot of money on the march.
5. (It, They) feeds hungry people all around the world.

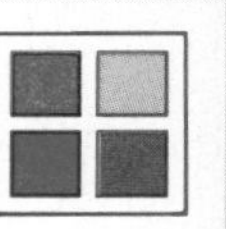

Possessive Nouns pages 194–195

Write possessive noun phrases to take the place of these word groups.

1. the house of the man
2. the friend of Joe
3. the arm of the girl
4. the son of Mr. Brown
5. the desk of Ms. Vega
6. the dish of the cat
7. the shoe of Dr. Choy
8. the office of Mrs. Ky
9. the brother of Jane
10. the room of Martha

Plural Possessive Nouns pages 196–197

Write plural possessive noun phrases to take the place of these word groups.

1. the shirts of the boys
2. the pens of the teachers
3. the fathers of the babies
4. the feet of the runners
5. the caps of the swimmers
6. the caves of the brown bears
7. the whistles of the coaches
8. the baseball of the players

Compounds pages 200–201

Match the words to make compound words. Then use the compound words in sentences.

1. back	**a.** paper
2. fly	**b.** brush
3. roof	**c.** yard
4. hair	**d.** lace
5. shoe	**e.** top

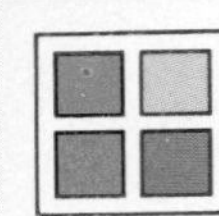

Prefixes pages 202–203

Find the word in each sentence that could begin with the prefix in ( ). Add the prefix to the word. Write the sentence.

1. Winona was happy. (un)
2. Her father wanted to build her new bike. (re)
3. She was certain that he could do it. (un)
4. She thought it might be possible. (im)
5. He connected the parts of the bike. (dis)

Suffixes pages 204–205

Use a word from the box to replace each group of words in ( ). Write the sentences.

adjustable	sailor	harmless	flexible	harmful

1. I like being a (person who sails).
2. I enjoy putting up the (able to be adjusted) sails.
3. I even like wearing my (able to be flexed) life jacket.
4. Usually the wind on our lake is (without harm).
5. My life jacket will protect me if the wind is strong enough to be (full of harm).

A Friendly Letter pages 206–207

Pretend your cousin Anita is coming to visit you. Write her a friendly letter. Tell Anita what she can expect to see and do in your town.

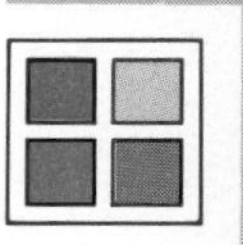

Envelopes pages 208–209

Use a ruler to draw an envelope on your paper. Then put this information on the correct parts of the envelope. Add capital letters and commas (,) where they are needed.

To: ms. pauline gordon
5522 hyde park blvd.
chicago IL 60637

From: carla lister
18 bond st.
aztec NM 87410

Writing a Thank You Note pages 212–213

Pretend you are writing to your friend Jake. You want to thank him for inviting you to his skating party. Write a thank you note to Jake.

Editing a Thank You Note pages 214–215

Read Ralph's thank you note. Notice the changes he made. Rewrite his letter.

207 texas street
max, Minnesota 55407
may 24 19--

Dear Grandma

Thank you for sending me the kite for my birthday. i will use it on the next windy day.

love
Ralph

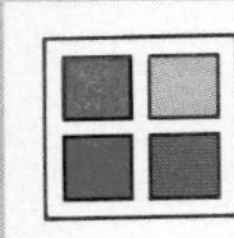

Mechanics Practice page 215

Rewrite these times and addresses correctly.

1. 1100 PM
2. 1015 AM
3. 545 AM
4. 230 PM
5. 339 Bleecker st
   new york NY 10011
6. 2817 field ave
   lawrence kansas 66044

Rhythm and Rhyme in Poetry pages 216–217

Read this poem. Answer the questions below.

The sea was galloping grey and white;
Christopher clutched his sixpence tight,
We clambered over the humping sand—
And Christopher held my hand.

A. A. Milne

1. Which lines in this poem rhyme?
2. How many strong beats does line 1 have?
3. Choose the line below that has the same number of strong beats as line 4 of the poem.
   The books are upon the shelf.
   It was raining all across the land.

Sound Words in Poetry pages 218–219

Read the poem. Then answer the questions.

Clickety-clack! It's coming closer.
Woo-oo-woo! It's nearer still.
With a whoosh of wind and a clang of metal
The train speeds over the hill.

1. List the sound words from this poem.
2. Which words in line 1 begin the same way?

UNIT 7

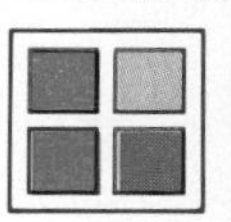

Present Time and Past Time Verbs pages 228–229

Tell whether the underlined verb in each sentence tells about present time or past time.

1. Timothy and Janice played on a Little League team last summer.
2. They practiced a lot.
3. Their coach showed them many tricks.
4. Now they play on our team at school.
5. Our team learns more from them every day.

Forms of Be pages 230–231

Choose the correct form of the word *be* in ( ). Then write the sentences.

1. I remember when I (were, was) just starting school.
2. The other students (were, was) afraid.
3. The teacher showed us our books and toys, and soon all the children (am, were) having fun.
4. In third grade we (are, am) learning more than we did then.
5. I (am, are) enjoying school more now.
6. The students in my class (is, are) learning how to write stories.
7. Our teacher (am, is) very nice.
8. My science book (are, is) very interesting.
9. I think that I (am, are) going to be a scientist.
10. My parents (are, is) both scientists.

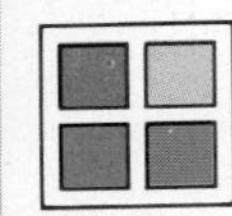

Irregular Verbs pages 232–233

Change the underlined verbs to the form shown in ( ). Write the sentences.

1. I begin my voice lesson. (past)
2. I sing all the notes in the scale. (past)
3. I sang these scales many times each day. (present)
4. My voice rang out clearly. (present)
5. I begin to learn difficult songs. (past with *have*)

Contractions with Not pages 234–235

Here is a list of groups of words. Make each underlined group of words into a contraction. Then use the new word groups in sentences.

1. I have not
2. She has not
3. He is not
4. They are not
5. We were not
6. Jo has not
7. Loki is not
8. Fred was not
9. I had not
10. The boys have not

Other Contractions pages 236–237

Rewrite these sentences. Make the underlined words into contractions.

1. I am going to meet my friend Alan.
2. He is going with me to hear bands in the park.
3. We hope they are good.
4. We are bringing a picnic lunch.
5. I am making a dessert for the picnic.

Encyclopedia pages 240–241

Use these encyclopedia volumes to answer these questions.

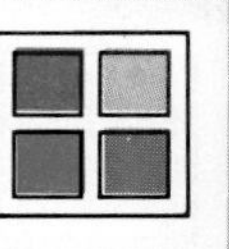

1. Would an article about Washington, D.C., be before or after information about whales?
2. In what volume would you find information about seagulls?
3. Would an article on bridges be in the same volume as an article about César Chavez?
4. In what volume would you find information about Oliver Wendell Holmes?
5. Would an article on kangaroos be in the same volume as information on lizards?

Notes and Outlines pages 242–245

Find an encyclopedia in your library. Look for information on one of the subjects below.

Seaweed	Mexico City
Weaving	Goats
Golda Meir	Paul Robeson

Read the article. Look for important facts. Take notes. Then use the outline form to put your notes in order.

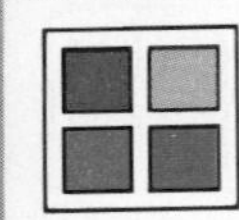

Writing a Report pages 246–247

Choose one of the topics below. Go to the library. Find information on the topic in a book or encyclopedia. Take notes on the information. Put your information in outline form. Then use your outline and notes to write a short report. Write a paragraph for each main topic in your outline.

Violins	Mary McLeod Bethune
Francis Scott Key	Soccer
Portland, Maine	Chief Joseph
Clouds	Diamonds
Puerto Rico	Rockets
Louisa May Alcott	Vultures

Editing a Report pages 248–249

Read this first paragraph of a report on the first zoos. Notice the editing marks. Rewrite the report, making all the corrections shown.

People in egypt were the first
to keep animals in zoos. They
began collecting groops (groups) of animals
more than three or four thousand
years ago. they collected antelopes,
baboons, and other wiled (wild) animals.
people in egypt uzed (used) these
animals for hunting.

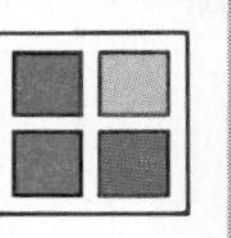

Mechanics Practice page 249

Rewrite these sentences. Put apostrophes (') where they belong.

1. Randy and Randys friend Jacob are camping out.
2. Theyre setting up their camp.
3. During the night Randy feels as though hes getting wet.
4. The two boys tents are leaking!
5. Jacobs sleeping bag is soaking wet.

A Magazine Article pages 250–253

Read the magazine article below. Then answer the questions about it.

> Tiny plants and animals live all around us. They are too small to see, but they are everywhere. They live in the soil, the air, and in rivers and oceans. They grow on other plants and animals, and some even live on you!
>
> These tiny plants and animals are called microbes, from the Greek words *micro,* meaning "small," and *bios,* meaning "life." So, *microbe* means "small life."
>
> *Lucia Anderson*

1. Is this article fiction or nonfiction?
2. Is the information about microbes true?
3. Did the author make up the word *microbe*?

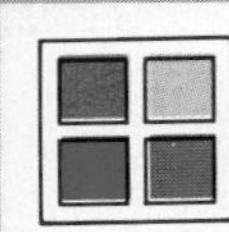

UNIT 8

Introductions pages 260–261

Write the introductions that are best. Choose one from each pair.

1. James, this is Lucy Stone.
   James, this is Lucy Stone, my cousin from Vermont.
2. Mother, this is Mr. Davies, my art teacher. He is teaching us to work with clay.
   Mother, I would like you to meet Mr. Davies.
3. Tony, I want you to meet my father. Tony is in my class.
   Dad, this is Tony Perez. He is in my class.
4. Grandma, this is Mr. Li, my piano teacher.
   Grandmother, I'd like you to meet Mr. Li.
5. Ms. Parsons, this is my new neighbor, Annette.
   Annette, meet Ms. Parsons.
6. Ms. Dale, this is Dr. Zahler. He writes books about science.
   Ms. Dale, this is Stan Zahler.

Telephone Messages pages 262–263

Take a message on this telephone call. Use today's date.

Hello. Is your mother in? This is Mrs. Perkins. I am calling to see if your mom can drive me to town tomorrow. It is 1:00 now. Could she call me back before 3:00? My number is 535-9200.

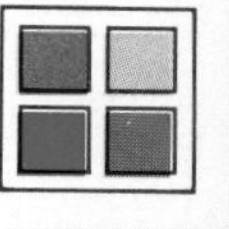

Thinking About What You Hear pages 266–267

Read each sentence below. Write *statement of fact* or *statement of opinion* for each one.

1. It took us a half-hour to drive to the woods for our campout.
2. It was fun to hike through the forest.
3. I think it is scary to sleep in the woods at night.
4. In the morning we cooked breakfast over the fire.
5. Food tastes better when it is eaten outdoors.

Test Directions pages 270–271

Write the name of the student who followed each direction correctly.

1. Circle the letter of the word that is an adjective.

Chris	Ned	Ana
a. red	**a.** red	**a.** red
b. see	**b.** see	**b.** see
c. I	**c.** I	**c.** I

2. Underline the prefix in each word.

Chris	Ned	Ana
unlike	unlike	unlike
redo	redo	redo
impolite	impolite	impolite

3. Fill in the circle by the word that is a pronoun.

Chris	Ned	Ana
○ fair	○ fair	○ fair
○ him	○ him	● him
● box	○ box	○ box

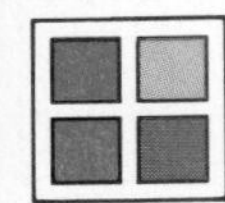

Maps pages 272–273

Look at this map. Then answer the questions.

1. How many different streets will Tim have to walk on to get to Diane's house?
2. If Tim wanted to cut through yards, could he get to Diane's house without crossing a street?
3. Is there a bridge between Tim's house and Diane's house?
4. If he followed the roads, could Tim get to Diane's house without crossing the railroad?

A Telephone Directory pages 274–275

Use these telephone book listings to answer the questions.

Sand – Solomon
Sand, Jeffrey 23 East Rd. **444-7654**
Saul, Jennifer 53 Forest Dr. **455-9890**
Sayer, Marc 455 High St. **435-8877**
Sears, Cindy 25 East Rd. **444-5858**
Silva, Maria 829 Noon Rd. **433-6556**

1. What is Jennifer Saul's address?
2. What is Maria Silva's telephone number?
3. Who lives at 455 High Street?
4. Which two people live on the same road?
5. Who has this telephone number: 435-8877?

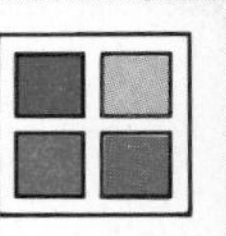

Writing and Editing a Book Report pages 278–283

Write a book report on a book you read this month. Tell the name of the book and the name of the author. Give some interesting facts about the book. Tell your opinion of the book. Then read the report you wrote. Have you written the book title correctly? Do your sentences begin and end correctly? Edit your report and rewrite it. Prepare note cards and give an oral report.

Mechanics Practice page 281

Rewrite these sentences. Write the titles correctly.

1. In school I talked about my favorite book, sweet and sour, by Carol Kendall.
2. Jim talked about the story called pinocchio.
3. Douglas said he likes the television show little house on the prairie.
4. He also enjoyed the book called little house in the big woods.
5. Margaret said that her favorite thing to read was a poem called how doth the little crocodile.

A Play pages 284–287

Read these statements about plays. Write whether each one is true or false.

1. A play has only one character.
2. A play can have one or more settings.
3. A play is meant to be acted out.
4. A play is mostly conversation among characters.
5. Stage directions tell the audience what to do.

INDEX

4 5 6 7 8 9 0 1